Designing Correctional
Organizations for Youths

Series on Massachusetts Youth Correction Reforms

Center for Criminal Justice
Harvard Law School

Designing Correctional Organizations for Youths:

Dilemmas of Subcultural Development

Craig A. McEwen
Bowdoin College

Center for Criminal Justice
Harvard Law School

Ballinger Publishing Company ● Cambridge, Mass.
A Subsidiary of J.B. Lippincott Company

 This book is printed on recycled paper.

Prepared under grant numbers 72-NI-99-00096, 73-NI-99-00556, and 74-NI-99-0176 in the National Institute of Law Enforcement and Criminal Justice, grant numbers 76-JN-99-0003 and 76-JJ-99-0452 in the National Institute of Juevenile Justice and Delinquency Prevention, both in the Law Enforcement Assistance Administration, U.S. Department of Justice, and under grant numbers 71-35X-905A1, 71-35X-905AO, 73C-060,231, 74C-084,2332, and 75C-047,2391 in the Massachusetts Committee on Criminal Justice, and with help from the Center for Criminal Justice using funds from Ford Foundation grant 690-0122. Points of view or opinions stated are those of the authors and do not necessarily represent the official position of the U.S. Department of Justice, the Massachusetts Committee on Criminal Justice or the Ford Foundation.

International Standard Book Number: 0-88410-789-2

Library of Congress Catalog Card Number: 77-27488

Printed in the United States of America

Library of Congress Cataloging in Publication Data

McEwen, Craig A.
   Designing correctional organizations for youths.

   (Series on Massachusetts youth correction reforms)
   Includes bibliographical references.
   1. Juvenile corrections—Massachusetts. 2. Community-based corrections—Massachusetts. 3. Subculture.
I. Harvard University. Center for Criminal justice. II. Title. III. Series.
HV9105.M4M2   364.6   77-27488
ISBN 0-88410-789-2

To Maggie

Contents

List of Tables

Foreword

During the seven-year period from 1969 to 1976, some of the most sweeping reforms in youth corrections in the United States took place in Massachusetts. The state's Department of Youth Services became a highly visible national symbol of a new approach to juvenile corrections through its repudiation of training schools and its advocacy of community-based services. Over the same period the study of these reforms by the Center for Criminal Justice, Harvard Law School, generated a detailed and extensive body of data about the processes of change and their impact. The five books that make up this series are based on that data. In a time of increasing concern about the extent and seriousness of youth crime, this work is of special importance. The books are intended not only to constitute a comprehensive case study but also to explore significant issues of theory and policy and to present an analytic record of experience that will serve as a useful guide to other states that seek to improve the effectiveness of their youth corrections system. More broadly, these books provide important insights into the process and problems of effecting change in human service agencies.

*　　　*　　　*

Traditional public training schools have been the focus of criticism for several decades, with attacks coming from three major sources. First, critics have argued that these institutions are partly responsible for high rates of recidivism because of their criminalizing effects on the young people who emerge from them. A second source of criticism has come from proponents of treatment ideologies. They argue that counseling and therapy should replace traditional custodial care, and that youthful offenders should be dealt with at home and in their communities. A third challenge to training schools has come from advocates of the civil rights of children, and has focused on due process, the "right to treatment," and the "right to be left alone." These challenges have put strains on the correctional systems in many states and have raised important questions about whether programs can help young people and still meet a community's demand for protection.

These questions were confronted during a period of crisis, reform, and reaction in Massachusetts correctional policy that made the state a unique site for observation and evaluation. It was at the beginning of this period that the Harvard Center for Criminal Justice inaugurated its study of the reform process. A brief review of the events surrounding the Massachusetts reforms will allow for a better perspective on the scope of this project.

* * *

A series of crises in youth correctional services in Massachusetts was followed in 1969 by the resignation of the long-time director of Youth Services who had strongly supported the use of traditional training schools. Recidivism rates for youth ranged from 40 to 70 percent, and investigations of the system, with accompanying newspaper coverage of its dramatic shortcomings, led civic and professional groups and the public to support reforms.

When Francis Sargent became governor in 1969, he expressed his strong support for reforming youth services. In the fall of that year he appointed a new commissioner, Dr. Jerome Miller, to head a reorganized Department of Youth Services. Miller took charge with a mandate from the legislative and executive branches of state government and from liberal reform groups to develop new programs, although the scope of the mandate was broad and undefined.

For the first two years Miller sought to create a humanized and therapeutic climate within the existing institutions. Visible symbols of the old system such as dress and haircut requirements were abandoned. This raised a storm of protest from old-line staff who resented such attacks on their absolute control. Miller's order not to strike a youth brought similar outcries. In the early months Miller's efforts were hampered by financial limitations and the tradition-minded bureaucracy he inherited. Nonetheless, by the spring of 1971 Miller and his new planning unit had prepared a reform plan which focused on decentralized, community-based treatment centers—both residential and nonresidential.

These moves were met with resistance from the adherents of the old philosophy. Many of them were close to influential legislators and community leaders in the small towns close to the training schools. And they had relationships with judges, probation officers, and public officials, many of whom shared their views about the proper function of the training schools. During his first two years, Miller was faced with two legislative investigations of his reforms.

Meanwhile, Miller decided that therapeutic communities could not be run successfully in the existing institutions, particularly in view of the resistance from old-guard personnel. In the most dramatic stage of the reform process, he moved to close the old training schools, to establish a network of decentralized community-based services, and virtually to end locked facilities for youth. He took steps to establish a structure more closely tied to community life: regionalization of services; new court liaisons; diagnostic and referral policies; individual case decisions; the monitoring of services increasingly purchased from private agencies; and staff development programs to reassign, retrain, or discharge former personnel.

Suddenly, in January 1973, after three hectic hears of change, Miller resigned to become the new director of Family and Children's Services in Illinois. He believed that administrators initiating major reforms invariably become expendable because the hostility that focuses on them creates a barrier to completing the process of reforms and that a new commissioner could best finish the job. When Miller left, financial and personnel problems had not yet been resolved, and a new system of residential and nonresidential services had not yet fully replaced the old.

Under Miller's successors as commissioner, Joseph Leavey and John Calhoun, the department has consolidated the new network of community-based programs and resolved many of its administrative problems. It has had to contend, however, with a sizable amount of public counterreaction, including strong pressure to increase the availability to the courts of secure facilities.

Massachusetts has demonstrated that radical changes in official ideology and programs can be achieved over a comparatively short period of time, but the traditional training school system that existed in Massachusetts is still the dominant pattern throughout the country. In light of this situation, it is clear that the Massachusetts reforms, and the political and organizational upheavals that accompanied them, have presented to policy-makers and scholars a rich opportunity to study a crucial issue in human services and to learn something as well about complex change in process.

The Center for Criminal Justice at Harvard Law School has taken advantage of this opportunity for the past seven years. This project was undertaken shortly after the Center was established. One of our principal goals in creating the Center was to engage in major empirical projects that would provide data and analytical insights to guide policy-makers in the administration of criminal justice. The work reflected in this series of books has been the largest by far of our projects. Under the leadership of Professor Lloyd Ohlin, a remarkable group of scholars—the authors of the books in this series—have combined their varied backgrounds and skills to make a major advance in knowledge and theory in a field that has traditionally been dominated by fads, fashions, and untested dogma. This collaborative effort by Ohlin, Miller, Coates, Feld, and McEwen had the benefit of the work of a fine supporting staff and profited from the advisory and critical roles played by other staff members of the Center, our Criminal Justice Fellows, and visiting Research Fellows.

Only time tells which intellectual undertakings have a major impact on the development of social institutions. I can only record my sense that this volume—and the others in the series—reflect a rare convergence of a fascinating and significant set of social changes with the tireless, objective and imaginative efforts of a unique group of scholars.

James Vorenberg
Harvard Law School

Preface

This project began in the winter of 1969/70 in anticipation of major reforms in the Massachusetts youth correctional system. From a personal standpoint it represented a fresh opportunity to study two important correctional problems previously explored to some degree in two separate projects: the process and impact of significant changes in correctional policy and the relationship between the organizational structure of correctional programs and peer-group subcultures among inmates. An earlier opportunity to study the first issue, change in correctional organizations, occurred from 1953 to 1956 when I directed a study at the University of Chicago of a major change in the Wisconsin prison probation and parole system as a consequence of transfer of corrections to the welfare system. This project, supported by the Russell Sage Foundation, was carried out with the assistance of Donnel M. Pappenfort and Herman Piven and, in the final year, Donald R. Cressey. It yielded many insights into problems of organizational change and the internal dynamics of prison life which have found reflection at various points in the present study. Extensive use has been made of the Wisconsin data to test the generalizability of new theoretical perspectives developed in the analysis of the Massachusetts data and reported most fully in the second book in the series, *A Theory of Social Reform*.

An earlier opportunity to undertake a comparative analysis of the second issue, relating to the effect of organizational differences on peer-group subcultures and inmate response to program intervention,

. occurred from 1957 to 1960 when I codirected with Richard A. Cloward at Columbia University a study of a public and private training school for boys in New York State. The results of this project were never fully developed, but it generated theoretical insights that were incorporated into our book on *Delinquency and Opportunity* (1960), and into the program of Mobilization for Youth project on the Lower East Side of Manhattan. The Massachusetts data has provided an excellent opportunity to explore much more intensively the sources of subcultural variation, and the books by Feld and McEwen report the results of this objective. In addition, more probing study of inmate response to programs was possible through the analysis of cohort data reported in *Diversity in a Youth Correctional System.*

Initial explorations in 1969, utilizing staff and fellows of the Center for Criminal Justice, led to intensive participant observation and formal interviewing of Department of Youth Services staff and youth in the summer of 1970. The direction of the total project crystallized when I was joined by my associates Alden Miller, late in 1970, and Robert Coates, in 1971. Barry Feld, who had been one of the observer-interviewers in 1970, directed a subculture study in selected institutional cottages in the summer of 1971. This type of study was extended to the community-based programs of the deinstitutionalized system by Craig McEwen in the summer of 1973. Barbara Stolz, who participated in the subculture study of the summer of 1971, began in 1972 a doctoral study of the state-level political process external to DYS. This study was complemented by a parallel dissertation analysis of organizational and political process in the central office of DYS by Arlette Klein.

In approaching the project as a whole, Miller, Coates and I developed a general conceptual framework, an observation guide that was employed throughout most of the study, and a system-oriented strategy of program evaluation. While we worked closely as a team, sharing most decisions in a collegial fashion, there was some specialization in terms of principal interest. I was particularly interested in the construction of a case analysis of the entire reform effort and its relevance to broader trends of correctional policy. Miller was especially interested in the system-wide analysis of the process of change, with an emphasis on the effectiveness of interest-group tactics. Coates was particularly concerned with issues of program evaluation in the context of active change and in the conceptualization of community-based corrections.

During the course of the Harvard study, seventeen separate data-gathering efforts took place, focusing on recidivism, program dynamics, the relations between youth and correctional staff in various

settings, and the politics of the reform and counterreform movements. These components of the overall study are shown in the
accompanying diagram in relation to the major historical events of
the reform. They combine variously in the present series to form the
perspectives from which the authors of the five books viewed the
day-to-day reform process in the Massachusetts youth correctional
system and in other systems that faced similar upheavals. Each book
has important implications for the study, promotion, or restraint of
change in other social-service settings as well. As briefly summarized
here, they range from the most comprehensive perspective to the
most particular.

Reforming Juvenile Corrections: The Massachusetts Experience
(Ohlin, Coates & Miller) provides a description and analysis of the
entire Massachusetts youth correctional reform process and a comparative assessment of the effectiveness of successive correctional
policies. The presentation sets the analysis in the context of ideological conflicts about youths in trouble. We discuss successive phases of
the reform process and the conditions leading to it, using an analytical structure that guides narrative development and critical discussion while employing data from all seventeen components of the
Harvard study. We thus seek to explain from a broad policy perspective not only why and how the changes occurred but what effect
they had on youth, staff, and other involved groups.

The series proceeds to a more detailed analysis of the process of
change. *A Theory of Social Reform: Correctional Change Processes
in Two States* (Miller, Ohlin & Coates) draws extensively on classic
sociological literature while using the events in Massachusetts and the
earlier correctional reform movement in Wisconsin to develop a conceptual model that identifies key interest-group constellations, their
critical characteristics and interrelationships, and the dimensions of
their impact upon correctional systems. Conclusions based on an
analysis of largely qualitative data are tested in the development of
a mathematical simulation. The book addresses policy issues center-
ing on ways to promote or hinder reform.

The diversity of programs developed during the reform years
offered a natural laboratory for the testing of policy. As some five
hundred youths moved through the complex network of Massachusetts correctional programs, including nonresidential programs, foster care, forestry, group homes, boarding schools, secure programs
and adult jails, the research staff followed and documented their
progress. In *Diversity in a Youth Correctional System: Handling
Delinquents in Massachusetts* (Coates, Miller & Ohlin), both the
short-run and long-run impact of such program sequences become

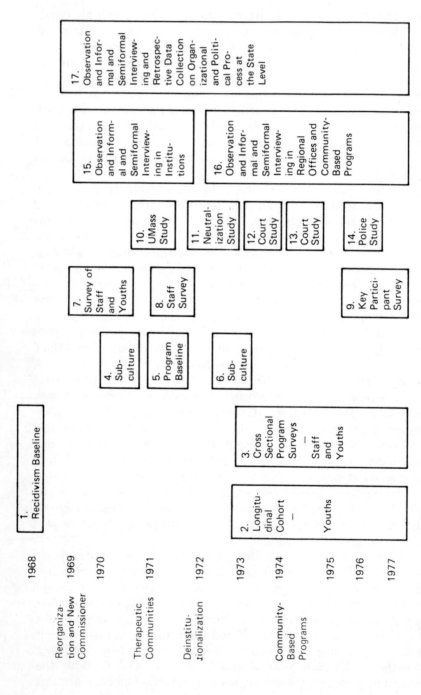

BLOCK PLAN OF STUDY CORRELATED WITH MAJOR CHANGES IN THE MASSACHUSETTS DEPARTMENT OF YOUTH SERVICES

Components of the Study

1. *Recidivism Baseline:* A study of offical records of youths paroled before the reforms to provide a comparison baseline for recidivism of youths passing through the new programs.

2. *Longitudinal Youth Cohort:* Repeated interviewing of youths at different points in their progress through the system from intake to return to the community, along with official records checks of recidivism for comparison with the recidivism baseline.

3. *Cross-Sectional Program Surveys, Staff and Youth:* Interviews to further characterize programs through which youth in the cohort had to pass.

4. *Subculture, 1971:* Interviewing and participant observation in selected programs before the closing of the institutions.

5. *Program Baseline:* Interviewing in institutions immediately prior to the closing.

6. *Subculture, 1973:* Interviewing and participant observation in selected programs after the closing of the institutions.

7. *Survey of Staff and Youths:* Interviewing in institutions during the first year after reorganization.

8. *Staff Survey:* Informal interviews of remaining staff in the institutions after most of them had already closed.

9. *Key Participant Survey:* Interviews of staff throughout the reform system after consolidation of the reforms.

10. *University of Massachusetts Study:* Interviews and observation at the University of Massachusetts conference used to place youths taken from the closing institutions.

11. *Neutralization Study:* Interviews with participants and observation of the process of setting up group homes in specific communities, during which attempts were made to neutralize community resistance.

12. *Court Study, 1973:* Interviews and observation to assess the interface between the courts and DYS.

13. *Court Study, 1974:* Continuation of Court Study of 1973.

14. *Policy Study:* Interviews, questionnaires, and observation to assess the interface between the police and potential DYS youth.

15. *Observation and Informal and Semiformal Interviewing in Institutions:* Monitoring of the day-to-day process.

16. *Observation and Informal and Semiformal Interviewing in Regional Offices and Community-Based Programs:* Monitoring of the day-to-day process.

17. *Observation and Informal and Semiformal Interviewing and Retrospective Data Collection of Organization and Political Processes at the State Level:* Monitoring of the day-to-day process.

clearly visible through quantitative analysis of longitudinal data characterized by approximately 2,500 variables. By synthesizing and cross-testing various theoretical perspectives on the youth correctional process, we were able to focus important policy issues concerning the quality of life within programs and the extent and quality of linkages to the community, all of which vitally affect the youths' future relationship to society.

A detailed look at the problems of both innovative and more traditional program settings for young offenders is provided in *Designing Correctional Organizations for Youths: Dilemmas of Subcultural Development* (McEwen). Using participant observation and survey methods the author contrasts ten institutional program settings for young people, with thirteen others that were part of a community-based system developed to replace the training school system. In calling upon a range of settings unusual in previous subcultural research, McEwen presents a detailed analysis of day-to-day interaction patterns that reflect different policies of community contact, egalitarianism, youth participation in decision-making, degree of supervision, and selection of youth with special background characteristics. These policies and patterns of interaction are then related to outcomes in youth subcultural beliefs, youth behavior, and the relations between youth and staff.

The final volume in the series, *Neutralizing Inmate Violence: Juvenile Offenders in Institutions* (Feld), focuses on a subset of ten program settings for youth, ranged across a custody-treatment continuum within the confines of training school institutions. In this more intensive look at a traditional group of institutions, also used for other comparative purposes in the preceding volume by McEwen, participant observation and survey methods are combined to examine in closer perspective the connection between the official correctional organization and inmate subcultures. The study explores ways of creating diverse patterns of official programs and subcultural responses within the confines of the same institution. Feld focuses sharply on policy issues concerning organizational means for the control of violence in institutional settings and contributes to more general theory of complex organizations.

The series thus offers an opportunity to examine a broad range of theoretical and practical concerns, the interrelationships of which are virtually impossible to perceive in a less comprehensive study. The project was originally designed to do this and was supplemented by special studies as new issues and problems developed in the reform process.

Since the Massachusetts study focused on controversial issues, every effort was made to encompass as wide a range of perspectives on these issues as possible. The theoretical structure of the project was designed to articulate the different interests that coalesced into support or criticism of various reform measures or their consequences. This led us to search out persons holding widely divergent views and, where necessary, to undertake special studies of some groups, like judges and police, to make sure their perspectives were adequately represented. Our own research staff was composed in such a way as to assure sympathetic understanding of opposing points of view. In fact we encountered the common research experience of staff identification with their respondents, particularly in the course of participant observation. This required special attention to the problem of achieving a balanced assessment over-all by having a variety of interviewers collect data on the same topics.

It should be kept in mind that problems of change and policy implementation in youth corrections have much in common with problems in other human-service organizations—adult corrections, mental health, retardation, and welfare social services. The theories and strategies of change, the methods of evaluating service systems and the development and implementation of new policies represent forms of knowledge and insight of equal utility and transferability to these other types of service organizations.

A large number of people have been involved in this study between its inception and the completion of the manuscripts in this series. In addition to Ohlin, Miller, Coates, Feld, McEwen, Stolz, and Klein, whose roles were described above, there has been a large field staff ranging at times up to twenty people. It is not possible to fully state our indebtedness to the dedication and enterprise the field staff displayed or to acknowledge fully their contribution. Here we can only list their names:

Nathaniel Ackerman
Henry J. Albach IV
Wendy S. Allen
Mark E. Ashburn
Ira M. Baline
William Bazzy
Bonnie B. Boswell
Judith H. Caldwell
Robert Chilvers
Roy Cramer
Diane C. Engster
Finn-Aage Engster
John R. Faith

Elizabeth Farrell
Robert Fitzgerald
John H. Fleming
Gail Garinger
David D. Garwood
Paula A. Garwood
Geoffrey Ginis
Preston B. Grandin
John Greenthal
Nancy Hall
Elinor C. Halprin
Kenneth Hausman
William Hill

Albert R. Johnson
Stewart W. Kemp
David R. King
Gwen Kinkaid
Neil Koslowe
Cheryl A. La Fleur
Thomas Manley
Jacqueline Miller
Andrea Mintz
Mary Morton
Fern Nesson
Susan Nyman
Gail A. Page
Linda Perle
Clifford Robinson
Wendell P. Russell, Jr.
Kurt L. Schmoke

Fern Selesnick
James R. Shea
Carol Sherman
Shelley Stahl
Mary Strohschein
Kip R. Sullivan
Hollis Sutherland
Arthur R. Swann
Blue Tabor
Eva Teichner
Christian S. Schley
Jane E. Tewksbury
John Troubh
Helene Whittaker
Elizabeth Williams
Anne Yates
Alma Young

Judith Auerbach and Jan Schreiber joined the project during the final year and a half as editors. Though special acknowledgment is included in the author's note to the individual volumes they edited, the wealth of experience and professionally sound judgment they brought to the overall project proved of enormous help in identifying and clarifying the special contributions of each of the books and the series as an articulated whole. Marion Coates did most of the computer programming after 1971 and brought to this task great patience and perservance in setting up and checking out complicated forms of data processing. An expert consulting team from the firm of Peat, Marwick, Mitchell and Co., led by Robert Nielson, undertook the very difficult task of a comparative cost analysis of the old and new correctional programs.

Secretaries who worked on the project included Christine Conniff, Deborah Cooper, Lorna Dumapias, James Franklin, Kathleen T. Gardner, Nancy Le Massena, Nancy J. March, Darnney L. Proudfoot, and Lucille Young.

Throughout the course of the project we received support and useful suggestions from Center staff members and directors of other projects at the Center. Most of all, however, we are deeply indebted to Professor James Vorenberg, Director of the Center. From the beginning Jim provided constant encouragement, criticism, and professional judgment, especially when troubleshooting was needed in periods of crisis. Rosanne Kumins, Administrative Assistant of the Center, could always be counted on for help in moving the project along through innumerable hazards, but she also managed our budgets and accounts despite the exasperating complexities of coordinating funds from different sources. I am personally grateful to Harvard Law School Dean Albert M. Sacks for his encouragement and generous grants of research leave so that I might remain deeply involved in the research effort.

Special assistance was provided by staff of the funding agencies, especially James Howell of the Office of Juvenile Justice and Delinquency Prevention, Law Enforcement Assistance Administration, U.S. Department of Justice, and Robert Cole and Karen Joerg of the Massachusetts Committee on Criminal Justice. The Massachusetts Office of the Commissioner of Probation, under the direction of Elliot Sands, Commissioner, Joseph Foley, Assistant Commissioner, and Mark Santapio, in charge of the records, was of great help in securing data on recidivism.

Obviously, the study could not have been done at all without the generous cooperation of the staff and youth of the Massachusetts Department of Youth Services throughout the project, with the constant support of Commissioner Jerome Miller, his successor Commissioner Joseph Leavey, and finally the present Commissioner John Calhoun.

Funding for the project came from several sources. It was begun using the Center's own funds from its original Ford Foundation grant. Beginning in 1971 the project was funded in large part by the Massachusetts Committee on Criminal Justice, and aided by matching funds from the Center's Ford Foundation grant. In 1972 additional funds were granted by the National Institute of Law Enforcement and Criminal Justice, Law Enforcement Assistance Administration, U.S. Department of Justice. This support was later taken over by the Office of Juvenile Justice and Delinquency Prevention, when that office was founded and eventually became the principal source of funds for the project as a whole in its final two years.

Lloyd E. Ohlin
Harvard Law School

Author's Note

Many people contributed to the larger project, of which this research is one part. I wish to acknowledge those who contributed especially to this book.

My primary debt is, of course, to the youths and staff people who cooperated so fully in this research project. Their cooperation would have been for naught, however, had it not been for the skillful and dedicated work of the five people who joined me in collecting data: Robert Chilvers, John Fleming, Gwen Kinkaid, Christian Schley, and Mary Strohschein. I hope that seeing some of their field notes in print will belatedly justify the sleep they lost in recording them so faithfully.

To Barry Feld and the field workers who joined him in the summer of 1971, I am also grateful. Their work provided an excellent foundation on which to build. They too will see their field notes sprinkled through the following pages.

My job of translating the mass of data into a finished manuscript was made easier by the able assistance of many people. Marion Coates at Harvard and Myron Curtis and Robert Jackson at Bowdoin assisted me with computer work. Louise Caron at Bowdoin unerringly turned my handwritten pages into typescript. Judith Auerbach's editorial skills and wise advice improved the manuscript greatly, as did the suggestions of George McEwen and the editorial staff at Ballinger, especially Sid Seamans.

Throughout the course of this project, Lloyd Ohlin and Alden Miller served as sounding boards for my ideas and provided me with constructive criticism and necessary deadlines as well as encouragement and support. They and other colleagues at the Center for Criminal Justice, especially Robert Coates and Walter Miller, taught me much while providing good fellowship. Similarly, my colleagues at Bowdoin were stimulating and supportive.

Finally, I wish to note that without the interruptions by Maggie, Ian, and Kirk McEwen, I would have completed this book somewhat more quickly but much less happily.

Designing Correctional
Organizations for Youths

Introduction

Over the past two hundred years, prisons, reformatories, and training schools for juveniles and adults have by and large failed in their mission to reform society's offenders while incarcerating them. Despite periodic reassessments and redirections of ideology and strategy, this failure has consistently been reflected in high and relatively unvarying rates of recidivism. This apparent inability to "correct" as large a proportion of inmates as desired may result from a lack of knowledge of how behavior that is defined as criminal should be reformed; from shifting values about defining criminal behavior itself; from a lack of resources and commitment; or from overly high expectations of the possibilities of shaping future conduct within an incarcerating environment.

Related to the broad failure of prisons to reform their inmates is a second failure—the dismal fact that prisons and training schools have rarely been able to create humane and manageable living conditions for those persons who are being punished by the denial of some degree of their liberty. Although decaying physical conditions, poor medical treatment, and staff brutality are slowly disappearing through the reform efforts of well-intentioned corrections administrators and under the pressure of litigation brought by inmates and concerned citizen groups, the day-to-day suspicion and hostility in staff-inmate relationships and the companion tensions, brutality, and exploitation among inmates typically remain untouched by these reforms.[1] These daily tensions, which are manifestations of the informal inmate underlife, or subculture, make the prison experience frightening and debilitating for most inmates and create serious prob-

1

lems of control and supervision for correctional staff and administrators. It is to the causes of this second failure and the variety of organizational strategies for responding to it that this book is addressed.

Reformers cannot hope to achieve all possible correctional goals simultaneously, and some correctional strategies appear to be inconsistent with others.[2] This book examines not only the organizational and population features that influence different aspects of inmate social structure, subculture, and behavior (inmate systems)[3] but also the balancing and compromises involved in selecting one kind of organizational structure rather than another. The purpose of this study is to explain the varying characteristics of inmate systems and to identify alternative methods of correctional organization that might be used to direct their development.

Drawing on observation and questionnaires, the inmate systems shared by delinquents in twenty-three widely varied correctional settings in Massachusetts are compared. These range from a punishment cottage in a training school, to several therapeutic communities in and out of a training school context, to two nonresidential programs in the open community. Elements of inmate subcultures such as norms about "ratting" and shared beliefs about the extent of staff trustworthiness, aspects of social structures such as patterns of leadership and of friendship formation among delinquents, and the frequency of such behavior as running away, fighting, and using drugs all differ substantially within this sample of programs from the Massachusetts Department of Youth Services.

The causes of these variations in inmate systems—the major focus of analysis in this book—are primarily differences in the *structure* of the correctional organizations, and only secondarily are they differences in the composition of the inmate populations. That both of these features are subject to directed changes (the former more than the latter) means that the research reported here has significant policy implications for correctional planners and administrators. In addition, it adds a new range of data and a refined mode of analysis to the extensive theoretical and empirical literature on informal inmate systems.

The deinstitutionalization of youth corrections in Massachusetts during the early 1970s provided a unique research opportunity to examine these practical, theoretical, and empirical issues. Despite a long history of research about informal inmate systems, radical innovation in penology has typically been so rare, scattered, and short-lived that systematic comparisons among widely differing correctional organizations and the inmate systems they contain has been impossible. Particularly absent from the study of inmate systems have been programs reflecting the most recent reform thrust in the field—community-based corrections. During Jerome Miller's brief tenure (October 1969 to January 1973) as commissioner of the Massachusetts Department of Youth Services (DYS), he facilitated the development, in two stages, of an unprecedented variety of correctional programs for delinquents. The opportunity to examine some of these programs allows for significant expansion of our knowledge about the nature and possibilities of organizational influence on the development of informal inmate systems.

THE POLICY IMPORTANCE OF INMATE SYSTEMS

Not everyone would agree that shaping the formation of inmate systems should be the major focus, or even a significant focus, of correctional policy. All too often in the past decade recidivism rates have served as the major criterion for judging the success or failure of correctional programs whose paramount goal has been rehabilitation; reducing recidivism rather than directing the development of inmate systems would seem to be the overriding concern of evaluators, policymakers, and administrators. One thus reads in the *New York Times* that:

> A controversial study has branded the city's multimillion-dollar criminal-rehabilitation and prison alternative programs "a failure" and has warned that these efforts, instead of reducing crime, may be adding to the problem. The report, prepared by the city's Criminal Justice Coordinating Council, disclosed that within one year of entering these programs, 41 percent of the enrolled adults and juveniles had been arrested again at least once.[4]

Robert Martinson, in his influential review of evaluations of correctional programs, asked "What works?" and concluded that nothing does because the evidence did not conclusively show lowered recidivism rates for any innovations when compared to traditional penal institutions.[5] Even such an eloquent spokesman for equity, justice, and humanity in corrections as Norval Morris could not completely sever rehabilitation and reduced recidivism from these other goals. After having proposed in some detail an experimental prison designed to be equitable, just, and humane, he concluded that "the most important test of the new institution will be the recidivism rates of its group as compared with that of the control group."[6] For the most part informal inmate subcultures and social systems have been viewed by correctional planners as relevant to their interests to the degree that they impede or contribute to the rehabilitation of inmates. Whatever their contribution to understanding or altering recidivism rates and to furthering or blocking rehabilitation, however, the study of inmate systems and attempts to influence their formation are important in their own right for both humanitarian and administrative reasons.

Thus, three important reasons continue to make the failure to shape inmate systems a problem at least as vital as (and, perhaps, related to) that of controlling recidivism, and the current feasibility of guiding inmate systems makes analysis of the means of doing so imperative.

Even those most concerned with the problem of recidivism and the possibility of rehabilitation have had to contend with informal inmate systems because they typically are thought to support resistance to meaningful participation in therapeutic programs. Under pressure from their peers and the norms of the "inmate code," prisoners frequently do not take job-training, psychotherapy, confrontation groups, or classroom education seriously, or even refuse to participate in such activities altogether. Those who do join in must either rationalize their involvement as "playing the game" in order to win parole, or else exist on the periphery of the core inmate social system. The subculturally supported resistance to treatment attempts in most prisons was immortalized in poetry on a cell wall by an anonymous California inmate:

The guard brought a duckett, on it it read—group counseling
    tomorrow.
Be their or you are dead.
The object of this meeting is as far as I can see is to squeal on each
    other.
The biggest fink goes free . . .

We are all hear together regardless of our crime.
And you can bet your cotton picking ass we're going to do some
    time.
So let's knock off this shit of talking to the man, and let him figure
It out for himself, the best way he can.[7]

The hope for effective rehabilitation programs within prisons and training schools or their alternatives rests in theory, therefore, on some degree of control over informal inmate systems. The degree of success in rehabilitation (as measured by recidivism) cannot be understood apart from comprehending the nature of the informal inmate systems that operate in correctional programs. To alter inmate systems may be to increase inmate involvement in some kinds of programs aimed at rehabilitation, but the linkage between such participation and ultimate success in "curing" criminals remains uncertain.

Not only is the linkage between the character of informal inmate systems and ultimate rates of recidivism unclear, but the data presented in the following chapters provide decisive evidence that what one considers a "good" or "bad" inmate subculture or social system must depend on the kind of rehabilitation or punishment (or other goal) intended. The conventional wisdom that the best inmate subculture is one that supports the view of prisoners as sick or in need of treatment or conversion to a new value system is thrown into doubt when looking at programs that promote or tolerate ties between inmates and community members. Clarifying the relationship between inmate systems and a variety of rehabilitation and custodial strategies should help guide future research about the relationships between individual and collective inmate responses to correctional organizations and the ultimate success of these offenders as law-abiding citizens.

Historically, many of these pressures and recurrent movements for prison reform have grown out of a highly influential tradition of concern with treating inmates humanely, a sharp contrast with the more prominent and hard-headed emphasis on effectiveness or even cost-effectiveness, which touts recidivism rates so prominently. Often infused with religious and moral zeal, this tradition has sometimes been as concerned with saving prisoners from their own sinfulness as with protecting them from the abuse of others. Philadelphia's Walnut Street Jail, an early target for Quaker reform, was described in about 1780 as "a scene or promiscuous and unrestricted intercourse, and universal riot and debauchery" among the inmates.[8] It was in order to prevent such activities—considered inimical to penitence and reformation as well as inherently evil—that prison reformers in Pennsylvania designed the "separate and silent" penitentiary to eliminate informal inmate social systems altogether by preventing any relations among prisoners.

A major force in this reform effort, the Philadelphia Society for Alleviating the Miseries of Public Prisons, founded in 1776, was primarily intended to relieve "the physical suffering of prisoners" and to reduce the severity of prison punishment.[9] Similar concerns later prompted the abandonment of the "separate and silent system" because of its deleterious effects on the mental and physical conditions of prisoners. Continued humanitarian pressures over the years still yield improvements in the minimum physical conditions of prisons and considerable moderation in the severity and arbitrariness of prison discipline. In addition, contemporary prison reformers, like their predecessors, continue to be horrified by aspects of inmate systems involving sexual assaults, murders, and alcohol and drug use. Dramatic instances of such subculturally supported activity often receive brief but intense and widespread publicity, and they have considerable emotional impact on many citizens. Prison riots, which at least in part may grow out of challenges to the informal inmate social structure brought on by attempts to change correctional policy or administration, bring prisons under public scrutiny.[10] News coverage of such aspects of inmate systems, thus, often places enormous, if short-lived, pressure on policy-makers to bring about correctional change.

Many argue that penal philosophy has now reached a point where placement in prison is viewed as punishment enough; prisons themselves are no longer expected to administer punishment to inmates.[11] As we shall see, despite the vast improvements in the quality of official treatment of prisoners, these humanitarian concerns remain relevant to inmates today both because of the inhumane consequences of inmate systems and because of the kinds of control techniques that are sometimes used to overcome these inmate systems. Control over the shape inmate systems take *can* serve—in an obviously limited way—as a liberating force for prisoners; it has the potential to allow them at least to live in training schools, prisons, or their alternatives, free from fear of one another. Some of the controls over inmate systems can also be viewed as brainwashing or psychological coercion, and may to some appear far worse than their alternatives. The tradeoffs between the terrors of the inmate systems themselves and the manipulative character of some of the organizational strategies used to counter them are among the costs and benefits to be described and assessed in the following chapters.

The long history and significant impact of humanitarian concern with the quality of inmates' lives should not be an embarrassment today to policy-makers who may be accused of coddling criminals and delinquents. Instead, it should be a legitimate and effective counter to such politically threatening accusations, particularly when viewed together with the third major reason for studying and trying to direct inmate systems.

Informal inmate systems are of acute concern to correctional practitioners because they typically make the work of correctional administration a needlessly difficult and unsuccessful task. Day-to-day correctional practices and policies probably have been swayed less over the past two hundred years by reports of high or low recidivism than they have by events reflecting or growing out of informal inmate social life. Most prison and training school administrators and their employees live in the present, combatting daily crises and trying to solve immediate problems. Measures of recidivism do not assist them at all in this struggle; they are concerned not with the criminal activities of those people who have long since departed their institutions but with the maintenance of order and security within the current population.

From the perspective of the administrator or correctional employee, informal inmate systems are extremely important because, by understanding them, one can better predict inmate behavior in response to the prison regime. Administrators act at their peril if they ignore the inmate social structure or inmate expectations when they promulgate rules, mete out discipline, or organize therapeutic work or education activities. Considerable sociological research documents the unofficial recognition of this need and the consequent corruption of official authority that results from compromises with informal inmate leaders. These bargains ultimately give officials at least a share—with some inmates—of the control of the institutions they oversee.[12]

The nature of inmate systems, therefore, exerts both indirect and direct pressure on correctional policy and practice. By influencing the utilization and perhaps the ultimate success of rehabilitation programs, by shaping the lives of prisoners and making them the focus of humanitarian concerns, and by forcing recognition and compromise from guards and wardens, informal inmate systems have enormous practical importance in prisons, training schools, and wherever else people have their freedom limited by the state.

These three reasons make the examination of inmate systems crucial and suggest that concern with their form should take a more explicit and central position in correctional policy-making and planning. That more official attention in the form of program evaluations has been paid to recidivism rates than to the characteristics of inmate systems may be a consequence of the recent primacy given to rehabilitation in American penology. But that primacy is changing, and so with it may be the attention accorded to organizing correctional facilities in order to direct the development of inmate systems.

CHANGING PRIORITIES IN THE GOALS
OF CORRECTIONS: IMPLICATIONS
FOR DIRECTING INMATE SYSTEMS

The political and philosophical context for examining the inter-
mingling of inmate systems and humanitarian goals, administrative
ease, recidivism rates, and rehabilitation has undergone a rapid and
significant change in the early 1970s that promises to have a lasting
but as yet undetermined effect on the future of correctional policy.
The increasing abandonment of rehabilitation as the central correctional goal may reduce the overriding preoccupation with recidivism
rates as an indication of correctional failure, but it may also further
mask the failure to make training schools and prisons governable and
livable. Disillusionment with rehabilitation is shared both by critics
appalled by its capacity to do evil in the name of good intention and
by those who see it softening punishment and reducing the deterrent
capacity of the criminal law. In a field where the notions of reform,
rehabilitation, and humane treatment have for so long been inextricably linked in contrast to punishment, custody, and brutality, it
is possible that wise moderation of the commitment to rehabilitation
will disarm the strong forces for humanity in their continuing
struggle with the advocates of harsh punishment. It could also bring
subsiding demands and potential for radical reorganization of institutions, which continue by and large to promote inhumane and
disorderly inmate systems.

The rehabilitation ideal became official doctrine with the adoption of the National Prison Association's Declaration of Principles
in 1870. In the 1970s, at the point of its fullest implementation, the
rehabilitative doctrine faces a rapid decline in adherents. The director
of the Federal Bureau of Prisons, Norman Carlson, for example, now
admits:

> Rehabilitation has been seen as the basic reason for incarceration, as well
> as for probation and parole. The medical model that evolved—a model that
> implied offenders were sick and could be cured of crime by a treatment
> program—was unrealistic. Rehabilitation was associated with humaneness
> and we forgot that most inmates are not sick, that we do not know the
> causes of crime, and that we have developed no sure cures.[13]

Support for replacing rehabilitation as the ultimate correctional goal
comes from prisoner's rights groups, academicians, and practitioners
of widely varied political persuasions.[14] In Maine it has received legal
sanction in a revised Criminal Code eliminating minimum-maximum

sentences, parole boards, and parole in favor of judicially determined fixed-length sentences. These radical statutory changes were justified with the conclusion that though "educational, vocational, and other programs may still be offered prisoners, . . . the realization that there is no known program that can act as a 'cure' for criminality makes it irrational to rely on program participation as some sign of rehabilitation."[15] Other states, such as California, have followed Maine's example. The rush from rehabilitation is not a fleeting event but may set the direction for adult and, perhaps, youth corrections for years to come.

This retreat has been precipitated by the convergence of a number of trends and events: accumulating evidence that recidivism rates rarely change, whatever the intensity of therapeutic endeavor; continued awareness that inmate systems even in many relatively benign settings promote resistance to treatment efforts; the growing opinion that rehabilitation softens punishment and increases crime rates; and a deluge of court cases by prisoners challenging the right of officials to hold them indefinitely or "treat" them against their wills. The fundamental assumption noted by Carlson, that rehabilitation is humane, was thrown into doubt particularly by prisoners' resistance —informally and through litigation—to attempts to treat them against their wills. But it is now very clear as well that if rehabilitation is not necessarily humane, simply being humane is not necessarily rehabilitating.

Some of the forces leading to the retreat from rehabilitation may therefore have severed once and for all two separable if not wholly independent goals. As a consequence, the pursuit of correctional reorganization with both humanitarian and management concerns as paramount may proceed at the same time that "correction"— reform, rehabilitation, and treatment—are made opportunities within, rather than *the* purpose of, penal institutions.

Whatever its contribution to the lowering of recidivism rates, however, the rehabilitation philosophy as translated into organizational practice has at times had moderate to dramatic impact on the character of informal inmate systems in institutions. The comparative research of Street, Vinter, and Perrow, Berk, Cline, and Feld, among others, and the case studies of McCorkle, Elias, and Bixby, Empey and his colleagues, Studt, Goldenberg, and others have described or measured treatment or rehabilitation philosophy and practice and found it associated with changes in the typical informal inmate system, including reduced hostilities between inmates and staff and among inmates.[16] These findings make clear the variability and mutability of inmate systems, a sharp contrast to the earlier conclusion of Sykes and Messinger: "Despite the number and diversity of prison populations, observers of such groups have reported only one strikingly pervasive value system.[17]

Prompted by the rehabilitationist philosophy, recent modest innovations in correctional organization thus have sporadically shown effects on the organization and tenor of inmate life. A decline in the rehabilitationist spirit and concomitant increases in punitiveness could therefore slow the further development of such innovative programs unless they can be justified on independent humanitarian and management grounds.

INMATE SYSTEMS AND
SOCIOLOGICAL THEORY

Dominating this book is a practical concern with how and with what consequences correctional organizations can be altered to shape the emergence of inmate systems. The examination of these practical issues, however, is grounded in sociological theory and research about the nature and causes of inmate systems, about formal organizations, and, to a lesser extent, about delinquent subcultures. At the same time that this study can contribute to resolving an important policy issue, it may also thus add to the solution of a theoretical problem that has concerned sociologists for over twenty years. The uniqueness of the comparative data from the twenty-three programs examined here provides an unparalleled opportunity to help resolve this argument about the origins of inmate systems. In brief, the debate is between those who claim that inmate systems are indigenous to the total institutions where they flourish—that inmates create them as collective solutions to the pains of imprisonment that jeopardize their sense of self[18]—and those who argue instead that inmate systems represent little more than an extension into the institutions of the criminal and lower social class values, beliefs, and roles that prisoners had learned prior to their imprisonment.[19]

That sociologists should find it worth asking why so much hostility and "evil conduct" occurred in prison was probably a product of the full flowering in the 1950s and 1960s of the rehabilitation philosophy. Inmate hostility toward guards and resistance to their demands probably was no surprise to early jailors. It was entirely comprehensible that people who were perceived as vicious criminals, kept against their wills in cold, damp, and foul prisons and subjected to brutal abuse, would resent and threaten their captors and attempt to make their own lives more tolerable by violating rules. Only with the somewhat accelerated efforts in recent years to make living conditions more humane and "to do good" for inmates by "treating" and "helping" them could one be even moderately surprised by recalcitrance of prisoners. But sociologists became curious, and when Sykes and Messinger in 1960 pointed out the need "to know why inmate society is there," they launched a theoretical debate about inmate systems that continues unabated.[20]

When I began my research I was strongly influenced by Sykes and Messinger's functional theory, which linked the privations imposed on prisoners with their collective responses to the prison or training school regime. Institutions that took away people's liberty, goods and services, autonomy, heterosexual relationships, and personal security generated the value systems and roles which comprised inmate systems and which inmates called upon to compensate for their losses. Giallombardo's reasoning paralleled my own implicit expectations as I began my research:

> The inmate informal social system can be eliminated when the goals of the institution are modified to mitigate the deprivation of imprisonment. . . .
> If we reduce the deprivations, inmate society will be more congenial to treatment efforts.[21]

At the start of my field work in 1973 I expected to find a relatively benign set of inmate systems in what was essentially a rehabilitation-oriented system. Although I anticipated pockets of punitive and custodial resistance to exist, I hypothesized that the generally increased freedom of community programs should eliminate the needs informal inmate systems filled and, thus, the systems themselves.

My field experience challenged by reliance on the functionalist explanation: I was struck particularly by the comparison of two programs for adolescent boys which differed significantly in the freedom accorded residents, although both were considerably freer than conventional training schools or prisons. In the more closed institution, boys were confined by locked doors and screened windows to one floor of a building; additionally, during the waking hours they were frequently locked in one or two large indoor recreation rooms; their outdoor recreation area was surrounded by a high fence topped with barbed wire. Many of the boys could on occasion, however, go out on leaves of varying lengths, visits home, or to jobs. In the more open setting, the boys had almost full run of the building and grounds and could, usually with perfunctory permission, go home or elsewhere in the community. In both settings the boys wore their own clothing, could keep books, records, and stereo sets in their rooms; in both they were on a relaxed first-name basis with most staff members. Nevertheless, despite the differences in the two programs and despite their differences from traditional training school cottages where privations were generally much greater, the inmate systems were strikingly alike and generally quite similar to those in the traditional cottages. It seemed to me that many of the common characteristics of inmate systems in these programs derived from the similar age, sex, and social class backgrounds of their residents.

A little later, when I began actually to count objective privations in the programs under study, one of the programs that displayed the most privation—censorship of mail, general refusal of contact with relatives and friends, loss of privacy and restriction of possessions, public ceremonies of humiliation, heavily supervised and regimented days—had no distinct informal inmate system. Instead, in this therapeutic community youths were integrated into the official organizational structure, and they accepted with only rare challenge the organizationally imposed culture. What were viewed with resentment as privations in other settings were here accepted and even endorsed by the youths. Something appeared to be occurring that was inadequately accounted for by what I understood the functional theory of Sykes and Messinger to mean.

A reexamination was in order. First, the common assumption that Sykes and Messinger's approach implies that inmate systems have their origins indigenous to the prison or training school is a misleading interpretation of their theory in particular and of functional theories in general. In closing their seminal article, Sykes and Messinger asked whether "the values of prisoners represent something created *de novo*, or a selection and intensification of values flourishing in certain segments of the free society?"[22] Their point was not that the features of inmate systems are necessarily unique to prison settings; rather their theory suggested that the continued presence of similar inmate value systems in similar prison settings can, in part, be understood in terms of the functions these systems serve for inmates given the conditions they are required to endure.

In essence, therefore, there is no real conflict between Sykes and Messinger's theory and that of Irwin and Cressey, who argued that informal inmate systems are composed in large part of norms, values, and roles carried into training schools and prisons from the larger society. Inmate systems should thus vary with the composition of the inmate population on central variables such as sex, social class, and criminal experience and orientation, because these variables broadly predict differences in the kinds of experience inmates bring with them. It is these shared backgrounds that will then guide inmate adaptations to almost unvarying conditions of imprisonment.

When viewed in this light, the purportedly competing theories of

Sykes and Messinger and of Irwin and Cressey together call attention
to the fact that inmate systems are responses and adaptations to the
particular conditions of incarceration that prisoners encounter, and
are based on guidelines derived from shared, imported values, beliefs,
perceptions, and roles. Certainly inmates experience in varying
degrees the pains of imprisonment. There are, however, differences
between the objective conditions of imprisonment and inmate perceptions of them. In fact, the ways in which the conditions of imprisonment are perceived is a function of the inmates' experiences,
beliefs, and values; inmate subcultures define some of the conditions
of incarceration as deprivations, just as much as these subcultures
are responses to prison hardships.

Sykes and Messinger's great contribution lies in their explication
of the social psychological processes involved in the development
and maintenance of inmate systems, while Irwin and Cressey's lies
in their identification of some of the sources from which inmates will
draw in adapting to correctional organizations. But these two theories
—either separately or integrated—are not adequate explanations of
variations in inmate systems. The functionalist view tends to separate
inadequately the dependent variables (inmate subculture and perceptions) from independent variables (sense of deprivation as perceived by inmates); and the importation view falls short of explaining
why particular responses and values are selected from the vast repertoire of learned behavior that inmates carry into training schools and
prisons with them, and may imply less mutability of inmate response
than is actually the case.

One way of overcoming the inadequacies of these theories, while
at the same time using their insights, is to look directly at the structure and practice of correctional organizations to see how they reward
or punish inmates and create or foreclose opportunities for them.
These organizational characteristics affect the initial selection and
the ultimate utility and lifespan of the imported adaptations. One can
thus attempt to identify the objective characteristics of those settings
to which inmates must respond, as well as the measurable traits of
inmate populations that indicate shared experiences or values relevant
to adapting to a correctional institution. These two sets of variables—
several dimensions of organizational structure and practice and
aggregate features of the inmate populations—serve as the independent variables in this study. That these features are enormously and
uniquely variable is one of the major hallmarks of the deinstitutionalized system of youth corrections created in Massachusetts in the
early 1970s. That variety makes the following analysis possible.

An overview of the diversity of correctional organizations created by the two-stage revolution in youth corrections initiated by Jerome Miller in Massachusetts in thus the major focus of Chapter 1. After briefly tracing the history of Miller's reform efforts, it describes those programs of our study that emerged first in the "reformed" training schools, and then later in communities across the state. The methods of gathering and analyzing data about the twenty-three organizations and their staff members and youthful participants are also described. Description turns to analysis in this first chapter in an explanation of the inadequacy for this study of the usual custom of typing organizations by their goals; instead, key analytic dimensions of correctional organization and practice are described. Finally, two of the most unique characteristics of Miller's revolutionary closing of the training schools are examined in detail: (1) the diversity of population composition; and (2) the degree of contact allowed between young inmates and members of the free community. It is this latter organizational dimension, in part, that makes the Massachusetts DYS a community-based correctional system.

Chapters 2, 3, and 4 are divided into analyses of what emerged as rather distinct and separable elements of inmate systems. As noted earlier, the data make clear that the notion of a "good" or a "bad" inmate system is far too simple to correspond to the variety of correctional organizations, goals, and theories. Just as important, the data make it evident that inmate systems are not monolithic entities. Inmate perceptions of staff members are quite distinct, for example, from other values and beliefs prisoners may hold; variations among programs in inmate relations with staff members are the focus of analysis in Chapter 2, while differences in the remaining elements of inmate subcultures are the object of study in Chapter 3. Finally, differences in the structure of relationships among youths and their perceptions of one another are analyzed in the first part of Chapter 4, while variations in patterns of troublesome behavior—fighting, drug use, and running away—are explained in the last half of that chapter.

In the process of directing the development of inmate systems, one may alter some of these elements without touching others. Because the different dimensions of correctional organization weigh differently on the diverse aspects of inmate systems, they are introduced as they become relevant to the analysis. Having already described inmate population characteristics and the community contact dimension in Chapter 1, the equality dimension is discussed in Chapter 2 and the participation and supervision dimensions are covered in Chapter 3.

At the close of each of these three major data-analysis chapters, the implications of the findings for sociological theories about inmate systems are summed up in a cumulative fashion. These summaries reinforce and build on the theoretical groundwork; they are more clearly directed to an audience of scholars interested in the theoretical and empirical issues examined in this book. These summaries also begin assessing the implications of the data for correctional policy, a topic addressed more fully in Chapter 5. Each organizational dimension is examined separately (including the different aspects of population composition), and suggestions are presented for the implications each has for directing the nature of inmate systems in particular programs and, more tentatively, for the achievement of other correctional goals in these organizations.

A strong argument is made for the creation of more egalitarian correctional organizations, and then a fork in the policy road is pointed out: one direction leads to high levels of community contact, and the other runs to high levels of participation or supervision. Some questions are also raised about the applicability of these varying modes of correctional organization to different kinds of inmate populations, and about the implications of the data for the design of whole correctional systems.

Faced with the high probability of the continued use of imprisonment as a punishment in the United States, what organizational forms might denial of freedom take? The answers that conclude this book would do much, I believe, to make the lives of inmates better, the work of officials easier and more rewarding, and the task and technique of corrections more consistent with democratic and humanitarian principles.

NOTES

1. The speed at which these prison conditions are disappearing is glacial, at best. As Gordon Hawkins in *The Prison: Policy and Practice* (Chicago: University of Chicago Press, 1976), pp. 42-43, notes, about half the people in maximum-security prisons in the United States are housed in edifices built before 1900. The overcrowding of current outdated facilities suggests, however, the opportunity for radical and rapid change; new facilities are needed (to *replace*, not supplement, those now in use). These might well be designed, for example, in ways to foster the kinds of organizational innovations described in this book.

For descriptions of inmate subcultures and staff-inmate relationships, see for example, Donald Clemmer, *The Prison Community* (New York: Holt, Rinehart, and Winston, 1940); Gresham Sykes, *The Society of Captives: A Study of a Maximum Security Institution* (Princeton, N.J.: Princeton University Press, 1958); Gresham Sykes and Sheldon Messinger, "The Inmate Social System," in *Theoretical Studies in Social Organization of the Prison*, Richard Cloward, et al. (New York: Social Science Research Council, 1960), pp. 5-19; Sethard Fisher, "Social Organization in a Correctional Community," *Pacific Sociological Review* 4 (Fall 1961): 87-93; Howard Polsky, *Cottage Six—The Social System of Delinquent Boys in Residential Treatment* (New York: Wiley, 1966); Rose Giallombardo, *The Social World of Imprisoned Girls: A Comparative Study of Institutions for Juvenile Delinquents* (New York: Wiley, 1974).

2. See, for example, Donald Cressey, "Limitations on Organization of Treatment in the Modern Prison," in *Theoretical Studies in Social Organization of the Prison*, Richard Cloward et al. (New York: Social Science Research Council, 1960), pp. 78-110, and Lloyd E. Ohlin, "Correctional Strategies in Conflict," *Proceedings of the American Philosophical Society* 118 (June 1974): 248-53.

3. Throughout this book I shall use the general term "inmate system" to refer to subcultures, social structures, and behavior patterns of inmates—youths in correctional settings.

4. Selwyn Raab, "City Prison Reform Plan Called Failure," *New York Times*, August 18, 1975, p. 1.

5. Robert Martinson, "What Works?—Questions and Answers about Prison Reform," *The Public Interest* 35 (Spring 1974): 22-54.

6. Norval Morris, *The Future of Imprisonment* (Chicago: University of Chicago Press, 1974), p. 121.

7. Quoted by Gene Kassebaum, David Ward, and Daniel Wilner in *Prison Treatment and Parole Survival: An Empirical Assessment* (New York: Wiley, 1971), pp. v-vi.

8. F.C. Gray, *Prison Discipline in America*, quoted in Edwin Sutherland and Donald Cressey, *Criminology*, 8th ed. (Philadelphia: Lippincott, 1970), p. 483.

9. Sutherland and Cressey, *Criminology*, p. 484.

10. Richard Wilsnack, "Explaining Collective Violence in Prisons: Problems and Possibilities," in *Prison Violence*, ed. Albert Cohen, George Cole, and Robert Bailey (Lexington, Mass.: D.C. Heath, 1976), pp. 61-74.

11. Humanitarian values have generally seemed to carry more weight than punitive goals in the long-term drift of penal policy. Nevertheless, punitive views cannot be ignored, for they set real, though changing, limits on the degree of possible humanitarian reform.

12. See, in particular, Sykes, *Society of Captives*.

13. Norman Carlson, "A More Balanced Correctional Philosophy," *FBI Law Enforcement Bulletin* 46 (January 1977): 23.

14. See, for example, the publications of the National Federal Prisoner Rights Project, Leavenworth, Kansas. Recent popular and scholarly accounts arguing somewhat similar points include: American Friends Service Committee, *Struggle for Justice* (New York: Hill and Wang, 1971); Morris, *Future of Imprisonment*; Hawkins, *The Prison*; David Fogel, ". . . We Are the Living Proof . . .": *The Justice Model for Corrections* (Cincinnati: Anderson, 1975); Ernest Van den Haag, *Punishing Criminals: Concerning a Very Old and Painful Question* (New York: Basic Books, 1975).

15. Maine Criminal Law Revision Commission, "Introduction, Participants, Authorization, Table of Contents, to Accompany Proposed Maine Criminal

Code" (Augusta, Maine Legislative Document No. 314 [107th week], 1975), p. 5.

16. For examples of the comparative research, see David Street, Robert Vinter, and Charles Perrow, *Organization for Treatment: A Comparative Study of Institutions for Delinquents* (New York: Free Press, 1966); Hugh Cline, "The Determinants of Normative Patterns in Correctional Institutions," *Scandinavian Studies in Criminology*, Vol. 2, ed. Nils Christie (London: Tavistock, 1968), pp. 173-84; Richard Berk, "Organizational Goals and Inmate Organization," *American Journal of Sociology* 71 (March 1966): 522-34; Barry Feld, *Neutralizing Inmate Violence: Juvenile Offenders in Institutions* (Cambridge, Mass.: Ballinger, 1977) (in this series).

For examples of case studies, see Lloyd McCorkle, Albert Elias, and F. Lovell Bixby, *The Highfields Story: An Experimental Treatment Project for Youthful Offenders* (New York: Holt, 1958); Lamar Empey and Maynard Erickson, *The Provo Experiment: Evaluating Community Control of Delinquency* (Lexington, Mass.: D.C. Heath, 1972); Lamar Empey and Stephen Lubeck, *The Silverlake Experiment: Testing Delinquency Theory and Community Intervention* (Chicago: Aldine, 1971); Elliot Studt, Sheldon Messinger, and Thomas Wilson, *C-Unit: Search for Community in Prison* (New York: Russell Sage, 1968).

For a thorough review and re-analysis of the empirical research in this field, see Craig McEwen, "Subculture, Social Structure, and Behavior in Community-Based Correctional Settings: A Comparative Analysis of Thirteen Programs for Juveniles," unpublished Ph.D. dissertation, Harvard University, 1975.

17. Sykes and Messinger, "Inmate Social System," p. 5.

18. This theory is attributed to Sykes and Messinger, "Inmate Social System." See also Sykes, *Society of Captives;* Sheldon Messinger, "Issues in the Study of the Social System of Prison Inmates," *Issues in Criminology* 4 (Fall 1969): 133-44. Erving Goffman, among others, is also often included in this camp—see *Asylums: Essays on the Social Situation of Mental Patients and Other Inmates* (Garden City, N.Y.: Anchor Books, 1961).

19. John Irwin and Donald Cressey, "Thieves, Convicts and the Inmate Culture," in *The Other Side: Perspectives on Deviance*, ed. Howard Becker (New York: Free Press, 1964), pp. 225-45, get credit for the importation theory.

20. Sykes and Messinger, "Inmate Social System," p. 12.

For some of the most recent research that tests the importation and functional theories, see, for example, Ronald Akers, Norman Hayner, and Werner Gruninger, "Homosexual and Drug Behavior in Prison: A Test of the Functional and Importation Models of the Inmate System," *Social Problems* 21 (1974): 412-22; and Desmond Ellis, Harold Grasmick, and Bernard Gilman, "Violence in Prisons: A Sociological Analysis," *American Journal of Sociology* 80 (July 1974): 16-43.

21. Giallombardo, *Social World of Imprisoned Girls*, p. 12.

22. Sykes and Messinger, "Inmate Social System," p. 17.

※ *Chapter 1*

Taking Corrections to the Community

The revolution in youth corrections in Massachusetts led by Commissioner Jerome Miller was not fundamentally an expression of a radical new vision of correctional goals; rather, it was an affirmation of the twin themes of rehabilitation and humanity that had been integrated into the ideology of progressive correctional officials across the country by 1970. By giving these common themes the highest priority and by pressing the Department of Youth Services (DYS) to achieve them, Miller wrought sweeping changes in the structure and practice of youth corrections in Massachusetts. This chapter focuses on a descriptive overview of these reforms, and introduces an analytic framework for assessing the differing impacts they had on the inmate systems of delinquent youths.

Since deinstitutionalization and the development of community-based corrections have been generally viewed as the most significant of the DYS reforms, this chapter also takes up in detail the analytic dimension most closely related to this perspective—community contact, the integration in practice of community and corrections in the programs under study. Later chapters will describe in detail the three remaining dimensions of organizational variation.

The vastly increased variety in the composition of inmate populations under the new DYS policy of dispersal of youths and diversification of programs is important to an understanding of inmate systems. This chapter will also introduce, therefore, a series of variables that gauge this variation. To provide a background for this description and the initial analysis of program variation, the recent changes in Massachusetts youth corrections will be reviewed, and then the nature of the research reported in this study will be discussed.

THE RESEARCH SETTING: A BRIEF HISTORY OF DYS REFORMS

Soon after his arrival in 1969 as the new commissioner of the Department of Youth Services, Jerome Miller started translating his broad mandate for reform into more concrete goals and into specific directives to the various staffs of the much-criticized training schools. As commissioner he announced that he planned to humanize the treatment of offenders and to build therapeutic communities within the existing institutional facilities. To implement these goals, Miller issued a series of edicts to staff members of the institutions: youths were permitted to wear their hair as they chose and to wear their own clothing rather than institutional garb. He forbade the practice of marching in silent formation and prohibited the use of corporal punishment and "strip cells." Miller even allowed eligible youths to carry their own cigarettes rather than be forced to receive them as rewards from staff members. All of these directives struck heavily at the sense of authority jealously guarded by many institutional staff members; a large proportion of these men and women protested and resisted the changes.

Miller encountered similar resistance to his attempts to develop a new therapeutic orientation within the institutions. Impressed by the model of a therapeutic community developed by Maxwell Jones, Miller introduced institutional staff to the concept in a series of training sessions and then encouraged them to develop such communities within the institutional cottages, each of which was to be run with considerable autonomy. Although some of the younger staff members in particular were enthusiastic about these new plans, which called for more democratic relationships between staff members and youths, many DYS employees resisted out of discomfort, uncertainty, or ideological disagreement. Implementing the steps leading to the organization of therapeutic communities thus was as uneven as was obedience to Miller's other orders.

After about a year and a half of experience with this resistance and faced with increasing dissension and declining morale on the part of staff, Miller judged that these unevenly implemented reform efforts had failed to meet his hopes for a humane and effective system of rehabilitation. He then moved abruptly to close the training schools altogether and to encourage simultaneously the development of a network of community-based programs, state-funded but run largely by private groups.

The task of deinstitutionalization was easy enough, but certainly controversial; over a number of months Miller simply moved the youths out of training schools. He left some staff behind to care for the empty buildings, placed others in an expanded but decentralized (into seven regions) DYS bureaucracy, and encouraged some to become staff members of the privately run facilities that were opening their doors to DYS youths under contract with the state. This rapid and nearly spontaneous deinstitutionalization was not universally popular. Miller's authority to initiate these changes was questioned, as was his wisdom in closing the old institutions. Administrative difficulties soon emerged as well. Persistent problems arose in the location, creation, evaluation, and payment of the scores of facilities providing services, in the process of placing youths in these diverse places, and in the administration of such a decentralized system.

The extent of the changes that emerged from Miller's revolution can be grasped by a brief look at the juvenile correctional system in Massachusetts before and after deinstitutionalization. In 1971 a tour of programs for delinquents in Massachusetts would still have been relatively simple. Youths were housed in four short-term detention centers, three training schools, and in a small program at Topsfield, a complex that had once been a novitiate. The concentration of facilities was a misleading indicator of the degree of variation in programming, however, for by that summer a number of training school cottages—each housing from twenty to forty boys or girls—had been made autonomous and were no longer integrated into the daily regimen of the larger institutions. In addition, the small coeducational program at Topsfield had just begun. Nevertheless, the institutional location of these varied cottages and programs made for similar visual impressions. Two-story buildings with dormitories or individual rooms upstairs, living area downstairs, and lockers in the basement (in the boys' cottages only) served, with variations, as the training school cottages. Other buildings on the grounds housed the schools, kitchens, administrative offices, and the vocational trades shops. The young residents of these facilities were all under the direction of the Department of Youth Services (as adjudicated delinquents or as juveniles awaiting a court hearing).

By 1973 the logistics of visiting programs for juvenile delinquents in Massachusetts had become vastly more complex because of the decentralization of service. The physical settings of the nearly two hundred programs utilized by DYS for placement reflected the enormous diversity of programming available. A ranch-style house in a suburb, one floor of a YMCA building, sections of one of the still-used detention centers, a large room in a commercial building on a busy urban street, a sprawling modern brick complex in a quiet rural setting, a large frame house in a declining urban neighborhood, and the cars of the staff members (in a nonresidential program) were among the varied settings for the thirteen community-based programs we studied in 1973. The number of youths in these programs ranged from eight to about seventy, and the populations were extremely varied in composition. Five of the thirteen programs were coeducational, and four of the thirteen had large percentages of residents who were not officially delinquent but had been referred by another state agency (typically the Department of Social Services) or were privately supported.[a] Generally, this range in size and composition mirrored the total range of programs used by DYS in 1973 to handle groups of young people.[1]

COLLECTING THE DATA

Both the process and product of the revolution in youth corrections in Massachusetts created extraordinary possibilities for policy-relevant social research. Although the ultimate course of this revolution was uncharted when Miller arrived in Massachusetts in 1969, the Center for Criminal Justice at Harvard Law School began what became a massive study of nearly all facets of the reform process. The development of this far-reaching research project and its many segments are described in the Preface. The subculture studies reported together here were important elements of that project and were intended to yield intensive qualitative as well as quantitative data about the day-to-day operation of a limited number of programs and the experiences of youths in them. As Ohlin noted, these studies of the nature of inmate subculture were to help gauge "the penetration and impact of the reform measures" Miller was promoting.[2]

The research for this subculture study was designed to collect comparable sets of data through intensive participant observation and questioning in ten training school cottages during the early stages of reform (summer 1971) and later in another small sample of fully reformed (as it turned out, wholly new) programs in the summer of 1973.

Feld and co-workers undertook the first study in ten cottages

---

[a]See the Appendix for more detailed descriptions of the thirteen community-based programs in our sample, and Feld, *Neutralizing Inmate Violence* (in this series) for detailed portraits of the ten training school cottages.

(from three institutions) chosen to reflect the broad range of imple- mentation of the new guidelines issued by Miller. Five field workers spent five weeks each in two different programs as participant ob- servers. At the end of each day they recorded the day's events as they remembered or had noted them down at the time. Rather than preparing free narratives, the field workers reported their observations on precoded forms that identified particular categories of interest, such as actions of youth leaders, troublesome incidents, staff-inmate relations, population changes, argot, and so on. Nearly two thousand pages of field notes resulted from the two studies. In addition, youths and staff members completed lengthy questionnaires and were interviewed briefly.

In the summer of 1973 five new field workers and I made up the second research team, observing thirteen new programs.[3] These pro- grams were selected on the basis of information available from DYS and from the first-hand experience of others in the Harvard research project. In choosing a sample we tried to include as wide a range as possible of correctional strategies, population mixes, and locations. We excluded programs that contained fewer than five youths from DYS, had little or no contact between members, or specialized in handling the problems of children eleven years or under. We followed essentially the same procedures as did Feld, and used modified ver- sions of data-collection instruments he had adopted. Changes in some of the questionnaire items and observational categories reflected, for example, the new possibilities for contact between youths and com- munity members.

Administrators, youths, and staff members were extremely coop- erative. We generally explained ourselves as people helping to write a book about "kids in trouble," and that role allowed us to bridge the gulf that sometimes existed between youths and staff members. Both groups tested us, and most of us had awkward moments when youths pressed us to intervene on their behalf with staff, or when staff mem- bers queried us about the behavior or whereabouts of the youths.

In several programs, some youths remained suspicious, particularly a few of the black residents who, for example, refused to fill out questionnaires or to be interviewed by the white field workers. Never was the resistance so widespread, however, as to bias the data seri- ously. Collecting both questionnaire and observational data helped both to overcome the general methodological limitation of either method and to compensate for particular problems in the collection of one kind of data or the other. That the two kinds of data drew strikingly similar pictures of youth responses to their correctional organizations makes me confident that the limited flaws in data collection in no way misdirect the analysis and interpretation. The use of direct field observation proved to be particularly vital in this organizational analysis because it allowed direct measurement of organizational structure and practice, which is impossible through interviews or questionnaires alone.[4]

PROGRAM PATTERNS: A DESCRIPTIVE OVERVIEW

Early in our research we had to establish whether the community programs as a group were substantially different from the cottages in the reformed training schools. The only clear contrast was in the level of contact between community members and youths, but a number of so-called community programs were as isolated from their surroundings as were virtually all the training school cottages. In fact there was at least moderate variation along each of the analytic dimensions—to be described in the following section—among programs located in both the training school and community settings.

Rather than clustering together as community-based *versus* training school, therefore, the programs fall generally into three different but not very distinct groups based on some of their scores on the analytic dimensions: (1) institutional programs; (2) group-process programs (therapeutic communities, concept houses, guided-group interaction programs); and (3) open-community programs. A description of these clusters—rather than of each program separately—should serve to orient the reader more fully to the correctional world we are about to enter (also see Appendix).

Of the programs we observed, twelve can be loosely described as institutional in character. They were almost all housed in imposing edifices, and the residents were integrated into a diverse routine of activities designed and directed by a highly differentiated staff of professionals and nonprofessionals. Although this broad description would seem to encompass all of the ten training school cottages studied in 1971, it in fact includes only the six that had not become almost autonomous therapeutic units under Miller's reform pressure. Five of these six—Cottage 8, Westview, and Elms for boys, and Putnam and Clara Barton for girls—were fully integrated into the daily routine of the larger institutions. Although by 1971 the trade and educational programs and the counseling program were attenuated by the changing focus of the Miller administration, some activities in each of these areas took place in addition to summer recreation in each of the institutional cottages.

Thus the twenty-five to forty-five residents of these five cottages engaged in daily routines involving several hours in the morning or afternoon at work in the laundry or the kitchen or at the remedial education courses (the schools were out of session during the summer) that were run outside the cottages themselves. For example, Westview furnished the kitchen crew for the Lyman School, and the residents of this cottage were divided into two shifts to prepare the three meals, serve them, and clean up after them. Youths spent much of their free time talking, watching television, reading comics, or playing basketball or softball outside in the recreation area. A few of these activities, along with rare visits to a drive-in movie or some other outing, were organized by staff members.

The boys slept in second-floor dormitories containing about twenty-five beds and overlooked by a guard-post; they kept their belongings in individual lockers in the basements of the cottages. With informal staff escort, they walked (no longer marched) to a separate dining facility for their three meals and were usually delivered a small snack in the evenings. By contrast, the girls were all locked into their small single rooms at night, provided with buckets for emergencies. Although they could mix with residents of other cottages during the daily range of institutional activities, the girls ate their meals inside their own cottages.

Cottage 8, Westview, and Elms were staffed by several sets of cottage parents, couples usually in their fifties. They were joined by a counselor, and their work was supplemented as in the girls' institution by instructors in the trades, by teachers, and by a miscellany of other personnel. While the boys in the cottages could have "mothers," the girls were prohibited "fathers"; the staff at Putnam and Clara Barton were all women and again predominantly middle-aged.

Cottage 9, the punishment cottage at the Shirley Industrial School for Boys, was the sixth of the traditional institutional units in the training schools. Although its residents were not at all integrated into the daily life of the school, the cottage itself was an integral part of the institutional regime, serving as the specialized discipline unit. Boys who had run away or fought too often (or fought with the wrong people) were sent there for periods of one to three weeks or sometimes longer, and there they stayed with no outside contact except some outdated magazines and with the hope that their television would be fixed. Staffed by strong men only, the cottage itself was reinforced with wire mesh screens on windows, locked doors, and backed by a fenced-in (but never used) recreation yard. The boys in Cottage 9 had no program, but sat around all day, interrupted only by the three meals brought in to their dining room and by morning and afternoon "hopper calls" to the basement toilets.

The community-based, institutional programs offer a much greater diversity of style, location, routine, staffing and program than the six traditional cottages.[b] Regiment and Shelter, like Cottage 9, were part of a larger system for short-term custody, but their function was to detain their charges pending a hearing or disposition. Regiment held up to twenty-one boys, and Shelter up to seven girls. A single floor of a recreation building in a small city housed the boys at Regiment in small single rooms, and a large urban row house served the girls.

In Regiment, the bulk of the program rested on about seventeen young men who worked in alternating shifts keeping the boys active in a wide range of recreational activities both inside and outside the building.[5] All boys were required to participate in these activities and were lined up, counted off, and marched to and from their games and from their meals, which were served in one section of a public cafeteria downstairs. At Shelter, in contrast, the girls had much free time to sleep, talk, crochet, or listen to records while the four professional staff members devoted their efforts to working on the girls' court cases and health and family problems and locating placements for those girls who were ultimately committed to DYS.

Warning, Reward, Mother, and Fatigue were closer than these two detention centers to being community versions of the traditional training school cottages. All four were located in imposing brick buildings, which added to their institutional character, and all had accredited schools, professional social workers, and recreation specialists who claimed portions of each youth's day.

At Fatigue, a decaying building housed a summer population of only twenty-five boys who were attended to by a young staff of six male child-care workers, four teachers (three of them women), a male social worker, an administrator, and a cook. Together they tried to exhaust their charges with activities. The boys spent the morning hours in school and the afternoon and evenings in recreation, including frequent long trips to beaches for boating, swimming, and picnics. Although officially requiring staff approval, the boys were almost completely free to come and go as they pleased, and many took the opportunity to explore the city, go to stores, visit friends, and occasionally, visit families. Most of the boys there had no official record of delinquency but were referred there by social welfare agencies as children needing long-term residential care because of family problems.

[b]Although the official names of the training school cottages have been retained, the thirteen programs of the 1973 research have all been given fictitious titles as agreed in arranging for the observations with program directors. The names of youths and staff members in all excerpts from field notes have, of course, been changed.

By contrast, Warning was a secure setting for boys, enclosed behind the locked doors and screened windows of one of the remaining DYS institutions—a detention center. All its thirty-five or so residents had been committed to DYS by the courts. Although a recreation specialist, teacher, social worker, and court liaison workers were all kept busy, the major chores of supervision and counseling went to the twenty or so men—many of whom were ex-offenders—who divided the three shifts. Each day some residents were out on escorted or unescorted furloughs, in court, or in one of the educational or recreational activities, but large numbers remained to congregate for hours at a time around the color TV and the pool table, whiling away the hot summer hours.

Reward housed about sixty girls, and Mother held about twenty-seven. In both places, most of the referrals came from social work agencies.[6] Both programs had their array of social worker, teachers, and recreational leaders during the day; in addition, Mother had fourteen house mothers who split three shifts in three living units, while at Reward each living unit of about twelve girls had one nun as the permanent house mother.[7] The activities at Reward were highly structured, and mixed the girls from the separate units during mealtime and in a summer program of academic, recreational, and beauty classes, segregating them in their individual units most evenings. Life at Mother was more unstructured: recreational activities were planned sporadically, and much time during the day and evening was taken up with television, conversations, and individual activities.

In contrast to these diverse institutional programs, eight of the twenty-three programs used group-treatment techniques, and their programs centered generally around these activities. Commissioner Miller provided the first impetus toward the emergence of such programs when he brought Maxwell Jones, the originator of the therapeutic community concept, to Massachusetts for several training sessions with training school staff members. Implementation of the model varied considerably, however, within the training schools, and only four of the programs studied in 1971—"I Belong," Topsfield, Shirley, and Sunset—could be said to have developed something akin to a therapeutic community. Even among these programs, variation was enormous; Sunset cottage, for example, had eliminated its once daily small-group sessions and held community-meetings only sporadically due to staff shortages during the summer of observation. Shirley, "I Belong," and Topsfield, in contrast, held one or more group sessions each day.

In 1973 a number of privately sponsored programs were also using variations on the therapeutic community model. Of the programs we studied in 1973, Primal, Confront, Group, and Open House all employed group therapy sessions and community meetings and tried quite explicitly, like their training school counterparts, to influence the shape of informal inmate systems so that peer pressure would work in the direction of staff-supported treatment goals. These four programs used techniques that varied from intensive group confrontation sessions at the two concept houses—Primal and Confront—to much quieter and milder guided-group interaction and positive peer culture sessions at Group and Open House.[8] While group sessions were at least an everyday affair at the first three, they were much more sporadic at Open House, whose residents spent considerable time away from the program in the outside community.

Most staff members in these eight programs entered into these group meetings—attacking, questioning, cajoling, and occasionally taking criticism. Except at Open House and Sunset, the programs actually revolved around these community or small-group sessions. In the group-treatment programs, staff members tended to be younger, the rules more relaxed, and the activities more limited in scope and self-contained than in the programs in the institutional cluster. Housing arrangements and daily routines varied so immensely as to defy brief description. Some youths lived in cottages identical to Elms or Cottage 8, others in suburban ranch houses; some had single rooms, while others were crowded into boys' and girls' dormitories. Program populations also varied in size from the eight at "I Belong" to seventy at Primal, and from an all-male composition (Sunset, Shirley, "I Belong," and Group) to coeducational in the remaining programs.

Finally, three programs represented the most distinctive products of the deinstitutionalization process set in motion by Miller's administration. These were Drop-in, Pick-up, and Pair. The first two were nonresidential programs that brought as many as twenty-five boys and girls (Drop-in) and about fifteen boys (Pick-up) together for ten to fifteen hours a week in a variety of group recreational activities arranged by the six men who staffed Pick-up and the two men and two women who worked at Drop-in. Trips to the beach, work on putting together bicycles, boat excursions, or visits to concerts all provided a context in which informal individual counseling could take place. Staff in both programs also intervened with an individual youth's parents, teachers, or with court officials.

Pair was also open to the outside community, but in a different way since it was a residential program for eight to twelve youths, evenly divided between boys and girls. Each resident was paired off with a college student counselor of the same sex with whom he or she was expected to spend considerable time. Living together in a vacant fraternity house during the summer, the participants spent much time off on their own and in various combinations. Open House, described above as one of the group-treatment programs, also allowed its residents almost completely free access to the small city in which it was located.

ANALYZING CORRECTIONAL
ORGANIZATIONS: FROM
GOALS TO STRUCTURE
AND PRACTICE

The field experience of this research project and its mass of qualitative and quantitative data made it clear that the two prominent theories of inmate systems were by themselves inadequate for analyzing the variation in subcultures, organizations, and inmate populations that characterized the twenty-three programs of this study. Another theoretical perspective—drawn from the sociological study of formal organizations as well as an occasional piece in the literature of corrections—opened the way, however, to a more fruitful approach.

Broadly speaking, this theoretical perspective focuses on the manner in which the opportunities and rewards and the constraints and punishments in organizations influence the kinds of adaptations that members (here, inmates in particular) make to the organizations. Cloward, and to some degree McCleery, thus argued that elements of inmate systems are reinforced by line officers and administrators in prisons.[9] By opening or closing opportunities for moderately cooperative inmate leaders and by encouraging beliefs or norms such as "do your own time," the officers can effectively maintain relative quiet and stability in the population despite patterned and frequent violations of many rules. The traditional inmate system works on behalf of staff as well as against them, just as it does for inmates.

In a much more far-reaching comparative analysis of formal organizations, Etzioni typed them according to their compliance structures—compounds of the type of power wielded by those in high organizational positions and the kind of orientation toward the organization shared by lower participants.[10] In the prison structure, staff members are the higher participants and the inmates are the lower participants. Prisons are *coercive* organizations in this scheme because of the coercive power of staff and the alienated orientation of inmates. The coercive type contrasts with *utilitarian* types—such as most business organizations, where power is remunerative and the involvement of lower participants is calculative—and *normative* organizations—such as churches, where the power is normative and the involvement moral. Etzioni argued that the alienation of inmates in prisons is in part, a response to the unequal distribution of power in such organizations.

Etzioni proposed a series of hypotheses about the lower participants' degree of cohesion, leadership structure, and sharing of values with higher participants in the three organizational types described above. Translated into the terms of this book, Etzioni's work appears at first to offer a useful independent variable—organizational type—to explain variations in our dependent variable—the character of inmate systems. On second glance, however, it is clear that because the organizational types are based in part on participants' (here, inmates') responses to the organization, use of the typology to explain inmate response would involve circular reasoning. Nonetheless, the provocative discussion of the links between the nature of official power and different dimensions of lower participants' responses to it identifies relationships that are often quite similar to those appearing in the next three chapters. Etzioni's discussion of the independent variation of different aspects of lower participants' responses also reinforces my own conclusion that it is essential to treat elements of subcultures and social structures separately rather than merely as parts of monolithic inmate systems.

In addition, Etzioni's work, like that of McCleery and Cloward, reminds us that it is necessary to examine the details of organizational structure as well as the inmate perceptions of prison experience if inmate systems (or the adaptations of any lower participants to an organization) are to be understood. From the point of view of these theorists, therefore, differences in the manner in which power, rewards, and punishments are distributed within organizations will be related to variations in the content and structure of inmate systems. Differences in organizational goals are frequently indicators of different organizational structures, but it is the structures themselves that directly affect the actions and perceptions of the lower participants.

With this orientation, therefore, I turned from an initial preoccupation with classifying organizations by their goals to a search for ways to characterize the power and opportunity structures of the twenty-three programs. Many of the programs we had observed were very different from the more traditional cottages in our own sample, as well as from the congregate prisons about which so much is written. But how? In what ways? With these general contrasts and questions in mind, I began to list specific organizational characteristics (for example, percentage of staff members under thirty years old) that might make a difference in the way staff members and youths, or youths themselves, perceived one another and interacted. The list grew and variables began to fall together in comprehensible dimensions. As they did, they were combined into scales to measure these dimensions. Though most of this work was intuitive, statistical tools such as factor analysis, multidimensional scaling, hierarchical clustering, and Guttman scaling also helped me to discover how these many tangible differences fit together. I kept testing the utility of the developing dimensions and the scales used to measure them by seeing how well they worked in explaining variations in aspects of inmate systems. This was inductive analysis, and it precluded reliance on tests of statistical significance.

Four dimensions and scales to measure them emerged from this sorting of organizational characteristics: (1) community contact; (2) equality; (3) participation; and (4) supervision. Each of them describes an aspect of the way an organization interacts with or acts upon its clients. It is these points of contact that presumably most directly influence the perceptions inmates have of the organization, one another, and themselves, as well as the way they perceive the opportunities they have for action within the organization. The organizational characteristics summarized by these dimensions encourage or discourage particular adaptations drawn from the repertoire of each inmate population, or they may suggest or impose wholly new modes of response. These four dimensions may thus be viewed in terms of the degree to which they restrict in some way the opportunities for youths to generate their own adaptations to the organization and the extent to which they create opportunities for staff members to influence the form of the individual and collective adaptation made by youths.

Community Contact. Community contact is the first and most obvious of these dimensions and measures the extent to which the organization allows and encourages contact between youths and members of the free community. The conception of community-based corrections and the sharp distinction in our sample between closed institutions and, for example, nonresidential programs made such a dimension inevitable. Community contact has important implications for the extent of leverage or control staff members can exert over youths within the program. The community contact scale that measures variation along this dimension will be discussed later in this chapter.

Equality. The second dimension, equality, primarily reflects an organization's openness toward, and encouragement of, informal contact and relationships between inmates and staff members.

Equality is obviously never fully attained in any setting where some are freer than others to go and come as they please; perhaps it is more appropriate to think here of varying degrees of *inequality* between staff and inmates. The key in terms of inmate systems is the amount of social distance an organization builds into relationships between staff and inmates. It is important here to remember that the distance between inmates and professional and paternalistic therapists may be just as great as it is between inmates and cold, authoritarian guards. Equality provides opportunities for staff to influence inmates rather than coerce them, and it is ultimately the basis for any organizational direction of development of inmate systems.

Part of the scale measuring equality also gauges the extent to which organizations promote coordination and consistency among staff members. Time and again one reads of the great variation in the way prison guards handle their roles, and we saw similar variety in some of our sample of programs. Such variation and inconsistency should both increase the opportunities for an inmate system to develop and decrease the collective force of staff influence (although perhaps increasing the influence of a few individuals). As described in the next chapter, along with the discussion of the equality dimension, the high correlation of staff coordination with staff-youth equality led to their merger in one dimension and in one scale.

Participation. The next dimension gauges the extent to which a correctional program encourages or requires the participation of most or all youths in the work and decisions of the organization. It identifies the extent of opportunities for inmates to share with staff the responsibility for running or making decisions about the organization.

Although the equality and participation dimensions emerged from the data, there is clear precedent for them. They are implicit in the description of the "collaborative institution" recommended in 1968 by the President's Commission on Law Enforcement and the Administration of Justice.[11] Weinberg and other analysts of prisons and training schools have spoken of bureaucratized guards and staff on one hand and inmates on the other as separate castes, implying organizational support of formalized relationships that stand at one pole of an equality dimension.[12] The traditional emphasis on the total power of prison officials as well as the classification of correctional institutions as coercive organizations both highlight one pole of the participation dimension. The stark contrasts on these two dimensions between traditional prisons and some of the programs we observed helped make the isolation of the equality and participation dimensions easier.

Supervision. The fourth dimension to appear in the analysis was supervision. It measures the extent to which the organization keeps track of and orders the relationships among youths. By engaging youths in attractive but officially sanctioned and carefully monitored activity, the opportunity for informal interaction to occur among youths is decreased. Early in the field research I was impressed by the way some programs kept youths active in school, therapy, recreation, and so on, while others left them with considerable free time during which they clustered together out of range and control of staff. That the latter rather than the former situation appears common in congregate prisons where traditional inmate systems flourish, reinforced the importance of this dimension.

Two additional variables—size and ratio of inmates (or clients) to staff—often appear in organizational analysis, especially of human service organizations. Initially I saw them as related to the supervision dimension, assuming larger size and larger ratios of inmates to staff would reduce the supervisory capacity of the organization. I still believe they do, but the two variables are not highly correlated with the variables composing the scale measuring variation along the supervision dimension and thus were not included in it. Presumably, their impact is relatively independent of the organizational features reflected in this scale; in theory, nonetheless, decreases in size and inmate/staff ratio should make the task of supervision easier and might affect other organizational features and inmate systems as well. These two variables therefore are included separately in the following analysis of inmate systems.

These four dimensions of organizational structure and practice are thus the key analytic instruments—along with size, inmate/staff ratio, and selected characteristics of inmate populations—in the attempt in the following three chapters to dissect the sources of variation in significant components of inmate systems. To approach organizations in terms of such dimensions, however, contrasts quite sharply with the more conventional approach to analyzing differences among correctional organizations: using typologies relying on a program's most prominent goals or purposes, typically custody/punishment versus rehabilitation/treatment. Because such typologies have served so well and continue to dominate both empirical, theoretical and policy analyses in corrections, it is worth considering where their inadequacies lie.

A major point of the corrections literature has been that competing goals in corrections have prevented the full implementation of treatment aims; thus, goal variations are not necessarily reflected in variations in organizational structure and practice. Just such a recognition led Giallombardo to argue that "the structural form of the informal social system evolved by female juvenile offenders" will be the same "irrespective of the goals of the formal organization."[13] Such a strong statement is unsupported by the data of this study, but it is an unsurprising conclusion to draw if one relies only on official statements of goals to differentiate organizations. Even more important is the recognition that an enormous variety of organizational structures exist for achieving broadly similar goals, and these organizational mechanisms, rather than the goals, are the shaping influences of informal inmate systems.

Not only is the correlation between organizational goals and organizational structure imperfect, but the causal relationship between the two is doubtful. The model—implicit or explicit—in works emphasizing typologies of organizational goals is that organizational leaders decide on a set of goals, select the best means of implementing them, and then design the organizational structure accordingly. Although such rational planning is indeed conceivable, a more plausible model for some kinds of organizations is that goals and organizational structures develop almost simultaneously and in interaction with one another, but are not wholly dependent on one another. Traditions of organizational structure—such as the typical congregate prison—evolve and have lives of their own irrespective of the changes in penal philosophy and goals that are influenced by broad trends in societal values. Organizational forms may be adopted without a clear understanding of the precise goals they are meant to advance, while goals may be advocated with little or no awareness of the most effective organizational strategies for their achievement.

The variety of rehabilitative and custodial programs now in operation defies simple categorization. More finely tuned and updated analysis of goals may be one possible solution to the problem of an outdated goal typology, but it is an inadequate one. In this study we originally tried to bring the typology up to date by combining the traditional custody-rehabilitation dichotomy with one that divides programs according to their high or low emphasis on community contact. The resultant fourfold classification of programs into custody, rehabilitation, reintegration, and advocacy goals did very little, however, to advance understanding of the variations in inmate systems among these same programs.

Even greater refinements in defining organizational goals bring one nearer the possibilities of more exact measurements of organizational practice—thus, equality is a likely goal of most programs that exhibit it. Reliance on good typologies, however refined, still creates pressures to analyze organizations as wholes rather than to examine the variables that characterize them. The major problem of typologies by goals therefore remains: they treat organizations as units and tend to assume similar structures among organizations with the same goals. Where such concomitance is high, the goal typology serves adequately; but, as is increasingly the case in corrections, when the correlation between particular goals and specific structures declines, goal typologies lose their power.

Although the four analytic dimensions described above have great advantages over goal typologies, their use presents one serious disadvantage. The dimensions are variables that slice across organizations and cut the same programs in different ways. By contrast, in assigning a single goal to each program, each organization maintains its wholeness even if its particular identity is somewhat obscured. Instead of comparing the organizations as wholes with one another, this study looks mainly at relationships among variables—that is, organizational dimensions and elements of informal inmate systems. In the process, however, the programs tend to lose even their attenuated "goal-grouped" identities. To alleviate this problem, therefore, the last chapter attempts to suggest ways in which the variables fit back together, and what consequences this has for inmate systems.

Although in a broad sense organizational goals such as rehabilitation, custody, or community reintegration are not very useful in defining the organizational variations that relate to differences among inmate systems, these goals are extremely important in understanding the process of correctional change and the general direction of correctional systems and organizations. While neither commitment to rehabilitation nor to humanitarian goals distinguishes adequately among programs—particularly in the community-based system—the dedication to these principles was a major force in creating the varied programs under study. Much research and policy discussion thus will continue to focus on the range of general correctional goals. The analytic dimensions introduced in this chapter make it easier, however, to examine the imperfect relationships between these essentially abstract conceptions of purpose and the relatively specific aspects of organizational structure and practices that directly affect inmate systems.

MEASURING ORGANIZATIONAL STRUCTURE AND PRACTICE

The task of measuring program variation along the four dimensions of organizational structure presents us with a problem that has long plagued students of organizations. Heydebrand distinguishes direct from indirect methods of assessing organizational characteristics.[14] The indirect method rests on the *perceptions* of the organization described by samples of members or by informants in questionnaires or interviews, while the direct method involves the observation of "analytical or structural properties" such as proportion of employees in administrative positions or size or degree of functional complexity.

For a number of reasons direct measures have been relied on in this study. First, indirect measures have a special potential for inaccuracy—what staff members believe an organization is doing may differ substantially from actual practice. Fully involved people often lose their perspective. Second, direct measures of organizational variables suggest more clearly than do indirect measures the policy implications of the analysis. Structural characteristics in organizations are more changeable than are human perceptions; if the staff perception of the level of coordination and cooperation among staff is inversely related to the likelihood of some unwanted outcome (such as high rates of inmate escape), it would be less clear what steps one might take to resolve the problem than if the outcome were associated inversely with the frequency of staff meetings or the level of role differentiation among staff.

A third reason for rejecting indirect measures of organizational traits in this study is that such measures are more clearly intertwined with the dependent variables (the character of inmate systems) than are direct organizational measures. Staff perceptions are influenced by the structure of the organization, the composition of the youth population, and the nature of youths' response to the staff and organization as well as by their own experiences and values. The youths' perceptions of the organization are shaped as well by the character of the youths' subculture. In either case, to employ measures of independent variables that are strongly influenced by the dependent variable would be to increase the danger of circularity in the analysis.

Nonetheless some of the direct measures employed here run afoul of the same problem because they are derived from observations of patterns of staff behavior that are similarly influenced by youths' responses. Practices such as holding daily community meetings or encouraging youths to address staff members by their first names indicate what one might call normative properties of organizations— the operating principles or assumptions—of the program. Organizational norms—often derived from more general goals—are key factors in directing and regulating relationships among members and in setting the tone for individual and collective definitions of the organization. These norms must be inferred from patterns of behavior. Fortunately, in our sample these patterns were often made clearer by official oral or written statements of program policy or by the obvious acquiescence of program officials to the practices of their co-workers.

Scales to measure each of the four dimensions of organizational variation were thus composed from organizational properties reported by our observers in their field notes or by the programs in their own literature. The items of each scale were scored simply by assigning a 1 if the property was absent and a 3 if it were present in a program. On occasion (indicated in the description of each scale) a score of 2 was assigned when a clear need for an intermediate value arose. The items were equally weighted and summed to achieve the scale scores.[15]

In constructing the scales some properties that seemed on their face to be valid measures of the dimensions in questions were dropped from the scales because they correlated poorly with other properties. Obviously, however, despite such refinements, these scales are only rough measures that reflect in part the particular (and limited) characteristics of the programs in this sample. They nonetheless give an indication of the important general dimensions of organizational variation that make a difference in the nature of informal inmate systems.

COMMUNITY CONTACT

Advocates of community corrections generally believe that offenders cannot be taught how to behave normally when placed in an abnormal environment such as a training school or prison, and that correction can take place best in free communities.[16] The idea of reforming people among their neighbors is an old one, set aside temporarily by the "discovery of the asylum."[17] Prisons and training schools have created the problem that community-based corrections is being reinvented to solve: the challenge of transferring people from separation to incorporation into free society.

At least some of the unstated or seldom stated sociological assumptions undergirding community corrections can be identified.[18] Community-based corrections rests on a recognition that people's actions are at least in part the product of alterable social pressures and that these derive in part from the social networks in which people are enmeshed. It is grounded then on the assumption that social control inheres fundamentally in the ongoing social relationships in which people are engaged. In making this assumption it plays down the belief that the key sources of social control in the free community arise from the threat of official sanctions through law or from the individual's internalization of values and norms.

The emphasis on the controlling force of social relationships suggests, for example, that the basic changes that aging or maturation tend to bring about in human relationships (from student to employee; from dependent child to independent provider for a family) are among the essential forces at work in youth corrections. To the degree that correctional programs work successfully with individuals to restructure these social relationships and perhaps to speed up the maturation process, the greater their immediate success will be. In addition, restructuring relationships may have long-term effects because these relationships will have continuing impact on youths after correctional treatment ends. Jobs, friendships, school settings and family ties will provide socially acceptable rewards for former offenders. These mechanisms for promoting law-abiding conduct are natural and continuing forces of control for all law-abiding citizens.

Community corrections may hold more promise for rehabilitation than have previous correctional ideologies that rested either on faith in moral or religious conversion, psychological treatment, resocialization, or deterrence through aversion to punishment such as loss of freedom. Community corrections in small doses (such as work- or school-release programs) also tests whether people can make a satisfactory adjustment to the community after living in a confined or isolated setting. Each day an ex-offender is involved in the lawful affairs of the outside world gives increasing evidence of satisfactory reformation or reintegration; these signs of success, in turn, may be used by parole boards or correctional decision-makers (or conceivably by the offender himself) as cues in making decisions about whether or not to release an individual from state supervision.

Behind the exploration of correctional use of community controls and the exploitation of the free society as a testing ground for offenders lurks the same goal that has guided correctional philosophy if not practice for so long—rehabilitation or treatment. In quest of that general goal, the Massachusetts DYS set in motion far-reaching organizational changes over which the department could maintain little control when it deinstitutionalized the youth corrections system. Amateurs and professionals across the state set to work constructing programs to rehabilitate delinquents. Out of the hands of centralized, bureaucratized decision-makers responsible for large institutions, new mechanisms for reaching the goal of rehabilitation were introduced.[19] Some but not all of the new community programs were based upon the sociological assumptions about community-based corrections.

In practice, thus, community corrections for young offenders in Massachusetts has meant the replacement of a few large, isolated state-run institutions with scores of privately run programs dispersed throughout the state. It has not inevitably meant that youths have much *if any* contact with local residents, relatives, employers, friends, or teachers. In fact, the widely varying degrees of contact between inmates and members of the free community is one of the most striking characteristics of the community-based system. No simple typology of reintegration and rehabilitation goals can capture the diversity of these programs.

From our observations of these diverse community programs, it was evident that regardless of a program's emphasis on community intervention as a goal, when community contact occurred it removed youths at least temporarily from the direct influence and supervision of program staff members, and in many cases—because each youth had a different set of community contacts—removed youths from interaction with one another. In addition, in many instances contact with members of the community allowed youths an opportunity to choose or maintain relationships that were unavailable in closed programs. These bonds lessened the importance of relationships within the program, and, at least potentially, provided reinforcement for perspectives and beliefs inconsistent with those officially promulgated. These factors in particular seemed relevant to the character of inmate social organization and interaction and to the extent of impact that the programs and their staff members might have on the character of the inmate systems.

Ultimately, thus, we came to view the *community* component of the revolutionized youth corrections system as an organizational dimension indicating the degree to which the program allowed for contact between inmates and citizens regardless of the goals or purposes of that contact, the location of the program, or its ultimate objectives.[20] Whatever the grand design of Commissioner Miller's policy of deinstitutionalization, one of its crucial consequences as far as inmate systems are concerned appears to have been the varied extent of youth-community contact it allowed.

The immense contrasts in the degree to which participants in the twenty-three programs were encouraged to move back and forth between the worlds outside their programs and those inside them is evident from two extracts from our field notes. One typical entry by a field worker at Open House listed the whereabouts of the seven residents one morning:

Alex off at school
Joe off to the car wash to work
Sandra at the key punch job
Betty in the kitchen

Jim working with the lawn mower in the yard
Three staff members are going to pick up Fran from her boyfriend's house
    where she has been on the run
Henry is in bed

Clearly some limits were placed on contacts between Open House residents and members of the community, but they did not approach those evident at Primal:

> During the staff meeting, some of the staff were going through the letters the kids were about to receive, giving them a rather cursory reading. Someone said that Simon was making a request for a letter to his girlfriend who had just had a miscarriage with his baby. Linda and Art were angry, and wanted to know how he found out about the miscarriage. After suggesting possible negligence on the part of Dale and Sandy (program members) in not screening Simon's letters closely enough, they decided that it was probably during one of the sneak phone calls he had made from the hospital when he had his tonsils out. Anyway, they complained, he should never have been allowed to find out about the miscarriage, and no, they decided, he can't send a letter.

Five variables were selected to measure more systematically the degree of organizational support for youth-community contact, as shown in Table 1–1. Each is examined in detail below.

Live at Home. The first variable in Table 1–1 indicates whether or not the program was residential in nature. Clearly the only two nonresidential programs, Drop-in and Pick-up, had far less contact time with their clientele and on balance loomed much less large in the lives of their participants than did the residential programs.

Sign-Out Privilege. The second community-contact variable indicates whether or not a program granted a majority of youths the considerable freedom to come and go in the local community without supervision—that is, the opportunity to sign out. Neither Topsfield nor any of the training school cottages granted their residents such a privilege; the rural settings of these programs made the logistics of such visits impossible even if they had been viewed as desirable. The community-based programs, by and large, were located where such visits were feasible. Of these programs this freedom was evident at Warning (where it was also most restricted by a system of limited passes), Fatigue, Pair, and Open House, in addition, of course, to Pick-up and Drop-in, which were nonresidential programs. Group, Confront, and Primal all had some arrangement for those residents

Table 1–1. Scores on Variables Composing the Community Contact Scale, by Program[a]

	Community Contact Variables					
	Live at Home	Sign-Out Privilege	Weekend Home Visits	Work Outside	School Outside	Total Community-Contact Score
Institutional Programs						
Cottage 8	1	1	3	3	1	9
Elms	1	1	3	1	1	7
Westview	1	1	3	1	1	7
Clara Barton	1	1	3	1	1	7
Putnam	1	1	3	3	1	9
Cottage 9	1	1	1	1	1	5
Regiment	1	1	1	1	1	5
Shelter	1	1	1	1	1	5
Warning	1	3	3	3	1	11
Fatigue	1	3	3	3	3	13
Mother	1	1	3	3	3	11
Reward	1	1	3	3	1	9
Group Treatment Programs						
"I Belong"	1	1	3	1	1	7
Topsfield	1	1	3	3	1	9
Shirley	1	1	3	3	1	9
Sunset	1	1	3	3	1	9
Primal	1	1	1	1	1	5
Confront	1	1	1	1	1	5
Group	1	1	2	3	3	10
Open House	1	3	3	3	3	13
Open Community Programs						
Drop-in	3	3	3	3	3	15
Pick-up	3	3	3	3	3	15
Pair	1	3	3	3	3	13

[a]Programs with a particular characteristic received a score of 3, and those without it a score of 1. Scores of 2 were assigned to programs where the trait was partially evident (see text).

who had showed considerable progress in the program to sign out in the later stages of their stay. The youths given this privilege constituted much less than a majority, however, and these programs were scored as not having a sign-out option. Like residing at home, the freedom to sign out maximized the likelihood that youths could build or maintain relationships of their own choosing or engage in activities that would serve to sustain self-conceptions and reduce the centrality of the correctional organization and its members in their lives.

Weekend Home Visits. A third variable indicating that the program facilitated youth-community contact was the presence or absence of the chance given to youths to visit home on occasional weekends. With the exception of Cottage 9, Shelter, and Regiment (the three institutional punishment or detention centers), and Confront and Primal (the two most intense group-therapy programs), all the programs encouraged and allowed cooperative participants to make periodic visits home. At Confront and Primal such visits occurred, but only for a very few youths toward the final stages of their residence in the program. Group—like Primal and Confront, part of the group-treatment cluster—was given an intermediate 2 score on this variable because of the unique way it handled home visits. Counselors called the youth's parents and made arrangements for pick-up and return, as they did at the other programs, but in addition, at Group a kind of contact was reached with the parents and youth, often in open discussion among residents and staff, about the restrictions to be placed on these visits. They were carefully circumscribed in order to prevent unsavory relationships and to restrict the chance for troublesome behavior to emerge. These carefully determined rules helped reinforce staff or program authority, or at least minimized the degree to which community contacts undercut it; thus, the intermediate score.

Work or School Outside. Families were not the only community members to whom youths might be released. Some programs were far more flexible than others in allowing their residents to take jobs outside the program or to attend community schools. The presence or absence of these two opportunities to have contacts beyond the program are the fourth and fifth variables in the community-contact scale shown in Table 1-1. Three of the institutional cottages—Clara Barton, Elms, and Westview—and all of the three institutional detention and punishment programs did not allow either of these external contacts, nor did "I Belong," Primal, and Confront during the major part of a youth's residence. At Primal and Confront only a youth who had completed months of residence (typically over one year) might take a job on "reentry" or "second stage"—a preliminary to graduation from the program. Cottage 8, Putnam, Sunset, Shirley, Topsfield, Reward, and Warning did not permit residents to attend local schools, although they each let several residents work at outside jobs. The remaining programs permitted both school attendance and employment.

As Table 1-1 indicates, not surprisingly, the open-community programs have the highest community-contact scores. Although both the institutional and group-treatment program clusters tend to allow considerably less contact between their residents and outsiders, a substantial variation remains within each cluster. Even some of the institutional cottages in the training schools as well as several of the cottages in the group-treatment cluster had made moderate strides toward community contact as defined here. It is just such crossing of broad categorical lines that makes necessary the analysis by organizational dimensions rather than by types.

Although the data about community contact give a sense of the differences and similarities among program organizations, the part played by community contact and by the other dimensions in shaping inmate systems will become clearer in the next three chapters. Undertaking that task, however, requires an introduction to the measurement of the second major set of independent variables in this analysis—the characteristics of youth populations. While the most obvious change in the Massachusetts system of youth corrections pertains to the new community-based system, Miller's reforms also created an unparalleled diversity in the composition of correctional populations.

VARIATION IN YOUTH POPULATIONS: THEORY AND MEASUREMENT

Although the patterns of inmate life in most U.S. prisons for adult male offenders are strikingly consistent, significant variations appear depending on the sex, race, and age composition of the offender population. Beginning with the early comparative work of Hayner, sociological observers have noted a less clearly differentiated set of argot roles and a less organized system of producing and distributing illicit goods and services in institutions for boys than in prisons for men.[21] On the other hand, younger males seem to place heavier emphasis on physical toughness and more frequently engage in physical violence and homosexual assaults than do older men.[22] The comparative work of Feld in this series, the case studies by Carroll of the role of black inmates in Rhode Island's prison, and work by Davidson on the organization of Chicano prisoners in San Quentin all stress the influence of racial and ethnic composition on the shape of emerging inmate systems.[23]

Behavioral differences that can be associated with age are not as evident between imprisoned women and girls as between men and boys; instead, females exhibit strikingly similar subcultures, which contrast sharply in many aspects with those of males.[24] Several observers have reported extensive and stable quasifamily systems with extensive differentiation of kinship roles—mother, father, uncle, aunt —in several large "families" encompassing much of the prison population. At the core of these systems are relatively unstable marriages that define homosexual relationships. This kind of social differentiation includes neither a clear inmate hierarchy nor a well-developed division of labor for providing illicit goods and services.[25] Unlike the subcultures among imprisoned males, the women's and girl's normative systems stress the value of social ties and the expression of sentiments.

Nevertheless, women and girls in prison, like similarly situated men and boys, distrust and dislike most of their fellow prisoners. Cooperation with prison staff is also roundly condemned, although the anti-informing ethic seems not to be such a central norm as it is for men and boys. Physical violence is not unknown among women and girls but appears generally to be less frequent than for males. Certainly physical strength and toughness or control over goods and services are not nearly as important as sources of power and prestige for females as they are for males.

This accumulation of research and theory clearly emphasizes the vital significance of different populations in shaping inmate systems, yet researchers have been plagued by the confounding effects of population composition and organizational variation in sorting out their relative importance in the formation of inmate systems. For example, it is common for the residents of more open or therapeutic programs to have been selected for participation because of the limited seriousness of their crimes or because of their previous conformity in prison programs. To the degree that differences exist, therefore, between the inmate systems of therapeutic and custodial programs, they may be explained by variations in inmate composition as well as by the differences in organizational goals, structure, and practice.

One common reaction to this confounding of variable sets has been to try to show comparability of populations in different institutions or cottages in order to argue convincingly that variations in inmate systems follow directly from differences in organizational goals or structure.[26] Alternatively one could presume essential comparability in organizational structure and infer that differences in inmate systems result from varying prisoner populations. Given the wide range of correctional organizations in our sample, we could not make the second assumption.

Similarly, the diversity in the populations of these programs made it evident that we could ignore this source of variation only at our peril. These populations ranged from all-male or all-female to coeducational; from selected "hard-core" offenders[27] (in intensive-care programs such as Warning, Confront, and Primal) to selected low-risk offenders (in nonresidential programs such as Drop-in and Pick-up); from all DYS youths to mixtures of delinquents with social service agency referrals and private patients; from age concentrations of 16 to 18 year olds to age ranges of 13 to 35 year olds; from all working- or lower-class youths to a mix of poorer youths with substantial numbers of middle- to upper-class young people;[28] and from white youths exclusively to balanced proportions of blacks and whites.

We could not argue for essential comparability of these populations, ignore their substantial variations, or control them away in cross-tabulations. Impossibility generates new assumptions and procedures, however, and rather than try to push them aside, we included population composition as a central variable in the empirical analysis. Instead of trying to eliminate the effects of population composition from those of organizational characteristics on inmate systems, we tried to determine how these two sets of variables acted with and upon one another in the creation of informal inmate systems.

In light of the past research on the effects of population characteristics on informal inmate systems and the unique and potentially influential features of the community-based youth populations, we chose eight variables to measure these traits, as shown in Table 1-2.[29] Three of the variables—the percentages of youths 16 years of age or older, of males, and of blacks—provide indicators of the factors most significant in differentiating inmate systems in traditional institutions from one another.[30]

Because Massachusetts has a relatively small minority population, the proportion of black youths may be less important in this analysis than in data drawn from other locations. No data on parental education, occupation, or income were collected in the 1971 sample, and therefore we could not introduce social-class composition as a variable. Given the backgrounds of people who commit the crimes that lead to arrest and imprisonment, however, this is rarely a variable in correctional studies. From field reports and the data gleaned in 1973, it appears that only the two privately operated concept houses— Primal and Confront—had a substantial infusion of middle- to upper-class youths.

The other five population variables, as Table 1-2 illustrates, all deal in one way or another with the extent, seriousness, or duration of the criminal careers of the youthful program participants. First, since not all programs in the community-based system relied exclu-

Table 1-2.   Inmate Population Characteristics, By Program (percentages)

	Percent 16 or over	Percent Male	Percent Black	Percent DYS	Percent First Offense Prior to Age 14	Percent DYS Youths with Prior Commitment	Percent DYS Youths Committed for Crime against Person	Percent DYS Juvenile Status Offense
Institutional Programs								
Cottage 8	87%	100%	27%	100%	60%	87%	23%	5%
Elms	58	100	31	100	59	90	22	9
Westview	59	100	18	100	62	62	18	15
Clara Barton	23	0	5	100	68	64	9	56
Putnam	35	0	11	100	58	58	3	54
Cottage 9	63	100	19	100	63	92	16	7
Regiment	39	100	10	100	45	11	9	22
Shelter	29	0	29	100	20	40	0	67
Warning	61	100	50	100	82	88	33	0
Fatigue	40	100	50	28	58	56	9	45
Mother	38	0	12	56	42	9	13	73
Reward	0	0	3	42	67	33	12	38
Group-Treatment Programs								
"I Belong"	25	100	25	100	75	50	28	14
Topsfield	73	44	25	100	33	87	0	39
Shirley	88	100	19	100	44	67	18	19
Sunset	53	100	14	100	87	73	14	5
Primal	59	71	3	48	81	65	20	21
Confront	61	60	8	64	40	40	25	17
Group	100	100	0	70	72	43	11	22
Open House	75	62	25	75	57	29	20	30

Open-Community
Programs

Drop-in	62	56	0	94	50	33	17	0
Pick-up	25	100	0	100	71	38	14	14
Pair	29	62	38	100	57	14	10	40

sively on DYS for their clients, the percentage of DYS youths in the total population was recorded.[31] The number of DYS youths in a program ranged from 100 percent in all the training school cottages and several of the 1973 programs to 28 percent in Fatigue. Using only the DYS youths as a base, four other percentages were computed on the basis of the youths' self-reports: the percentages of those committing their first official offense before age 14; of those with a previous commitment to DYS; of those currently committed for a crime against a person; and of those currently committed for a juvenile or status offense such as runaway or truancy. Using such measures, we hoped to find out what kinds of programs were dealing with particularly tractable or intractable youths and whether or not youth toughness would significantly affect the nature of the informal youth systems. One might suppose that programs with higher proportions of youths with more extensive or serious engagement in crime would share inmate systems that exhibit greater antagonism to staff, more suspicion and exploitation among youths, and stronger commitment to criminal values.

Some of the most crucial variables of any population comparison are unmeasureable, or are so close to the dependent variables (in this case, patterns of adjustment as manifested in relationships, attitudes, and behavior) that one cannot measure them as independent variables, at least in an essentially static study such as this one. The problem of the unmeasured variable particularly plagues researchers in the criminal justice system where police, judges, probation officers and others make judgments about the danger people pose to society, their commitment to a criminal way of life, or their degree of rehabilitation. Although populations may look either comparable or different in terms of demographic characteristics, there may be unmeasured, substantial differences or similarities among them that result from the intuitive decisions of the experienced men and women who run the criminal justice system. These screening processes may well produce meaningful differences in the populations.

A new complication was added to this old problem in the process of deinstitutionalizing youth corrections in Massachusetts, because in some instances (theoretically in all), youths were given a chance to look over one or more programs and to decide themselves which one to enter. Limited self-selection—other implications of which will be examined in later chapters—creates the likelihood that other intangibles (that is, unmeasured variables) will distinguish the youth populations. For the sake of this analysis, however, such speculation must necessarily be set aside.

Table 1–3 presents correlations of these eight population variables

Table 1-3. Correlations among Eight Population Characteristics (*N* = 23 programs)

	Percent 16 Years and Over	Percent Male	Percent Black	Percent From DYS	Percent Pre-14 Offense	Percent Prior Commitment	Percent Crime Against Person	Percent Juvenile Status Offense
Percentage of youths 16 years or older	—	.50	.06	.12	-.04	.41	.22	-.46
Percentage of male youths		—	.26	.19	.41	.35	.54	-.80
Percentage of black youths			—	.07	-.08	.31	.14	.01
Percentage of youths from DYS				—	-.06	.30	.04	-.30
Percentage of DYS youths committing first offense before age 14					—	.29	.49	-.48
Percentage of DYS youths with previous commitment						—	.30	-.43
Percentage of DYS youths committed for crimes against persons							—	-.70
Percentage of DYS youths committed for juvenile status offenses								—

and displays some interesting but unsurprising relationships. The two most striking correlations are between the percentage of DYS youths sent to the program on the basis of status offenses and: (1) the percentage of males in the program (*r* = -.80) (2) the percentage of youths committed for crimes against the person (*r* = -.70). The first relationship comments on both the nature of juvenile crime and the way our courts treat it; boys are far less likely than girls to come before the court on juvenile charges, and programs with more (or all) boys thus have fewer status offenders. The second relationship is partly a measurement artifact as well as a reflection of the same phenomenon: the more status offenders in a program, the fewer of any other kind of lawbreakers there will be. Higher percentages of boys also mean higher proportions of persons committed for offenses against the person (*r* = .54).

LEVEL OF COMMUNITY CONTACT AND YOUTH POPULATION CHARACTERISTICS

As Table 1-4 and similar tables of correlations between organizational dimensions and population characteristics in Chapters 2 and 3 show (see Tables 2-2 and 3-4), a striking feature of this sample of

Table 1-4. Correlations between Community Contact Scale and Population Characteristics

	For All Programs (N = 23)	For 1973 Programs Only (N = 13)
Percentage of youths 16 years or older	.01	.02
Percentage of male youths	.05	.22
Percentage of black youths	.12	.17
Percentage of youths from DYS	-.11	.11
Percentage of DYS youths committing first offense before age 14	.13	.30
Percentage of DYS youths with previous commitment	-.29	-.06
Percentage of DYS youths committed for crimes against persons	-.07	.02
Percentage of DYS youths committed for juvenile status offenses	-.03	.18

programs is the relative lack of confounding relationships between these two sets of variables. The correlations are generally very low; although it is clear that both youth populations and program organization vary considerably, they do not generally vary together. As noted earlier, there may be unmeasured variations among program populations that do relate both to organizational variations and inmate system differences. Nonetheless, the striking variety of combinations of people and places makes the task of analyzing their separate and joint impact on youth adaptations somewhat simpler.

TECHNIQUES OF DATA ANALYSIS

Two techniques have been used to describe the ways in which variables interact to shape inmate systems—correlation and multiple-regression analysis of quantified variables, and description and analysis of qualitative data. Although the former technique appears far more scientific, the two have much in common, particularly as used upon this set of data and for the purposes of this book. Their combination is particularly appropriate in a study that examines aspects of inmate subcultures. The individuals questioned served both as informants ("What do you think others would do?") and as respondents ("What do you believe?"), and their pooled answers to both kinds of queries give us different ways of looking at the essential features of informal subcultures and social organization. The richly detailed field observations collected during the many hours spent on-site provide another perspective on these inmate systems.

This combination of analytic methods is also particularly appropriate for handling our unwieldy sample of twenty-three programs. It is too large a group to allow detailed, qualitative descriptions and comparisons of each program, although it is small enough to make this a tempting proposition. Yet in juggling the cases during such comparisons, it is difficult to keep separate the twenty-two individual programs that are up in air while examining briefly the one momentarily in hand. Unfortunately for purposes of quantitative analysis, an N of twenty-three is quite small. My analysis will make moderate use of both approaches, therefore, in the belief that the richness of the comparisons along with the more systematic character of the quantitative analysis will reinforce one another and partially compensate for the weaknesses of using either approach by itself.

Multiple-regression analysis is a sophisticated statistical tool, but to understand its purpose is simple: to produce a mathematical equation so that scores on several independent variables (in this case the characteristics of the inmate populations and the dimensions of organizational variation) can be added up to produce the score on the dependent variable (inmate system characteristics such as the percentage of youths liking the staff) that actually occurs under those population and organizational conditions. That is, if we know the percentage of DYS youths, of status offenders, and so on in a program, and its community contact score, equality score, and so on, we can use the equation to tell us—under these conditions—what percentage of youths would like the staff. If we alter any of the conditions (independent variables), we change the predicted score on the dependent variable. If our equation were perfectly accurate, it would in practice allow us to say how many more youths would like staff members if we doubled, for example, the amount of community contact. But these regression equations (like most) are far from perfect, and the measures fed into them are not free of fault.

One measure of any equation's accuracy is the amount of variance it explains (R^2)—the proportion of the variation in the dependent variable accounted for by the combination of independent variables in the regression equation; thus an R^2 of 1.0 means that the regression equation is a perfect predictor, and proportions less than that indicate a decreasing power to predict the dependent variable. In a multiple-regression equation, some of the variables are weighted more heavily than others because some prove to be much more powerful predictors of the dependent variable than do others. As it happens, a few of the variables contribute so little to the prediction (as indicated by the relatively small size of their standardized regression coefficient), that they can be dropped entirely from the equation without significantly reducing its power of prediction.

The regression equations that appear in this study include only those variables remaining significant.[32] Although some of the technical aspects of the regressions are presented in the tables, the regressions are intended solely as descriptive and exploratory devices for identifying the combinations of variables that appear most crucial to understanding particular dimensions of informal inmate systems.[33] For those who only intend to skim the tables, the most important information is simply whether or not a variable (such as community contact) appears in the regression at all.

Keeping in mind the same goal of understanding inmate systems, the qualitative data drawn from the extensive field reports of the observers are examined to help illustrate, explain, and go beyond the regressions. The consistency between the field notes and the quantitative data are impressive. Even more important, the qualitative materials provide insights and highlight patterns and dimensions of behavior, subculture, and social structure that could never be obtained from preconstructed questionnaires—the source of virtually all the quantitative data on informal inmate systems.

SUMMARY

When the officials of the Massachusetts Department of Youth Services decided to close their training schools and take the task of youth corrections to the diverse communities of the state, they probably assumed that community programs were inherently less coercive, less depriving of fundamental rights, less harmful to self-conceptions, and consequently more humane than the institutions they replaced. We will indirectly examine these assumptions in subsequent chapters. They must, however, be looked at in a broader context than the simple contrast between training school cottages and community-based programs. Indeed, the movement of corrections to the community wrought significant changes in many of the fundamental characteristics of the correctional organizations available to youths. It was not solely an opening up of corrections to the community and communities to corrections. The move in fact did create new possibilities for programs to encourage greater contact between delinquent youths and community members than was already occurring in the reformed training school cottages. It also diversified enormously the composition of the youth populations in correctional programs. But though these were the major changes affecting inmate systems generated by deinstitutionalization, they were only part of a complex mix of organizational alterations, some of which had already started in the partially reformed training schools. These other vital dimensions of correctional organizations and variation—equality, participation, and supervision—will be described in the following chapters as we begin to explore piece by piece the several aspects of inmate social systems, subcultures, and behavior, as well as the nature and causes of their variation.

NOTES

1. The major exception to the representativeness of our sample was the purposeful exclusion of any program in which there was not regular contact and interaction among groups of five or more youths; clearly we could not study subcultures unless we had groups. As a consequence we left out all programs (all nonresidential) that relied on one-to-one casework, or advocacy between a staff person and a youth, and all foster homes.

2. Lloyd Ohlin, "Reform of Correctional Services for Youth: A Research Proposal," mimeographed (Cambridge: Center for Criminal Justice, Harvard Law

School, 1970), p. 47. The proposal is reprinted in somewhat modified form as "Organizational Reform in Correctional Agencies," in *Handbook of Criminology*, ed. Daniel Glaser (Chicago: Rand McNally, 1974), pp. 995–1020.

3. The nine field workers besides Feld and McEwen who participated in the two studies were all white, middle-class college graduates chosen from a large applicant pool. This group included five law students (all men), and four college graduates about to embark on graduate study in political science, journalism, law, and nursing (all women). All were trained briefly by reading and discussing materials on participant observation and by meeting frequently during the beginning of the field experience to discuss observations and problems.

4. For example, D.S. Pugh et al., "Dimensions of Organizational Structure," in *Comparative Organizations: The Results of Empirical Research*, ed. Wolf Heydebrand (Englewood Cliffs, N.J.: Prentice-Hall, 1973), pp. 441–70, measure organizational dimensions from information collected through interviews with organization executives acting as informants. Pugh notes that the data minimize "the employees' perceptions of the organizations," but deal only with "what is officially expected *should* be done, and what is in practice *allowed* to be done; it does not include what is *actually* done. . . ." Ibid., p. 444. The data used in this book were derived from first-hand observations of *actual* organizational *practice* and structure, and were not simply the pronouncements of organizational officials; thus we have avoided the limitations of the data used by Pugh and his colleagues.

5. Of all the programs in this set, Regiment is most out of place because of the nonbureaucratic nature of the staff structure.

6. Massachusetts defined "status offenses" such as runaway and truancy as delinquent throughout the course of this research. As a consequence, it was our impression that the girls who came from the courts (typically for status offenses) were little different from those referred by welfare agencies. This was less true for boys.

Status offenses were removed from the definition of delinquency in 1974 in Massachusetts. Runaways, truants, and so-called stubborn children are handled now by the Department of Social Services. Interestingly, given the placement policies of DYS, to the degree such youths are removed from the home, they may end up with—though not *as*—delinquents anyway.

7. Reward was the only program where lack of official cooperation seriously limited research efforts. Our observer was restricted to observation of one unit, and she had some difficulty freeing herself from supervision there.

8. A "concept house" is distinguished from other group-treatment programs or therapeutic communities by the explicit nature of the program ideology, which pervades all dimensions of program life. According to Barry Sugarman when describing one such program, "the 'concept' is the term most often used by Daytop residents and staff to refer to the Daytop community, the Daytop philosophy and ideals, and the Daytop methods of doing things." *Daytop Village: A Therapeutic Community* (New York: Holt, Rinehart, and Winston, 1974), p. 11.

9. Richard Cloward, "Social Control in the Prison," in *Theoretical Studies in Social Organization of the Prison*, ed. Richard Cloward et al. (New York: Social

Science Research Council, 1960), pp. 20–48; Richard McCleery, "Communication Patterns as Bases of Systems of Authority and Power," in ibid., pp. 49–77.

10. Amitai Etzioni, *A Comparative Analysis of Complex Organizations: On Power, Involvement, and Their Correlates* (Glencoe, Ill.: Free Press, 1961).

11. *Task Force Report: Corrections* (Washington, D.C.: U.S. Government Printing Office, 1967), pp. 46–50.

12. Kirson Weinberg, "Aspects of the Prison's Social Structure," *American Journal of Sociology* 47 (March 1942): 717–26.

13. Rose Giallombardo, *The Social World of Imprisoned Girls: A Comparative Study of Institutions for Juvenile Delinquents* (New York: Wiley, 1974), p. 12.

14. Wolf Heydebrand, "The Study of Organizations," in *Comparative Organizations: The Results of Empirical Research*, ed. Wolf Heydebrand (Englewood Cliffs, N.J.: Prentice-Hall, 1973), pp. 31–43.

15. Initially a larger pool of items was used, and items were eliminated from scales when they correlated poorly with other scale items and the total scale score. Factor analyses were also used, and the factors generally corresponded to the scales reported here; they ultimately led to the combination of two scales into the equality scale. In one or two cases I maintained the integrity of the scales reported here in the face of factor loadings suggesting otherwise for reasons of "face validity" and theory. Similarly the scales were analyzed for their Guttman scale properties and generally scale well in that regard, although the numbers of items in all but the equality scale are small. None of these methodological niceties adds substantially to understanding correctional organizations and inmate systems, however, so none of them is reported here.

16. For an exceptionally clear statement of one theory of community corrections, see Robert Coates, "Community-Based Corrections: Concept, Impact, Dangers," in *Juvenile Correctional Reform in Massachusetts*, Lloyd Ohlin, Alden Miller, and Robert Coates (Washington, D.C.: U.S. Government Printing Office, 1977), pp. 23–34.

17. David Rothman, *The Discovery of the Asylum: Social Order and Disorder in the New Republic* (Boston: Little, Brown, 1970).

18. This kind of theoretical approach lay behind the Chicago Area Project started in the 1930s under the leadership of Clifford Shaw. For an overview of this project and theory, see Solomon Kobrin, "The Chicago Area Project—A 25-Year Assessment," *Annals of the American Academy of Political and Social Science* 322 (March 1959): 20–29.

19. Other goals of community corrections include reducing the psychological scars incurred by separating people from society; involvement of a wider spectrum of citizens in coping with the problem of crime and increasing their awareness of their responsibility for, as well as of, the social costs of crime; and lowering costs through the use of available community resources (such as schools, workplaces, housing) rather than duplicating them expensively for an excluded few.

20. Other researchers who analyze the part these relationships play in facilitating community "reintegration" and ultimate "rehabilitation" of youths may approach community contact differently. Rather than viewing this dimension as

involving merely the degree the program has exclusive control over their members, such analysts would want to define the precise character and quality of community-youth contacts. The concern in this book, however, is with the relatively short-run effects of community contacts on informal youth systems. The other approach to community contact is more heavily emphasized in Coates, Miller, and Ohlin, *Diversity in a Youth Correctional System*, in this series.

21. Norman Hayner, "Washington State Correctional Institutions as Communities," *Social Forces* 21 (March 1943): 316-22.

22. See, for example, Sethard Fisher, "Social Organization in a Correctional Community," *Pacific Sociological Review* 4 (Fall 1961): 87-93; Howard Polsky, *Cottage Six: The Social System of Delinquent Boys in Residential Treatment* (New York: Russell Sage, 1962); Desmond Ellis, Harold Grasmick, and Bernard Gilman, "Violence in Prisons: A Sociological Analysis," *American Journal of Sociology* 80 (July 1974): 16-43; Ronald Akers, Norman Hayner, and Werner Gruninger, "Homosexual and Drug Behavior in Prison: A Test of the Functional and Importation Models of the Inmate System," *Social Problems* 21 (Winter 1974): 410-22.

23. Leo Carroll, *Hacks, Blacks, and Cons* (Lexington, Mass.: D.C. Heath, 1974); R. Theodore Davidson, *Chicano Prisoners: The Key to San Quentin* (New York: Holt, Rinehart and Winston, 1974); and Barry Feld, *Neutralizing Inmate Violence: Juvenile Offenders in Institutions* (Cambridge, Mass.: Ballinger, 1977), in this series.

24. Rose Giallombardo, *Society of Women: A Study of a Women's Prison* (New York: Wiley, 1966); Giallombardo, *Social World of Imprisoned Girls*; Barbara Carter, "Reform School Families," *Society* 11 (November-December 1973): 36-43. See also Esther Heffernan, *Making It in Prison: The Square, the Cool, and the Life* (Chicago: Aldine, 1965).

25. Giallombardo, *Society of Women*, pp. 173-75.

26. See, for example, David Street, Robert Vinter, and Charles Perrow, *Organization for Treatment: A Comparative Study of Institutions for Delinquents* (New York: Free Press, 1966) and Feld, *Neutralizing Inmate Violence*, in this series.

27. "Hard-core" has a double meaning. On the one hand, it means youths who have previously been in trouble with the law and have a substantial past record of court appearances or commitments to DYS. On the other hand, in the community-based system it means youths who have been in a number of programs, perhaps under the same commitment. Youths might repeatedly run away from or be thrown out of programs, necessitating placement in new programs. These, too, were troublesome youths.

28. Primal and Confront in particular took in private clients in their concept houses, and the rates, approaching $1,000 per month at one of them, effectively selected a well-to-do private clientele.

29. Although the choice of such population variables as these was clearly indicated by the weight of corrections research, I would not have been so ready to think in terms of them had it not been for the influence of Walter B. Miller's work on status class subcultures. See "Subculture, Social Reform and the 'Culture of Poverty,'" *Human Organization* 30 (Summer 1971): 111-25. The exten-

sive and important work Miller has done on this subject since that article is not yet published, but as his colleague at the Center for Criminal Justice, I learned much from him first hand.

30. Sex, race, and DYS referral distributions were computed using what we knew of the characteristics of the whole cottage or program populations. The remaining percentages were computed from the questionnaires and interviews and were based at times on not-so-random samples; from what we knew of these not interviewed, however, no serious bias is introduced into the population variables by using data from the samples rather than from the total population.

31. Here I do not differentiate between those youths who were committed to DYS and those who were referred. In 1973, youths came to DYS in two ways. Most had been adjudicated delinquent in a juvenile court and had been committed to DYS, which decided where to place them; a judge could not sentence a youth for a particular length of time or to a particular place. Other youths had been referred to DYS; in these cases the juvenile court prevailed upon a youth and his parents to agree to take part voluntarily in a DYS program and thus avoid an official court hearing and finding. In either case personnel in DYS were in charge of placing a youth in a particular program.

It should also be noted that a private or social-welfare referral did not necessarily indicate a life free of transgression. Many of the private patients, at Primal particularly, had committed crimes—especially drug offenses—but were undergoing treatment in lieu of prosecution or court finding. Many of the girls at Mother and Reward who had been referred by social-service agencies had family conflicts very similar to those of peers who had appeared in court as "stubborn children" or "runaways." The presence or absence of a DYS label may well exaggerate the differences between youths at most programs.

32. In fact, it was necessary because of the small number of cases ($N = 23$) to remove as many variables as possible from the equations. This was clearly essential after we ran fourteen random variables (chosen from a table of random numbers) to see how well they could predict the dependent variables. Typically multiple correlations were around .80, and the F ratio of one or more of the independent variables was statistically significant, and on one occasion so also was the F ratio of the entire equation.

Regressions with four or five independent random variables showed none of these problems. Given that need, we used the following process for eliminating variables. In doing so we were guided as much by theory and intuition as by impartial statistical judgments. Initially we ran all fourteen independent variables and progressively removed clusters of them which had low F ratios, low standardized regression coefficients, and low zero-order correlations with the dependent variable. At times we forced one rather than another variable into the equation when theory dictated; thus, for example, the equality and participation dimensions sometimes got in the way of one another since all high participation programs were also high equality programs (here lies the problem of multicollinearity); typically one would do as well statistically as the other in the final equation, but they could not stay together. We, and not the computer, chose the survivor; generally these surviving variables have F ratios statistically significant at the 0.05 level or better, but several were included despite lower levels of statistical significance. These are noted in the tables describing the regression equations.

33. Although we have used them throughout as rough guides for whether or not to include a variable in the final equation, we have not reported the significance levels of the F ratio for the total equation or for the F ratios of each independent variable (with the few exceptions described in note 32 above). These are inappropriate given the inductive and descriptive use of the regressions in this study.

 *Chapter 2*

Kids and Keepers: Inmate-Staff Relationships

The staff here suck; [they are] about as narrow-minded as a toothpick and sneaky.

Some staff are alright, and some suck, in plain English. Some are fair; you be fair to them, and they'll be fair to you. But its two out of three that sucks.

I think the staff are all really fine, good people. I get pissed of at 'em sometimes, but I think they're all really great people.

These disparate assessments by youths of the staff members in their correctional programs reflect significant variations among the twenty-three programs in our sample. The views differed among individuals, but more importantly they varied considerably among programs. An exploration of the importance of and reasons for these sharp differences in youth evaluations of staff members is the subject of this chapter.

The often-described tensions between the polar missions of modern corrections—to control convicted persons through the coercive power of the state and to rehabilitate prisoners through humane and "scientifically sound" treatment programs—leave practitioners and theorists uncertain about the "proper" inmate response to incarceration. Since the founding of penitentiaries in the United States, correctional practitioners have always been somewhat surprised that so many inmates distrust and resent their keepers. The humanitarian goals of the new prisons in the 1820s and the successive humanitarian reforms since that time in correctional institutions have to a large degree been carried out "for the good of prisoners"— for their mental and physical well-being and for their rehabilitation. Hostile responses by inmates to the men and women who administer these "reformed" and "helping" settings appear to reflect a resistance and ingratitude that require special explanation. R. Theodore Davidson writes, for example, that he was employed by prison officials at San Quentin "to see if an anthropologist could determine what subcultural factors were responsible for Mexican-American prisoners being excessively violent and excessively reluctant to participate in rehabilitation activities."[1]

Whereas San Quentin officials believed that the violence and recalcitrance of some inmates required special explanation, others have seen such responses as nearly inevitable in prisons and have held out little hope of widespread peace and cooperation among prisoners. Both Etzioni and Goffman, for example, theorized that coercive recruitment to an organization breeds initial hostility and resentment among those recruited (e.g. prisoners).[2] Correctional settings are inherently coercive in their recruitment—people are assigned to correctional programs under the coercive authority of the state, so alienation from the organization and hostility toward those who administer it naturally follows. Clearly the long history of prison reforms has done little to alter the coercive character of imprisonment. Prisoners are held against their wills, and that they resent both their captivity and their captors should be no surprise. In fact much of the extensive literature on the competition between contradictory correctional goals concedes that the coercive and custodial mission typically wins out; thus, even the San Quentin officials were apparently surprised not so much by resistance but by "excessive" resistance.[3]

It is not necessary to choose between the naive hope that good intentions of officials will generate inmate respect and the more pessimistic assumption that correctional programs, being inherently coercive in nature, will inevitably generate inmate hostility toward staff and program alike. Coercive recruitment may, in fact, generate *initial* hostility, suspicion, and resentment on the part of new inmates, but their experience in the correctional setting will act either to reinforce that initial response, moderate it, or even overcome it. When a prison regime is consistently harsh and coercive, initial inmate hostility and resentment are likely to be confirmed. But when that kind of regime is radically altered, initial inmate suspicion and hostility can be transformed into active support of the program and trusting relationships between prisoners and staff members.

Understanding the ultimate nature of staff-inmate relationships in correctional settings and the reasons for their variation provides a key to analyzing the whole tenor of life within these organizations. A wall of hostility between staff and inmates creates mutual stereo-types and prevents the development of positive controls based on friendship, respect, and trust. Instead, staff must rely on force and on unofficial remunerative controls, while inmates manipulate guards largely through the threat of individual and collective non-cooperation and violence.

Cut off from the staff by institutionally imposed barriers, inmates turn to each other to learn how to adapt. This turning inward creates inmate social and cultural systems that are sustained over time by the process of socialization. Such inmate systems directly affect the quality of life for inmates and the possibilities for most conventional forms of rehabilitation. Counseling and education in particular rely on some degree of mutual trust between participants, a trust that hostile staff-inmate relationships do not foster. In a hostile setting, ironically, staff power over inmates is reduced because staff members are not privy to the inmate subculture and to the system of mutual influence among inmates that almost inevitably develops.

Staff-youth relationships are given priority in the analysis in this chapter, but they are obviously intertwined with the character of the relationships among the youths themselves and with the nature of the youth subcultures. Youths define the character of their rela-tionships with staff members through interaction with one another, and ultimately these definitions may become widely shared by inmates and take on normative character; "never trust a screw" is the classic example from the inmate code.[4]

Perceptions of staff—particularly negative ones—may thus become part of an inmate subculture. The existence and nature of that sub-culture to begin with, however, is a function largely of official or organizational messages about the character of staff-inmate rela-tionships. Although inextricably tied to the content of inmate subculture and patterns of inmate relationships and behavior, the structure of staff-youth relationships provides a staring point for analysis.

THE STARTING POINT OF YOUTH PERCEPTIONS OF STAFF

At no point in our research were we able to observe the evolution of staff-youth relationships from the first day of a program. Almost every observer, however, noted recent arrivals to a program and their early patterns of response. These general patterns were almost always the same: a quiet, watchful approach toward both their peers and staff, close attachment to one or two other youths (at times, previous acquaintances), and reticence except when spoken to by staff members. The uncertainty and tentativeness of individual responses closely resemble the reactions of small groups described by McCorkle, Elias, and Bixby at Highfields:

> Since the [staff group] leader is, to the boy, a member of what frequently seems to him a hostile and unfriendly world, the boy is usually guarded and suspicious in his initial responses at the group sessions. As group members test the leader's role, hostilities and aggressions are directed at the world in general, at the administration of criminal justice in particular, and somewhat later, at the leader. Behavior becomes disorderly, discussions aimless, and it might seem to the outsider that little, if anything, is accomplished. In time, the behavior of the group becomes more orderly, and the group supports and reinforces the leader's earliest definition of the therapy situation. There is some examination and analysis of the testing operations of the group and individual members of the group. When the group participants have satisfied themselves about the therapist, they test one another in a similar manner.[5]

Striking exceptions to this pattern did occur in our sample, but they were rare and highly visible. One youth was participating skillfully in group meetings within a day after his arrival at Group, something that took other residents weeks to learn. Although most residents and staff were favorably impressed with this performance, it only confirmed the clinical director's earlier assessment that the boy was so "pre-shrunk" that the program could not help him; his long history of group therapy and individual psychotherapy had trained him for a role that he used skillfully in manipulating others.[6] For most other youths at Group and elsewhere it took considerably more time to define and adjust to new programs, particularly to those where considerable openness and trust between youths and staff members were expected.

Under the restructured Massachusetts DYS an intriguing technique for reducing the coercive character of recruitment was developed, and perhaps this practice lessened the initial suspicion of many youths toward the new programs and staff. In theory, at least, each youth committed by a court to DYS is given a limited range of programs from which to choose. The placement officer decides whether the range should include residential or nonresidential programs, and if residential, what the appropriate level of service and security is. How consistently such a practice is actually followed is unclear; the location, capacity, and number of equivalent programs obviously limit alternatives in many cases. We do not have evidence that the limited voluntarism of placement actually produces greater initial trust of staff or commitment to programs, but the provision of limited choices should moderate the coerciveness of placement in any correctional system.

During our observations in 1973 it was evident that a small but significant proportion of youths were able to vote with their feet by running away from programs they disliked. Although "splitees," as they were sometimes dubbed, were often—but not always—returned to the program of origin, they could convince DYS officials of a mistaken placement by persistent runs. Such a policy of assignment that takes account at least of the strongest feelings of distate for a program may have reduced the general level of initial hostility and distrust toward staff evident in the system as a whole. It certainly created substantial challenges for the programs that ultimately had to take in as residents the most frequent runaways from other programs.

Even with the mildly voluntaristic placement practices of the current Massachusetts DYS, youths came to programs uncertain about what to expect, suspicious of staff members, and resentful of their loss of freedom, however, limited that loss might be. Their early individual impressions of staff members were shaped by the behavior of staff toward them and others and by what these responses told them to expect in dealing with staff. Variations in the organizationally mandated features of staff roles, therefore, merit close analysis to see how they ultimately related to youth perceptions.

ORGANIZATIONAL SUPPORT FOR STAFF-YOUTH EQUALITY

None of the twenty-three programs in our study possessed the trappings of high-security—uniformed, armed guards, bars, and high walls. The physical and symbolic separation in prisons that are imposed by guns, uniforms, watchtowers, and bars underline the differences between guards (and by extension all staff) and inmates. Although these particular barriers did not divide staff members and youths in the programs we studied, other organizationally imposed divisions were evident in some programs and conspicuously absent in others.

Relatively stable individual and collective youth definitions of staff members and of their relationships to staff are strongly influenced by the presence or absence of these barriers. On the one hand, organizational arrangements and expectations that give staff members the unilateral power to command, humiliate, or physically contain youths widen the gulf between the two groups. As a consequence, such arrangements make it unlikely that youths will overcome their initial suspicions and view staff members as trustworthy, helpful, or friendly. On the other hand, organizational arrangements that carefully cultivate similarities between staff members and youths can create an atmosphere in which initial resistance of youths may be overcome.

It is the degree to which such organizational arrangements are present that determines where a program stands on the staff-youth equality scale. Staff-youth equality can never be complete in any correctional facility, of course, because the staff always represents, at least indirectly, the coercive authority of the state. As indicated in Chapter 1, high staff-youth equality means *relatively high* with respect to the distant, formal, and overtly coercive relationships, idealized in the bureaucratic role of correctional officer; equality means, in this context, less *inequality*, less social distance, less formality, less reliance on formal authority and controls.

Seven organizational traits were used to measure the degree of organizational support for staff-youth equality, as shown in Table 2-1 and detailed below.

Informal Address. First, programs were scored on whether or not participants were on a first-name basis with the program staff. In only two of the community-based programs—both institutional programs—were there instances of formality; at Fatigue the boys were expected to use "Mr.," "Miss," or "Mrs." in addressing their teachers, and at Reward the nuns were invariably addressed as "Sister," although many of the lay staff were called by their first names. In the institutional training school cottages—Cottages 8 and 9, Westview, Elms, Clara Barton, and Putnam—formal address of staff members was expected. At Cottage 9, staff often returned the formal address by the boys with contemptuous commands addressed to "boy," highlighting their superiority even more. At Westview one staff member made clear the relationship between staff and youths by requiring boys to respond "Here, *sir*" during roll call. Sunset and Shirley cottages, although both housing (at least in theory) their own therapeutic communities, also employed traditional house parents who were addressed formally, unlike the other program staff people in the programs. Topsfield and "I Belong" were completely freed from the old conventions, and informality of address prevailed.

No Isolation Cells. The second indicator of organization support for staff-youth equality is the first of four that illustrate the extent to which the staff role involved regulation and implicit humiliation of youths. Several of the training school cottages still had and used isolation cells; although their use had apparently decreased in frequency under the Miller administration, their mere presence and the threat of their use further emphasized the authoritarian and distant staff role. At Cottage 9, the Tombs, as the five by nine foot isolation cells were called, were in most frequent use, often to back up staff authority when it was challenged.

> Larry and Gil were fooling around, and Mr. Bartolo ordered Larry over to the table across the room. Larry walked over but was giving Mr. Evans some back talk in the process. Mr. Evans got out from the desk and grabbed Larry by the T-shirt and asked him what was bothering him. Mr. Evans shook him some and then slapped him openhanded in the face; he then took him out into the hallway and yelled at him a little more before taking him up into his tomb at 3:35 p.m. where Larry remained for the rest of the day.

Though less frequently used, isolation cells were still available at Cottage 8, Sunset, Clara Barton, and Putnam.

No Locks. The degree of staff-youth equality was also indicated by the presence or absence of locks intended to control free access from one part of a building to another, particularly to the living area. The constant ritual of locking and unlocking doors made obvious the monopoly staff had over keys and security, symbolizing staff-youth inequality. In the community-based programs, only Warning and Reward (both institutional programs) maintained some semblance of physical security through lock and key, and it was far more obvious in the former than the latter. Warning residents constantly had to ask staff members to open doors—to let them up to the gym, to go down to the school or cafeteria, or even at times to get back to their own rooms (which were periodically sealed off during the day to keep better track of the boys). Particularly for the many staff members who were former offenders themselves, this obligation to be a jailer was a difficult one: "Alex said the worst thing about the job was having to carry the keys, after having been on the other side. He said that every staff member felt bad when he left at the end of the day, knowing that kids were locked up inside in that crummy place." At Reward only the outer doors were locked and the girls were not barred from the remainder of the building. On the other hand, in both these programs staff members also escorted youths to activities outside the locked building; thus, staff opened up as well

Table 2-1. Scores on Variables Composing Equality Scale, by Program[a]

	Staff-Youth Equality Variables							Staff Equality Variables				
	Informal Address	No Isolation Cells	No Locks	Free Smoking	Free Clothing	Young Staff	Ex-resident Staff	Low Staff Differentiation	Shared Counseling Role	No Shift Identities	Regular Staff Meetings	Total Equality Score
Institutional Programs												
Cottage 8	1	1	1	3	1	1	1	1	1	1	1	13
Elms	1	3	1	3	1	1	1	1	1	1	1	15
Westview	1	3	1	1	1	1	1	1	1	1	1	13
Clara Barton	1	1	1	1	1	1	1	1	1	1	1	11
Putnam	1	1	1	1	1	1	1	1	1	1	1	11
Cottage 9	1	1	1	1	1	1	1	3	1	1	1	13
Regiment	3	3	3	3	3	3	1	3	3	3	3	31
Shelter	3	3	3	3	3	3	1	3	1	1	3	27
Warning	3	3	1	3	3	3	1	1	3	1	1	23
Fatigue	1	3	3	3	3	3	3	1	1	3	1	25
Mother	3	3	3	1	3	3	1	1	1	1	1	21
Reward	1	3	1	3	3	3	1	1	1	3	3	23
Group Treatment Programs												
"I Belong"	3	3	3	3	3	3	1	3	3	3	3	31
Topsfield	3	3	3	3	3	3	1	3	3	3	3	31
Shirley	1	3	3	3	1	3	1	1	1	1	1	21
Sunset	1	1	1	1	1	3	1	1	1	1	1	13
Primal	3	3	3	3	3	3	3	3	3	3	3	33
Confront	3	3	3	3	3	3	3	3	3	3	3	33
Group	3	3	3	3	3	3	3	3	3	3	3	33
Open House	3	3	3	3	3	3	1	3	3	1	3	29

Open-Community Programs

Drop-in	3	3	3	3	3	3	3	3	3	1	31
Pick-up	3	3	3	1	1	3	3	3	3	3	29
Pair	3	3	3	3	1	1	3	3	3	3	31

[a]Programs with a particular characteristic received a score of 3 and those without it a score of 1. Scores of 2 were assigned to programs where the trait was partially evident (see text).

as closed off opportunities, in contrast to a prison setting where the major task of guards is only to close them off.

Locks were widespread in all the institutional training school cottages, although they were conspicuously absent at three of the four group-treatment cottages: Shirley Cottage, "I Belong," and Topsfield. Typically, at the least, the doors to the institutional cottages were locked at night to prevent easy escape. The most extreme security was taken at the two girls' cottages where a central switchboard electronically locked all the girls' individual rooms at night and opened them in the morning. The observer noted that "the matrons are not supposed to open the door of a girl after she is bolted in for the night unless there is a man present; the girls all have pails for emergency use in their rooms."

Free Smoking. Programs were coded according to whether or not they placed limits on smoking, a highly and almost universally valued activity among the youths. The rituals of lighting up and of bumming cigarettes (particularly Kools) were ever present. Restrictions on smoking were thus particularly resented. Such restrictions were evident in one institutional community-based program, Mother, where the hourly distribution of cigarettes—one per girl depending on behavior during that period—was a central part of the abortive token economy. This restriction was a point of much contention between residents and staff, as it also was in the five institutional training school cottages that regulated smoking—Cottage 9, Westview, Sunset, Clara Barton, and Putnam. Smoking was prohibited at Cottage 9, although a watchman's log report indicated the frequency of violation and the resultant staff-youth conflict:

> Lucky and Striker were seen smoking in the dorm. Crooner was humming and singing and was told to shut up. He kept this up until the group from the central building was called in and started shifting the boys around. The hoppers [toilets] were in continuous use. This is the general rule when cigs and matches are hid and used in the dorm.

Four of the boys were put into the Tombs for smoking that night. At Clara Barton and Putnam some girls were designated nonsmokers because of their age or to punish them for violation of rules, and thus could only look on during the designated smoking breaks. At Westview, Elms, and Sunset, smoking was supposed to occur only in specific places and at particular times.

Free Clothing. The fifth organizationally mandated practice that related to the degree of separation between staff and youth roles was the presence or absence of a requirement that youths wear standard-issue, institutional garb ("baggies"). Although such a requirement had been struck down as an institutional rule by the Miller administration, all but two of the cottages—both group-treatment programs—still made residents wear baggies at least for the initial two weeks of their stay. Once they had proved themselves, youths could have the privilege of wearing their own clothes. Baggies were, however, the universal clothing in Cottage 9. None of the community programs required standard clothing.

Young Staff. The presence of a majority of staff members under thirty years of age was the sixth variable gauging staff-youth equality. Both this and the seventh variable were used as indicators of whether or not positive attempts were made to reach across the generational gulf that often separated youths and staff.[7]

Staff members typically were adults, often middle-aged, with different, generationally based experiences from those shared by the teenagers with whom they worked. The training schools particularly had large proportions of older staff members who were there partly because of their maturity to serve as cottage parents—and partly as a result of a long-standing civil service system. In contrast, the relative newness of community-based programs may have contributed to the youthfulness of their staff members. Whereas only Topsfield and "I Belong" (both new group treatment programs in 1971) of the 1971 system had a majority of staff under thirty, all but Pick-up in the community-based system had at least half of their staff members under thirty.

Ex-resident Staff. The presence of former youth offenders as staff members served as the seventh variable indicating staff-youth equality. A clear barrier to identification and communication across staff-youth lines is the typical caste-like separation between the two groups; this division presents serious symbolic implications for perceptions of equality while often reflecting important differences in world-view and experience. Typically there is no upward mobility for inmates—they never become staff members; the implicit official message to youths is that "you can never become one of us because of your tarnished identity; you are morally inferior." Just as important is the gap in experience enforced by these caste lines. People often believe that those who are best able to understand them are those who have had similar experiences, but the validity of the inmate experience both in the program and prior to it are repudiated by the caste system, which denies former offenders staff roles. Several of the programs we observed in the community-based system violated traditional assumptions of correctional organization, however, and employed one or more former program members. All but one of the eight regular staff members at Primal were successful graduates, while two of the Group staff and one each at Confront, Drop-in, and Fatigue were former members.[8] Although Warning employed a large contingent of adult ex-offenders, it did not hire any graduates of its own program, and thus was not so coded.

The scores on these seven variables for each program and the summed staff-youth equality scale are summarized in Table 2-1. The table shows that all the community-based programs were high in staff-youth equality compared to those training school cottages, which had not adopted the group-treatment model. Only the group-treatment programs in the training schools resembled the later community-based programs in their support for more egalitarian relationships between staff members and youths. The restrictive, paternalistic, and somewhat arbitrary traditions of the old institutions died hard, with the result that the training schools, despite considerable reforms by 1971, were still, in general, places where staff were staff and youths were children.

EQUALITY AND STAFF CONSISTENCY

Even where the lines between keepers and kept are most clearly drawn, staff members rarely maintain the formal distance from prisoners which their official role requires. The many instances in which inmates placed themselves in jeopardy with fellow inmates by giving aid and comfort to guards during the Attica rebellion was just one vivid example of the kinds of bonds that can develop, even given the more extreme organizational supports for inequality at a maximum security prison.[9] Given the low numbers of staff supervising large numbers of inmates in most prisons, and the very real but nonetheless imperfect official limits on staff power, staff members, in order to do their jobs, make compromises with inmates. As many analysts of the most caste-like prisons have noted, the prison order is a negotiated power-sharing arrangement in which guards overlook some rule violations in return for the maintenance of order by the prisoners themselves (generally, by those profiting most by the guards' actions).[10] Instrumental pressures toward such compromises must certainly be supplemented by expressive ones as well, at least for many personnel. During the monotonous day-to-day routine of institutional life, staff and inmates may come to view one another as people sharing similar experiences; formal and distant relationships break down under the burden of daily interchange.

These pressures result in a series of tenuous and informal bonds between some inmates and some staff members. Such bonds require violation of official rules by staff and introduce considerable variation in staff administration of rules and treatment of individuals. Observations in the programs in our sample that had low staff-youth equality followed a consistent pattern. "Mr. Smith allows kids to roam the cottage whereas Mr. Fredericks keeps them in one place"; each staff member had a special orientation toward the rules. Those staff members who compromised institutional rules usually covered themselves with the administration, but even higher officials lent tacit support on occasion to these compromises:

> Mr. Simmons does not see the prohibition against smoking, which is an institutional rule, as making much sense. The school rule is that the boys are not allowed to carry their own cigarettes and are only supposed to smoke at specified times during the day, when the masters hand out cigarettes to the boys. The rule at Elms is that kids can keep their own cigarettes but that they cannot smoke in specified areas and that they cannot carry cigarettes around the ground; Mr. Simmons told me that the School Superintendent knows of his transgression of the school rule but that he apparently condones it.

Staff members consciously used these compromises in the enforcement of rules as levers in the attempt to control youths:

> Mr. Gerard and Mr. Delkus on duty. Mr. Alex presiding. People are carrying more than their share of cigarettes and smoking outside of the areas, Mr. Alex says. So there will be no smoking in the cafeteria for the next week. Mr. Gerard says that there is too much abuse of the smoking rules in the cottage as well and backs up Alex's point, saying that it is actually a school rule that there is to be *no smoking on trade*, but the staff are sticking their necks out for the boys.

These inconsistencies themselves may well serve to increase distrust and resentment by inmates of staff members in general, although each inmate may see at least one staff member as an exception—the one who shows him or her some special interest or provides special favors or privileges. It also is likely to have subtle effects on youths' perceptions of their situation by making manipulation of staff members and attention to what they can get away with the focus of their activity. Rules become meaningless; and official definitions of the situation lose whatever value they might otherwise have had as reference points for youths seeking individually and collectively to define appropriate conduct in the correctional setting.

STAFF EQUALITY

Staff-youth inequalities thus are not alone in widening the gulf between staff and youths. Early in the analysis of the organizational divisions between the youths and staff members in our program sample, it became clear that this separation was simply one aspect of the more general phenomenon of differentiation and inequality within programs. The distribution among programs of a number of organizational features that promoted or hindered equality among staff members closely paralleled the distribution of traits related to staff-youth equality. Inequities among staff members appeared to foster further inconsistencies and conflicts in the staff administration of rules and to drive a larger wedge between staff and youths than did staff-youth inequality by itself.

Although youths often could discover one or two sympathetic staff members with whom they were able to establish close relatinships even in a highly differentiated program, the uncertainty about how they were expected to behave and the appearance of arbitrariness that resulted from inconsistencies engendered suspicion and disrespect. These inconsistencies further promoted a gaming and manipulative orientation toward staff and rules generally by creating frequent opportunities to beat the system by playing staff members off against one another. The general degree of staff differentiation and inequality within a program thus appears to play a significant role in staff-youth relationships by affecting the level of staff coordination and consistency in applying rules and interacting with individual youths.

Organizationally supported equality among staff members was gauged by four variables as shown in Table 2-1 and examined below.

Low Staff Differentiation. Each program was coded on the basis of the degree of staff differentiation. Every staff we observed was functionally differentiated to some degree, of course, but that degree varied considerably. For purposes here, a staff with low differentiation was one in which over four-fifths of the staff members devoted most of their time to similar activities and had similar responsibilities. Using this rough criterion, five of the institutional training school cottages—Cottage 8, Elms, Westview, Clara Barton and Putnam—and four of the institutional community programs—Warning,

Fatigue, Mother, and Reward—had highly differentiated staff organization; distinct positions for teachers, social workers, administrators, childcare workers or cottage parents and masters were defined in these programs and divided the staffs fairly evenly into distinct groups.

In addition, two of the training school cottages using the group-treatment model, Sunset and Shirley, had highly differentiated staffing patterns which carried over from the recently and not completely broken bond to the larger institution. Both, for example, still had several sets of cottage parents who served mainly in a supervisory capacity, as well as counselors and special summer teachers. In the remaining programs, staff roles were officially defined in varying ways, but in each one, in practice, most staff members shared most responsibilities; these programs did not employ many professional specialists or people who were designated specifically for supervisory capacities.

Shared Counseling Role. One of the most crucial responsibilities in a correctional program is the counseling function, and the degree to which it was shared by staff served as the second indicator of staff equality. Counseling requires at least some attempts at collaboration between youths and staff members, and thus sharply distinguishes counselors from those supervisors who serve exclusively as rule enforcers. By creating at least two distinct, and at many times conflicting, relationships to youths in a program, such role differentiation fostered staff conflict and inconsistency toward youths. Programs that encouraged all or most staff members to take on a counseling role therefore also encouraged greater staff equality and coordination.

Diffusion of the counseling role was evident in all the programs with low staff differentiation, except for Cottage 9 where no one did any counseling. In addition, Warning, although highly differentiated in other respects, encouraged all its staff members, particularly the men on the floor who comprised the bulk of the staff, to "rap" with kids about their problems. Their efforts were supplemented by social workers and legal advisers. In all the other highly differentiated programs, counseling was generally reserved for designated professionals—the cottage counselor in the training school cottages and the social worker in the community programs.

No Shift Differentiation. The existence of a sharp delineation between different shifts of staff members working at different hours was the third variable. Staff communication and coordination were severely limited by shift divisions because each shift had its own character and problems and because staff members seldom had time or opportunity to communicate information across shifts. For example, the young people who took turns working the overnight shift at Shelter had no activities or program to occupy the girls, no counseling responsibilities, and little knowledge of the girls' individual backgrounds and problems. As a consequence, they were forced to rely on threats much more heavily than did the day staff in their attempts to maintain some semblance of order. A log book was one device for communication and continuity across shifts, but entries in these books were typically rather cryptic and allowed for little interchange about appropriate strategies for working with the youths.

All of the training school cottages except those furthest from the institutional regime—"I Belong" and Topsfield—divided staff personnel into nonrotating shifts. Employees at Warning, Mother, Shelter, and Open House were similarly divided. In each program there were specifically designated night workers, while the other staff people were mainly on a nine-to-five schedule. Those programs which overcame shift identities did so short of requiring all staff to work twenty-four hour days. In many programs staff members rotated the night duty (and weekend duty) so that all staff members worked during the days at some point, even if all did not work at night. At Reward, distinctive shift identification was prevented because a majority of the staff people were members of a religious order and lived in the same complex of buildings the girls did. They were in and out constantly.

Regular Staff Meetings. Finally, programs were distinguished on the basis of the presence or absence of regular (at least weekly) meetings involving all staff. Several programs had meetings of social workers or of child-care workers but never combined all the different occupational categories into one meeting, while other programs never succeeded in bringing together staff members from different shifts. Limited participation in staff meetings implies distinctions among staff members and reduces the degree to which staff people share in decision-making and in understanding how others are interpreting rules or handling difficult youths and troublesome situations.

Although some degree of differential staff handling of youths and interpretation of rules was almost universal, programs with regular and inclusive staff meetings could reduce, if not eliminate, such problems. At Group, for example, the weekly staff group meeting provided a context for all staff members to support and challenge one another's actions and to work out standard modes of response to troublesome behavior. A major portion of one staff group, for example, was devoted to providing feedback to Paul, a new staff member who had been a resident of the program:

> Harris commented about the degree of Paul's involvement with the kids and said that he may have to work at establishing distance. Paul had said earlier that he wanted people to tell him when he was doing things wrong or when he did them right.

Weekly meetings of all staff were far from universal. Of the twenty-three programs, twelve scheduled such meetings regularly. All of the programs that used the group-treatment model—except Sunset—included staff meetings in the weekly schedule as did Reward, Regiment, Shelter, Pair, and Pick-up.

That staff agreement, coordination, and consistency were not always present was evident from our observations of programs with relatively low levels of staff equality. At Warning, for example, we watched internal conflict lead to a major staff reorganization soon after we left. The strife made staff expectations of one another and of residents even more uncertain there. Child-care workers at Mother resented their exclusion from the decision-making process, complained repeatedly, and undermined through inconsistent implementation a token economy system that had been imposed on them:

> Nancy talked about not being moved up into the higher ranks of Mother's staff and said that the ideas of those who run the place are not really the ideas of the younger staff. The social workers really don't know how these kids live—they ought to live up there for a while to see the problems of the house mothers.

Teachers at Fatigue disagreed with the model of the tough, aggressive male that they felt the child-care workers reinforced for the boys: "I wish they [child-care workers] wouldn't roughhouse with the boys that way. It only makes our job harder."

Youths exploited staff failures of communication and inconsistencies when such failures could make their lives easier. In Cottage 9, for example, the observer reported: "At lunch today, Mr. Andrews ordered Silvio to sit in Gabe's seat starting this evening, breaking up the troublesome Silvio-Rudy table. However, Mr. Andrews neglected to tell the evening shift of his intended change, and Silvio and Gabe both sat in their regular seats. They asked me [the observer] if I noticed that, and I told them I did." In addition to accepting joyfully but passively any staff errors in their favor, youths also took an active part in playing staff members off against one another.

PROGRAM EQUALITY AS A SINGLE DIMENSION

The high correlation between scores on the staff equality and staff-youth equality dimensions ($r = .94$) and the theoretical and practical significance of the underlying variable—the degree of organizational nondifferentiation and equality—led us to combine these measures into one large scale that measured organizationally supported *equality* for the remainder of the analysis (see Table 2-1).

Although an explanation of these closely associated variations in organizational differentiation is not the major purpose here, several probable causes of differences in organizational equality are worth noting. First, program size is likely to be related to the degree of equality; the larger the membership, the more highly differentiated and bureaucratized and the less egalitarian the organization is likely to be. Size creates its own problems of coordination and places burdens on the process of collective participation, which are typically alleviated by the development of administrative hierarchies. Increases in size also multiply the difficulty of supervising the lower members in a program; rules based on perceived administrative convenience as much as on notions of justice and fairness are substituted for more personal and persuasive supervision.

Functional complexity is a factor of some significance in creating differentiation. Those institutional programs that tried to do the most for their clients—to provide them, through their own staff, health services, education, counseling, vocational training—also had the most highly stratified and differentiated staffs.[11] Either more restricted service goals or substitution of community resources (schools, physicians/hospitals) for in-program service can decrease the complexity of tasks *and* the degree of staff differentiation and inequality within programs.

Increased staff equality seems likely to be related to anti-professionalism in a program, perhaps both as cause and consequence. Such anti-professional beliefs tend to equalize staff, as does a commitment to the humanistic notion that sincerity, understanding, openness, and commitment are the effective tools of human service, not professional training and credentials. But even anti-professionalism can create new elites and foster tension and rivalry within the staff. Warning, for example was premised on the belief that ex-felons could best communicate with and deter boys who were in repeated and serious trouble with the law. In this program the college-trained counselor was, thus, not the equal of his prison-educated colleague.

The nature of organizational sponsorship may also play a part in determining the degree of organizational equality. State-sponsored and state-run programs and institutions almost inevitably import bureaucracy through the civil service rules and procedures that govern their employees. Bureaucratic human service agencies may also tend to promote the most interpersonally effective personnel into supervisory positions, leaving a large proportion of novices and less competent oldtimers providing person-to-person service at any one time. Such a situation of bureaucratization and thinned-out talent contrasts sharply with the character of many of the private programs that existed in Massachusetts in 1971 and 1973. "A sense of mission" provided the staff members of many of the community programs and two of the training school cottages ("I Belong" and Topsfield)[12] with a shared staff commitment and concern that the civil service system of the state bureaucracy could not sustain. Although some of the more long-standing private service agencies whose programs we observed had mini-bureaucracies of their own, many of the newer and smaller programs were started by younger men and women whose commitment to an idea or to the need for human service sustained them in the face of the financial hardships, struggles over community locations, and uncertainty about survival, which characterized the early Massachusetts experience with community-based programs. These unintended hardships may have resulted in a natural selection process that ended in the survival of some of the most dedicated practitioners. Compared to the men and women who often choose civil service careers in part for the security they provide, these people were probably experimenters and risk takers. More systematic, slower, more bureaucratic change, which Miller's critics believe should have been undertaken in Massachusetts, might well have stifled this intangible but important excitement and commitment among program staff.

The unified equality dimension, summarized in Table 2-1, cuts across two of the three program clusters. Institutional programs varied radically in degree of equality, while two group-treatment programs scored substantially lower on this dimension than the other six in that cluster. By contrast, all the open-community programs had high equality scores.

PROGRAM EQUALITY AND
COMMUNITY CONTACT

Although the correlation between the community-contact and equality scales is low (r = .19), programs that encourage considerable contact between youths and members of the free community are also universally high on the equality scale.[13] Community contact creates pressures toward organizational support for equality between staff and youths and among staff for a number of reasons. Openness to the free community provides access to resources that a program might otherwise have to furnish itself, such as teaching, medical and psychological care, and job training. Less complex in function, therefore, the program requires less staff differentiation to carry on its work. Openness also reduces or eliminates many of the aspects of staff role that distinguish it so sharply from the youth role; keys, controls over clothing, restrictions on cigarette consumption—rules that sharply restrict individual liberties—are no longer possible. Rather than restrictive rules and roles that drive staff and youths apart, there are pressures for staff members to be like the youths in order to attract them to the program. Without a captive audience and forced to compete with more freely chosen associates in the community for the attention of program members, staff members must do all they can to make themselves and their program attractive. One apparent consequence of this pressure is considerably increased organizational support for staff-youth equalities.

PROGRAM ORGANIZATION AND
CHARACTERISTICS OF THE
YOUTH POPULATION

One might suppose that more egalitarian programs would be so organized because they have a more highly selected and tractable clientele. Two of the correlations between level of equality in a program and the characteristics of the programs' youth populations lend some support to this interpretation (see Table 2-2). Although most of the correlations do not differ much from zero, there is a moderate inverse relationship (r = -.52) between program equality and the proportion of DYS youths in the population who had previously been committed by a court to DYS, and a weak inverse relationship between equality and proportion of youths in the program from DYS (r = -.31).

The source of the first relationship is an unexplained difference

Table 2-2. Correlations between Equality Scale and Population Characteristics (*N* = 23 programs)

	Correlation
Percentage of youths 16 years or older	.04
Percentage of male youths	.08
Percentage of black youths	-.09
Percentage of youths from DYS	-.31
Percentage of DYS youths committing first offense before age 14	-.21
Percentage of DYS youths with previous commitment	-.52
Percentage of DYS youths committed for crimes against persons	-.02
Percentage of DYS youths committed for juvenile status offenses	-.02

between the training school and the community-based youth populations we studied. In the former an average of 73 percent of the residents reported a previous court commitment to DYS, while in the latter an average of only 38 percent of the participants did so. Because the training schools also had the least egalitarian programs, there is a relation between equality and the percentage of previously committed youths. Similar reasoning explains the second correlation. Only in the community-based system (generally more egalitarian) were there any programs that took on private referrals as well as youths sponsored by other social agencies. When only the community-based programs are examined, both these relationships disappear, suggesting that there is no inherent reason why egalitarian programs cannot be created for populations with higher proportions of recidivists or of DYS youths.[14]

STAFF PERCEPTIONS OF YOUTHS

Theoretically, several factors should be at work in producing program-by-program variations in staff attitudes toward their charges. First, organizational differences reflect differences in the ideologies of treatment that help guide the programs. These philosophies may shape the general outlook toward delinquents that staff members have, as well as act to draw people who share beliefs compatible with the organizational philosophy into staff positions. Second, the organizational rules and expectations about interaction between youths and staff will affect the kinds of experiences staff members have with youths, and thus their perceptions of youths. The degree of distance which staff people are constrained to feel as a consequence of their particular roles as well as the distance youths may expect from staff as a consequence of the official definition of staff and youth roles will significantly affect relationships and mutual perceptions. Perceptions that youths and staff have of one another are interdependent and develop through interaction, at least initially, before they are firmly set in the mold of subculturally-supported mutual stereotypes.

Third, the characteristics of the youths will themselves influence staff perceptions. The direct influence arises from the sorting process through which youths are allocated to programs with different treatment ideologies; to the degree that more hostile and dangerous youths are concentrated in some programs, for example, staff members in these programs are likely to perceive youths as more dangerous and hostile.

Staff members in each program were asked a number of questions to help assess their general views about delinquents as well as their perceptions of the particular youths in their programs. These items were accumulated together in two scales—one measuring staff trust of delinquents[15] and the other measuring staff belief that "their kids" were particularly difficult to work with.[16] Programs were then assigned scores corresponding to the proportions of their staff members who scored above the mid-point on these scales.

A regression of the scale measuring staff trust of delinquents on the several scales measuring organizational traits and the eight indicators of characteristics of the youth populations of each program (see Table 2–3) reveals that the equality scale contributes most heavily to the variance in staff trust of youths ($r = .78$). Other variables add only marginally to an explanation of this variation.

Both the ideological foundation for equalizing relationships within a correctional organization and the consequent relationships with youths served to support the higher degree of staff trust in more egalitarian programs. The almost universal resistance by staff members in the community-based system to use of the word delinquent (and their horror at seeing "hard-core delinquent"—even in quotation marks—in the questionnaire) suggest the ideological forces at work. Youths were *not* to be labeled and were to be given the benefit of the doubt both in these new programs and in those training school programs that broke with tradition. The emotional distance required by traditional staff roles fostered harsher judgments of youths—stereotypes—that were not checked by closer, more personal ties. In addition, as shall be seen in later chapters, this distance

Table 2-3. Multiple Regression on Independent Variables of Percentage of Program Staff with High Score on Trust of Delinquents Scale (*N* = 23 programs)[a]

Independent Variables	Zero-Order Correlation with Dependent Variable	Standardized Regression Coefficient	F Ratio
Percentage of youths 16 years or older	-.20		
Percentage of male youths	-.14		
Percentage of black youths	-.05		
Percentage of youths from DYS	-.30		
Percentage of DYS youths committing first offense before age 14	-.13		
Percentage of DYS youths with previous commitment	-.60		
Percentage of DYS youths committed for crimes against persons	-.18		
Percentage of DYS youths committed for juvenile status offenses	.15		
Program size	.22		
Youth-to-staff ratio	-.22		
Equality scale	.78	0.78	32.65
Community-contact scale	.38		
Participation scale	.30		
Supervision scale	.13		

[a]For the regression equation the multiple correlation = .78 (R^2 = .61), and the F ratio = 32.65 (with 1 and 21 degrees of freedom).

contributed to the development of informal inmate systems that promoted attitudes and behavior partially justifying staff suspicions of delinquents.

Although general staff perceptions of the character of delinquents and delinquency are best accounted for by variation in levels of program equality, perceptions of the recalcitrance of the youth population they must work with on a day-to-day basis can be explained by a combination of program and youth characteristics. The regression of this scale on organizational and population variables (see Table 2-4) is consistent with the notion that staff members take careful account of youth characteristics in making judgments about "their kids."

Variation in the proportions of youths over sixteen years of age and in the proportions of youths committed for offenses against the person were particularly associated with variation in staff perceptions in this regression. Staff members faced with older, physically larger

Table 2-4. Multiple Regression on Independent Variables of Percentage of Program Staff with High Score on "Difficult to Handle" Youth Population Scale (*N* = 23 programs)[a]

Independent Variables	Zero-Order Correlation with Dependent Variable	Standardized Regression Coefficient	F Ratio
Percentage of youths 16 years or older	.40	0.55	9.47
Percentage of male youths	.28		
Percentage of black youths	.39		
Percentage of youths from DYS	-.01		
Percentage of DYS youths committing first offense before age 14	.14		
Percentage of DYS youths with previous commitment	.43		
Percentage of DYS youths committed for crimes against persons	.48	.40	6.23
Percentage of DYS youths committed for juvenile status offenses	-.32		
Program size	.21		
Youth-to-staff ratio	.09		
Equality scale	-.19		
Community-contact scale	-.13		
Participation scale	-.25	-.53	9.18
Supervision scale	-.19		

[a]For the regression equation the multiple correlation = .74 (R^2 = .54), and the F ratio = 7.46 (with 3 and 19 degrees of freedom).

youths and with those who had in the past attacked other people understandably viewed their charges as more difficult.

Older youths are more mature physically and can be more difficult to handle. At Fatigue, for example, boys reaching sixteen were usually eased out of the program because of the threat they posed to other younger and usually smaller boys and to the staff. During our observation there the social workers were feverishly trying to place a sixteen-year-old boy who was built like a heavyweight boxer and who when angered could (and did) pick up smaller residents by the feet and pile-drive their heads into the floor. The staff members understandably gave him a wide berth; none of them engaged in horseplay with him and he followed his own schedule of activities. Similarly, youths with histories of crimes against persons are generally defined in our culture as being more serious offenders, and it is not surprising that programs with higher proportions of such people would be—all else being equal—the ones where staff viewed youths as more difficult.

Youth population characteristics were not alone, however, in explaining the variation in staff perceptions. The degree of youth participation in the organization added substantially to the regression. High participation scores (this scale, described briefly in Chapter 1, will be discussed in detail in the next chapter) were associated with low proportions of staff who viewed their youths as difficult to handle; this association is largely a consequence of the ideologies of the more participatory programs in our sample, which tended to view delinquents—even those in serious trouble— as having problems not so terribly different from those of other people. In addition, the willingness of staff members in these programs to give responsibility to youths reflected a general expectation that delinquents were competent and did not need to be managed by staff.

YOUTH PERCEPTIONS OF STAFF

Organizations that sustain barriers between youths and staff members and among staff vastly increase the possiblity of inconsistencies in staff behavior and tend to formalize relationships so that they are focused around rules. So goes part of the argument made earlier in ths chapter. Measures drawn from questionnaires administered to youths in 1971 and 1973 made possible a test of these assertions. In both questionnaires youths responded to the statement, "The staff doesn't treat each kid equally; they have favorites" and judged how frequently "one staff member will want you to do one thing and another staff member will want you to do just the opposite."[17] The answers to these items were scored, correlated ($r = .86$) and summed to create a scale measuring youth perceptions of staff consistency.

The percentage of youths in each program scoring above the midpoint of possible values on the perceived staff consistency scale was regressed on the set of independent variables (see Table 2-5). The degree of program equality emerges as the most powerful contributor to explaining variation in perceived staff consistency. The equality scale includes measures of several organizational mechanisms for developing staff coordination and consistency; a strong relationship between equality and perceived consistency of staff indicates that these organizational techniques work effectively.

The emergence of program size as the second independent variable in this equation adds to this interpretation. Increasing size was associated with decreases in the level of staff consistency as perceived by youths. Larger size, like inequality, made coordination

Table 2-5. Multiple Regression on Independent Variables of Percentage of Youths with High Score on Staff Consistency Scale (*N* = 23 programs)[a]

Independent Variables	Zero-Order Correlation with Dependent Variable	Standardized Regression Coefficient	F Ratio
Percentage of youths 16 years or older	-.25		
Percentage of male youths	-.09		
Percentage of black youths	.02		
Percentage of youths from DYS	.09		
Percentage of DYS youths committing first offense before age 14	-.17		
Percentage of DYS youths with previous commitment	-.62		
Percentage of DYS youths committed for crimes against persons	.12		
Percentage of DYS youths committed for juvenile status offenses	.11		
Program size	-.48	0.37	6.46
Youth-to-staff ratio	-.29		
Equality scale	.67	.61	16.95
Community-contact scale	.21		
Participation scale	.13		
Supervision scale	-.07		

[a]For the regression equation the multiple correlation = .76 (R^2 = .58), and the F ratio = 13.98 (with 2 and 20 degrees of freedom).

among staff members more difficult; there were typically more staff members whose conduct had to be brought into alignment toward more youths. Magnitude alone made coordination difficult. Each staff member was less likely to know each youth and each staff colleague's approach toward him when a program had many members than when it had few.

Typically, formal rules are made to solve the problems of inconsistency and lack of coordination in depersonalized settings with large populations. Yet we have already seen hints of the limitations of such a strategy in correctional settings. On the one hand, the philosophy of individualized treatment is inconsistent with bureaucratic handling of youths; on the other hand, where bureaucracy and universalistic rules exist, staff members must typically compromise them in order to cope with the informal inmate system that develops to counter this formal system. In either case, therefore, the bureaucratic solution is an inadequate one, and increases in program size promote problems of staff coordination and consistency.

One solution to the problem of staff inconsistency was to make the notion of individualized treatment (as opposed to universalistic application of rules) a basic tenet of the program ideology. Only under special conditions, examined in the next chapter, were such attempts successful. Where youths themselves accepted such a norm, however, they tolerated greater variation in staff conduct toward them. Primal went even further and supplemented this norm with another, that injustices were part of life and had to be accepted with minimal resistance. Thus, although staff activity was well coordinated at Primal and the problems of inconsistency few, the normative system into which youths were socialized there provided a back-up system. It moderated the effects of errors in staff judgment and of inconsistencies in their behavior on youths' loyalty to the program and on their sense of fairness and justice.

In addition to making judgments about the degree of staff consistency, youths were asked in the questionnaires to indicate which they believed was more important for them while they were in a program: "to obey the rules and not get into any trouble" or "to understand personal problems."

A regression on the set of independent variables of the percentage of youths in each program who chose the rule-oriented response confirms the expectation that organizationally supported staff distance from youths was translated into more formal rule-oriented relationships with youths (see Table 2-6). The negative signs and large size of the standardized regression coefficient for the equality scale (as well as its high negative correlation with the dependent variable— $r = -.79$) testify to its supreme importance for youth perceptions of staff. The lower the level of program equality, the more likely were youths to perceive staff as rule-oriented.

Similarly, the degree of youth participation in the program contributes to the regression equation. The greater the involvement of youths in providing therapy for their peers and in making decisions about activities and discipline, the less likely staff people were perceived to be rule-oriented—even holding constant the level of program equality. High youth participation blurred even further the lines between staff members and youths and reduced the degree to which staff alone had to act as divisive rule-enforcers in a program.

These two characteristics of program organization are joined by one measure of youth population characteristics in the final regression. Programs with higher proportions of boys were, with other variables held constant, likely to have higher percentages of youths who viewed staff members as rule-oriented.[18] Most plausibly this pattern arose from culturally based differences in the willingness of boys and girls to express feelings and emotions and admit to having problems.

Table 2-6.   Multiple Regression on Independent Variables of Percentage of Youths Perceiving Staff as Rule-Oriented (*N* = 23 programs)[a]

Independent Variables	Zero-Order Correlation with Dependent Variable	Standardized Regression Coefficient	F Ratio
Percentage of youths 16 years or older	.05	0.24	3.86[b]
Percentage of male youths	.15		
Percentage of black youths	.00		
Percentage of youths from DYS	.39		
Percentage of DYS youths committing first offense before age 14	.11		
Percentage of DYS youths with previous commitment	.38		
Percentage of DYS youths committed for crimes against persons	-.03		
Percentage of DYS youths committed for juvenile status offenses	-.12		
Program size	.03		
Youth-to-staff ratio	.09		
Equality scale	-.79	-.67	24.02
Community-contact scale	-.05		
Participation scale	-.56	-.27	3.85[b]
Supervision scale	-.41		

[a]For the regression equation the multiple correlation = .85 (R^2 = .77), and the *F* ratio = 16.58 (with 3 and 19 degrees of freedom).

[b]These *F* ratios are significant at the 0.10 level.

Staff members in programs where males predominate may thus find youths to be resistant to attempts at counseling. Rebuffed in attempts to show their personal interest and concern through a conventional counseling relationship, staff members consequently are likely to be viewed by resistant boys as being (and may, in fact, become) "rule oriented," an orientation more in accord with the boys' view of themselves and of their proper relationship to staff members.

Finally, two items in the questionnaire tapped general youth evaluations of staff members. Responses to these questions were weighted equally and added together to create a scale measuring youth perceptions of staff concern and trustworthiness.[19] A regression of this measure on program and youth characteristics (see Table 2-7) makes clear that the degree of organizationally supported equality is the best predictor of general youth attitudes toward staff and that no other variables add significantly to the explanation. Where fewer barriers were imposed by the organization between

Table 2-7. Multiple Regression on Independent Variables of Percentage of Youths with High Scores on Perceived Staff Concern and Trustworthiness Scale (N = 23 programs)[a]

Independent Variables	Zero-Order Correlation with Dependent Variable	Standardized Regression Coefficient	F Ratio
Percentage of youths 16 years or older	-.11		
Percentage of male youths	-.04		
Percentage of black youths	-.21		
Percentage of youths from DYS	-.33		
Percentage of DYS youths committing first offense before age 14	-.08		
Percentage of DYS youths with previous commitment	-.52		
Percentage of DYS youths committed for crimes against persons	.00		
Percentage of DYS youths committed for juvenile status offenses	.11		
Program size	-.05		
Youth-to-staff ratio	-.12		
Equality scale	.66	.66	16.50
Community-contact scale	.18		
Participation scale	.31		
Supervision scale	.27		

[a]For the regression equation the multiple correlation = .66 (R^2 = .44), and the F ratio = 16.50 (with 1 and 21 degrees of freedom).

youths and staff members, youths viewed staff more positively. It is also important to note that the correlation between staff trust of delinquents in general and positive youth assessment of staff members is high (r = .77). As one would expect, the program-by-program judgments staff members and youths make of one another appear to be reciprocal.

While there was considerable variation from program to program in the proportion of youths who trusted staff members, it is striking that the general level of youth trust in staff members was high. Only 40 percent of the boys in Cottage 9 and 48 percent of the girls in Putnam scored above the possible scale midpoint, but from 60 percent to 100 percent of the youths in the remaining programs did so, for an overall program average of 85 percent. There are several plausible explanations for these generally positive views of staff.

First, the range of programs from which we drew our sample did not represent the whole continuum of organizational support for staff-inmate equality or inequality. In fact, although Cottage 9 came close to being at the least egalitarian end of the continuum, it had been affected by the Miller reforms and was not as brutal and de-humanizing as some youth and adult prisons reputedly are or have been.

Second, some people are able to transcend the limits placed upon them by their organizationally ordained roles and can bridge the gaps between youths and staff members. At Cottage 9, for example, an observer reported that one of the cottage masters spent most of the day playing cards with a group of about six youths. "He generally plays with kids the most [of all the staff members], but two others also do. By and large, the rest of the staff members maintain much higher distance." The ability of a few staff members to show interest in the youths and to communicate some semblance of warmth and affection may do much to make up for the more formal relations of their co-workers.

Third, in programs where inequality is high, youths often find reliance upon their peers particularly unpalatable. Mutual exploitation and distrust typically characterize most youth relationships in such settings. The development of relationships with the most accessible staff members, even if fleeting, may therefore provide both satisfaction and protection not elsewhere available; youths will evaluate positively even a benign and distant staff simply because of the contrast to their negative judgments of their peers. The nature of these relationships among youths and the kind of effect they have on program life will be examined in detail in Chapter 4.

It is not surprising given these favorable general assessments of staff performance that on the average 81 percent of youths in the twenty-three programs reported that they had at least one staff member with whom they could talk about their problems. Variation from 56 to 100 percent existed among the programs, however, and a regression of these percentages on the set of dependent variables (see Table 2-8) ultimately shows that three organizational characteristics help explain the extent to which youths found confidants among the staff. The degree of youth participation in the program was the most important factor for two particular reasons. First, high levels of equality were a prerequisite for high levels of participation, and the combination of the two brought youths into repeated, close contact with some staff members, making likely the emergence of close counseling relationships. Second, those programs

Table 2-8. Multiple Regression on Independent Variables of Percentage of Youths Having One or More Staff with Whom to Talk (N = 23 programs)[a]

Independent Variables	Zero-Order Correlation with Dependent Variable	Standardized Regression Coefficient	F Ratio
Percentage of youths 16 years or older	.27		
Percentage of male youths	.16		
Percentage of black youths	.14		
Percentage of youths from DYS	-.23		
Percentage of DYS Youths committing first offense before age 14	.04		
Percentage of DYS youths with previous commitment	-.02		
Percentage of DYS youths committed for crimes against persons	.10		
Percentage of DYS youths committed for juvenile status offenses	.05		
Program size	-.21		
Youth-to-staff ratio	-.25	-0.39	4.97
Equality scale	.43		
Community-contact scale	-.09		
Participation scale	.60	.49	7.88
Supervision scale	.37	.32	2.93[b]

[a]For the regression equation the multiple correlation = .71 (R^2 = .51), and the F ratio = 6.55 (with 3 and 19 degrees of freedom).
[b]This F ratio is significant at the 0.10 level.

with high participation scores tended to be strongly oriented toward a conception of their clientele as "kids with personal problems" and were particularly successful at creating normative pressure for youths to open up to staff members and to one another about these difficulties.

The reasons for the substantial positive coefficient for a scale measuring staff supervision over relationships among youths remains less clear.[20] (This scale, introduced in Chapter 1, is described in detail in Chapter 3.) It may be, however, that given similar levels of participation and equality, higher levels of supervision engage staff even more fully in activities and, to some degree, in the lives of youths. Supervision as defined here increases staff interaction with youths and may also symbolize to youths a concern for their individual and collective well-being on the part of staff. By bringing staff members and youths together, supervision, like equality and participation, creates greater opportunities for the development of counseling relationships.

The ratio of youths to staff members expectedly has a negative standardized coefficient in this regression, suggesting that in programs where many youths contend for the ears of only a few staff members, smaller proportions will find confidants. Program size may also, indirectly, be a key variable in determining the degree to which social bonds are actually created to link individual staff members with individual youths. All the programs we observed were relatively small, so variations on this variable in our data are limited. Moderate increases in program size would tend to exacerbate problems of control and supervision, however, and progressively remove staff from intensive interaction with youths to positions on the periphery of the youth world. The same phenomenon should generally occur when the ratio of youths to staff is high regardless of program size.[21] When that ratio is high *and* program size is very large (no programs with this combination were in our sample), the problems of establishing any close youth-staff relationships would be increased enormously.

RANKING OR RAPPING: THE CONTENT AND QUALITY OF STAFF-YOUTH RELATIONSHIPS

Egalitarian relationships between youths and staff members are not all alike; the degree of community contact that a program allows substantially affects the leverage staff members have over youths and subtly alters the context of these egalitarian relationships. When youths are relatively free to roam the communities on their own, as they were in many nonresidential programs and in some residential programs we observed—particularly Drop-in, Pick-up, Open House, Fatigue, and Pair—program staff members had to compete with the attractions of these communities for the attention of their members. Staff members and program peers were no longer the only possible partners in social intercourse for youths; other, more freely chosen sources of gratification were available.

As community contact increases, therefore, there is decreasing control by staff over the whole range of rewards and punishments affecting the conduct and beliefs of youths in their programs. Staff people run the risk of losing the trust, respect, or attention of youths by pushing them too hard to reject beliefs or practices for which they receive support elsewhere. Staff members must repeatedly decide when intervention is worth the risk of alienating youths.

To compensate for this competitive disadvantage, staff members who are supposed to be the equals of youths are pressured to become like them and to refrain from judging them harshly for their misbehavior. Punishment threatens rapport and tends to push youths away from the program and from staff members. Staff members must become equal to the youths on the terms set by the youths, or the youths will see little return from investing in relationships with staff.

The nature of pressures toward staff adoption of youth standards was clearest at Drop-in, a nonresidential program that expected its participants to stop in voluntarily and join its activities. With organizational resources at a minimum, the control that staff exerted over the youths' conduct was limited, as indicated in the following incident:

> On a trip back from an outing a couple of boys started giving everyone "the finger" from the back window and calling out obscenities. The staff member who was driving said nothing. There was a lot of finger giving and name calling from the van. One white guy who they harrassed . . . called something back and then made a point to follow us. The kids were somewhat concerned that he might be a "pig" and one of them took out his blade. Another flashed it round and started sharpening it to use against the guy in the car behind them. At a later point this car turned off and the kids relaxed.

Despite serious misgivings toward the kinds of attitudes and behavior described here, staff members were unwilling to jeopardize the fragile staff-youth bond by intervening.

Instead the staff members felt more comfortable exploiting elements of the youth culture they shared with program participants in order to cement the bonds more firmly:

> Last night five staff members took about eight kids to see some movies outdoors in a public park. One staff member explained to [our observer] that since the group was controllable and one of the kids had some "grass" with him, they decided to get some beer and let the kids have a good time. The group handled it well and no troubles arose. The staff member said the kids were very open about their feelings and all had fun.

Since the staff recognized that if rumors of this event reached Drop-in's higher administrators their jobs and the program might be in jeopardy, they unhappily reported it themselves and promised to exercise better judgment in the future.

> The kids were upset about the staff going to tell the "higher-ups" about

last night. The staff generally expressed disappointment that they would not be able to smoke and drink together with the kids again but hoped that the kids would still be as open with them.

Official constraints ultimately limited the degree to which the staff members could engage with the youths on their level, and thus may have restricted the development of intimacy and trust in staff-youth relationships. Nonetheless, the tenuous link between youths and staff at Drop-in and other open community programs placed considerable pressure on the staff to overlook some misconduct by youths.

Organizational support for community contact was also typically associated with staff recognition that youths had to live in and cope with their communities. First-hand staff awareness of these communities and of the kinds of pressures they placed on youths made staff members less sanguine about the possibility of significant value change and more prone to endorse or at least tolerate what they considered to be the least harmful aspects of street values and behavior.

The compromises and direct appeals to youth values that were required of staff in programs with high levels of community contact often resembled the corruption of authority and the cross-caste camaraderie evident in the least egalitarian programs. In these programs, too, staff competed for the residents' attention and obedience. But here the competition was with a youth caste that was separated and—to a very limited extent—unified by its inferior status in the organization. The need to maintain institutional order led staff people to bargain across these lines, typically utilizing highly individualized waivers of rules in exchange for a semblance of allegiance and order. Individual staff members also, at least in programs for boys, joined in the "ranking" (vociferous scapegoating) on occasion to demonstrate they understood and were, in fact, just some of the boys.

Themes of alleged homosexuality, compromised masculine identity, and family slurs were common in day-to-day conversation among the boys in the least egalitarian programs, and many staff members joined in on occasion. The message, a repeated and seemingly effective one, was that although staff members might be the masters (the official title of some in the traditional cottage) they were also not so different from the boys. The fact that most of the nonprofessional staff members were recruited from a milieu similar to that from which most of the boys came must have made such gestures of solidarity quite natural. Yet these gestures showing that staff shared a masculine subculture also underlined the absurdity of rules against swearing, which staff members enforced. Apparently this cross-caste identification was more difficult for the women working in the girls' cottages because they were not observed to enter into the girls' banter.

It is clear from this analysis that community contact specifically, and equality generally, create pressures for compromises in staff control and considerably limit imposition of staff or program standards and values on youths. Two organizational levers, however, may offer some advantage to programs in their competition with the free community. First, programs can attract youths to the extent that they offer desirable and unusual activities. Second, programs may threaten implicitly the youths with removal to something worse for failure to meet staff expectations.

It is unlikely, however, that many permanent options will be available for youths who have been placed in open programs unless the alternatives are other equally open programs; such programs tend to include youths whose crimes are less serious and who are for the most part first offenders. More restrictive treatment of these youths is likely to be considered unwise regardless of their in-program conformity. Temporary detention such as that reported in the Provo experiment may be a suitable alternative.[22] Transfer out of a program becomes a threat, however, only to the degree that the youths believe the program they are in to be particularly attractive. In programs with high community contact the key lever staff people have in their struggle to influence the behavior of program members thus is the attractiveness of the activities they offer and their own appeal as concerned adults.

CONCLUSIONS AND SUMMARY: IMPLICATIONS FOR THEORY AND POLICY

A lingering practical and theoretical concern at the center of correctional practice and organizational theory has been whether people coerced into joining an organization, as are prisoners, can ever come to respect, trust, or like those who hold them against their wills. On the one hand, correctional practitioners who wish to help their clients hold out the hope that captives will ultimately appreciate them and the work they do for them. On the other hand, organizational theories such as Etzioni's open the possibility that such conversions of alienated and coerced recruits can occur through socialization; Etzioni, however, can only discover an obscure example of such a process.[23] Indeed, our data and those of others cited in this chapter hint strongly that the initial orientation of individuals entering any—even the most benign—correctional setting is one of hostility, or at least suspicion. Even reducing the element of coercion by allowing youths (or adults) to participate in deciding which of a limited variety of correctional alternatives they will choose is not likely to eliminate altogether such suspicions.

Yet the data in this chapter make clear that hostility and suspicion need not remain the dominant perception youths have of staff. Through interaction with their peers, youths may come to a collectively defined and shared stance supporting hostility toward staff, or they may collectively and individually be persuaded that such views are unjustified.

The data presented in this chapter provide convincing evidence that the key to overcoming the natural hostility and suspicion of prisoners toward those who keep them involuntarily in prisons, training schools, or community-based programs is the creation of relatively high levels of equality between staff and youths and among the staff members themselves. More bureaucratic (differentiated and hierarchical) correctional programs that encourage staff to assert clear authority over their inmates and to treat them impersonally and routinely are ones in which the social distance between staff and prisoners will remain high, mutual regard low, and personal relationships between members of the two groups few.

The manner in which a correctional setting is organized thus has a significant impact on the way prisoners translate their initial distrust of staff members into more lasting impressions. The kinds of specific organizational mechanisms that have this effect are identified in the combined scale that measures organizational equality. Varying levels of organizational equality also affect other aspects of youth life and the possibilities for further organizational variation. These patterns will be explored in the next chapters, and their theoretical implications will become more apparent.

From a policy perspective the benefits of introducing greater equality into correctional programs must be weighed against the costs. Fostering trust and encouraging close bonds between inmates and staff members may be important ends in themselves. Building such relationships must be at the foundation of any effort to humanize correctional institutions and to make them effective instruments of control and rehabilitation. The authoritarian, impersonal (but corrupted) role of correctional staff in most conventional institutions—while simply reflecting correctional policy and, perhaps more deeply, societal values—is at the heart of the problem of dehumanization and internal disorder. Increased equality between inmates and staff must, therefore, be one of the first steps in efforts to achieve humanization and administrative control.

Yet one cannot propose methods to bring about humanization and internal order without also considering other paramount—even if mistakenly so—correctional goals: punishment and deterrence, rehabilitation, and reintegration into the community. How do more or less equality and more or less positive staff-youth relationships contribute to the accomplishment of these goals? The answer is not a simple one, as the discussion of equality and control in programs with high community contact illustrates. The following chapters will explore the relationships of program equality to other dimensions of organizational variation and to the nature of youth norms, attitudes, relationships, and behavior. Only after this examination can the complexity of the trade-offs involved in altering dimensions of correctional organization be more thoroughly understood.

NOTES

1. *Chicano Prisoners: The Key to San Quentin* (New York: Holt, Rinehart, and Winston, 1974), p. 1.
2. Amitai Etzioni, *A Comparative Analysis of Complex Organizations: On Power, Involvement and Their Correlates* (Glencoe, Ill.: Free Press, 1961); Erving Goffman, "On the Characteristics of Total Institutions," in *Asylums: Essays on the Social Situation of Mental Patients and Other Inmates* (Garden City, N.Y.: Doubleday, Anchor, 1961), pp. 1–124.
3. Not all inmates need demonstrate such resistance. It is evident that some proportion of inmates believe they deserve punishment, accept their incarceration, and identify with guards and officials. Professional criminals may tend to feel somewhat similarly, although they clearly do not identify with guards. Generally, however, convicted persons seem to view *their* own incarceration as unjust or arbitrary. See Jonathan Casper, *American Criminal Justice: The Defendant's Perspective* (Englewood Cliffs, N.J.: Prentice-Hall, 1972).
4. Gresham Sykes and Sheldon Messinger, "The Inmate Social System," in *Theoretical Studies in Social Organization of the Prison*, ed. Richard Cloward, et al. (New York: Social Science Research Council, 1960), p. 8.
5. *The Highfields Story: An Experimental Treatment Project for Youthful Offenders* (New York: Henry Holt, 1958), p. 75. A rather similar description of testing and change emerges from Ira Goldenberg's description of a rather differently (un)structured living arrangement for older boys in *Build Me a Mountain: Youth Poverty and the Creation of New Settings* (Cambridge, Mass.: MIT Press, 1971).
6. Within two weeks he ran away; he was bored with the program and reported, when he was finally located after several days absence, that he wanted to go to another program.

7. Typically the differences between staff and youth positions are reinforced because the persons occupying them belong to nonoverlapping social categories. The recent history of prison rebellions particularly underlines the racial and rural-urban divisions between inmates and staff members. As Mattick observed, youthful, urban, politically conscious minority-group prisoners are "regularly delivered into the hands of a predominantly white, rural, conservative, ruling caste in the prisons." See Hans Mattick, "The Prosaic Sources of Prison Violence," in *Criminal Behavior and Social Systems: Contributions of American Sociology*, ed. Anthony Guenther, 2d ed. (Chicago: Rand McNally, 1976), p. 538.

These divisions, though evident in the Massachusetts juvenile correctional programs, appeared less important than the presence or absence of wide age differences between staff members and youths. A major reason for this was that only about 17 percent of the youths in the programs we observed were black or had Spanish surnames. Although racial divisions were important in relationships among youths, they were less significant in staff-youth interaction. Nevertheless, black youths in several of the training school cottages did complain about racial bias by white staff members—as did at least one white youth about a black staff member.

8. At Confront all the regular staff members in the group-living program were graduates of the program. Because that was a formal job requirement, however, prospective employees entered as members for a training period. Only one staff member came (was sent by DYS) as a regular member and later was added to the staff.

9. See, for example, New York State Special Commission on Attica, *Attica: The Official Report of the New York State Special Commission on Attica* (New York: Bantam Books, 1972), pp. 157, 168, 175-76, 178.

10. See, for example, Gresham Sykes, *Society of Captives: A Study of a Maximum Security Prison* (Princeton, N.J.: Princeton University Press, 1958). Also, Mattick observes that the reinforcement of caste lines between staff and inmates in many prisons by the factors of race and political awareness makes the establishment of negotiated compromises more difficult ("Prison Violence," pp. 537-38).

11. Among the institutional community programs, however, staff-youth equality was much higher (scores 11-13) than in the equivalent training school cottages (scores 5-9).

12. The staff members for "I Belong" were drawn from newer and younger members of the Shirley School's employees; they developed the program design for "I Belong" themselves after a series of training programs by an outside consultant. Topsfield's staff, though also younger on the whole, was not so clearly self-selected; in fact it and the program terminated soon after the observations were completed due to growing staff conflict.

13. The low correlation is obviously a result of the fact that many of the programs with high levels of equality are very low in community contact. Community contact requires significant equality within the program, but equality does not depend on such contact.

14. For the thirteen community-based programs, only the correlation be-

tween the equality scale and the percentage of DYS youths who have previous records is .01, while the equality scale has a .29 correlation with percentage of youths from DYS.

15. In both 1971 and 1973, staff members were asked to "strongly agree," "agree," "50–50" (volunteered), "disagree," or "strongly disagree" with the following statements: "Most delinquents [kids in trouble] can't be trusted"; "The problem with delinquents [kids in trouble] is that they haven't learned to treat adults with respect and obedience"; "Unless you take precautions delinquents [kids in trouble] may attack you." Throughout the 1973 questionnaire I substituted "kids in trouble" for "delinquent" (with one exception in note 16) because of the nearly universal staff hostility to the term "delinquent" in the community-based system. Responses were scored from 1 to 5 and summed to compose the scale. The average correlation between these scale items is .33. The midpoint of the possible scale values served as the cutoff point between high and low scores. In this and all the following inmate system scales, missing scores were estimated to be the average score on all other scale items; fortunately, missing values were infrequent—never more than 5 percent on any scale item.

16. Staff members were asked to estimate: "How many of the DYS kids are 'hard-core delinquents'"; and "How many of the DYS kids pose serious control and management problems?" In the 1971 study these estimates took the form of estimates of percentages: "none," "less than 10 percent," "10–25 percent," "25–50 percent," "50–75 percent," "over 75 percent." Because of the small size of some programs and of DYS populations in 1973, the estimates were simplified to "none," "a few," "most," or "all." Feld's categories were equated with mine in the following fashion": none = none; a few = less than 10 percent, 10–25 percent, and 25–50 percent; most = 50–75 percent; and all = over 75 percent. The correlation between items is .43. The scores on these two items were summed, and the midpoint of the possible scale values served as the cutoff between high and low scores.

17. To the first item, youths responded "strongly agree," "agree," "50–50" (volunteered), "disagree," or "strongly disagree," while in the second item they chose from "most of the time," "some of the time," "a little of the time," "none of the time." The former responses were scored 1, 2, 3, 4, 5, respectively, and the latter were scored 1, 2, 4, 5. The correlation between these scale items is .86. The midpoint of possible scale values served as the cutoff between high and low scores.

18. This relationship holds true at the individual level of analysis as well. Forty-six percent of the boys as opposed to 36 percent of the girls thought staff to be most interested in having them "obey the rules and stay out of trouble."

19. Youths were asked to "strongly agree," "agree," "50–50" (volunteered), "disagree," or "strongly disagree" with the statement: "The adults here don't really care what happens to you, they're only doing a job." In addition, they were asked to indicate whether they thought "most of the staff can be trusted" or "you can't be too careful when you deal with the staff," and whether they would say that most of the staff in the program "usually help kids" or "usually

look out for themselves." Responses to the first item were scored from 1 to 5 and the latter two were scored 5 and 1, respectively. The variables constituting this scale average a .51 correlation with one another. The item scores were summed to get the scale score, and the midpoint of the possible scale values was used as the cutoff point between high and low scores.

20. This scale does not gauge coercive supervision, which divides staff and youths, but rather the organized sponsorship of activities, which leaves youths with little opportunity to evolve their own activities and informal organization.

21. One must be cautious in making absolute judgments about the effect of youth-to-staff ratios because in some highly participatory programs such as Primal, youths take on so many staff duties that the ratio is, for all practical purposes, greatly reduced.

22. Lamar Empey and Maynard Erickson report that youths in the Pinehills program could be placed in temporary detention when their recalcitrance passed certain limits. This experience helped teach that noncooperation had costs and underlined the relative freedom of the Pinehills program. See *The Provo Experiment: Evaluating Community Control of Delinquency* (Lexington, Mass.: D.C. Heath, 1972), pp. 51–53; and see also their general discussion of control in community programs, pp. 66–71.

23. He notes that the first Janizaries became loyal Moslem bodyguards as adults, although they were the kidnapped children of Christians (*Complex Organizations*, p. 152).

Chapter 3

Dime-Dropping and Pulling a Cover: Youth Subcultures

Don't be a dime dropper [informer]. . . . Like suppose a fork is missing and they [blame it on] you, just do your time [in an isolation cell] and when you come out, your friend would do that for you.

During "pull-ups" at the house meeting. Gert stood up and asked, "Is everyone aware of Amanda Jones?" Gert proceeded to suggest that Amanda was not taking her "shotdown" [demotion in house structure] seriously.

Informing on other inmates is a crucial and recurrent issue that youths must face in correctional programs. Like many other forms of conduct, informing is judged by youths with reference to their collective expectations about appropriate behavior. Because these collective definitions influence, but do not dictate, youths' self-conceptions and choices of action in the correctional program and, perhaps, after leaving it, the source and substance of youth subcultures is of immense importance to the maintenance of order in these programs, the achievement of some rehabilitative goals, and the establishment of humane program conditions for participants.

Consequently, correctional officials and reformers have, on occasion, contended for control of the content of these subcultures in the hope of creating a supportive network for their own efforts. Prison democracies, positive peer cultures, and therapeutic communities have been explicitly planned and implemented to turn subcultures to the benefit of staff and, presumably, prisoners and youths. Successful manipulation of youth subcultures appears to be achieved, however, at a cost measured in terms of sacrificed societal values and unachieved correctional goals. The nature of the mechanisms that involve youths in the official correctional organization, their influence upon youth subcultures, and their costs are the focus of this chapter.

Delinquents are not blank slates upon which the correctional experience etches identities, norms, values, and orientations. They are young people who have been socialized into a culture (probably several subcultures), who have developed modes of perceiving and judging the world, and who are enmeshed in networks of social relationships. These social bonds anchor each youth's identity, norms, and values by linking that youth to others who share and reinforce similar beliefs.

Rarely are these social networks carried intact into correctional institutions, however.[1] More typically each youth is pried loose from bonds in the community and left to develop new ties with a set of strangers in the correctional program. It is to these strangers—peers and staff members—that the youth must turn for reference points with which to compare individual judgments about appropriate behavior.

Correctional programs typically draw large portions of their clientele from relatively homogenous pools of young male or female lower-income urban dwellers. If youths choose their peers as their points of reference, therefore, expectations and world views common among people with these characteristics are likely to become the collectively supported basis for perceptions and action. In many correctional settings the social characteristics of the offender population thus determine, in large part, the content of shared youth values and norms.[2]

In typical training schools, youths choose other youths as reference points less because they are positively attracted to one another than because they have no other alternative given the organizationally mandated distance between them and staff members. High levels of equality are thus necessary in a program before youths can be expected to turn to staff members as significant sources of guidance. But equality is not sufficient by itself to give staff the ability to shape youth subcultures. Program support for community contact, although occurring in the context of high equality, for example, often permits youths to maintain social contacts that help sustain their individual values.

The result of high community contact is that both other youths and staff exert far less influence over an individual's definitions of his or her situation; collective life as a whole is less developed and distinctive than in more closed programs. The movement to truly community-based corrections programs, while facilitating greater equality between youths and staff and increasing the extent of youth-community contact, lessens the power that programs hold over the shared values and norms of their participation.

Two other organizational characteristics contribute significantly to the variation among programs in the degree to which official standards and beliefs are collectively adopted and shared by youths: (1) the organizational facilitation of youth participation in planning and operating the program; and (2) staff supervision over youth relationships and activities. In the context of a given level of program equality, these two dimensions of organization, along with the degree of community contact permitted, indicate the extent to which youths are subject to staff control and influence and free from the debilitating pressures of informal inmate system.

THE ORGANIZATION OF YOUTH PARTICIPATION

The extent to which youths are given structured opportunities to influence decisions and to take part in carrying out the work of the organization will influence the emergence of collective youth definitions of the situation. Discussions of what the organization should be like and how youths (and staff) should behave can become a structured part of the program in which staff members and youths jointly engage. Such opportunities—which are typically created by group and "community" meetings—reduce the extent to which the correctional experience is imposed on youths. Instead, youths have a continuing responsibility for creating, within clearly defined limits, their own rules and program. Their experiences are in part of their own making and cannot readily be blamed on staff. Structured youth participation in making and enforcing rules and carrying on the program also exposes staff to interaction among youths and the tentative values and norms emerging from such interaction. This exposure creates opportunities for staff people to influence the development of youth subcultures. The institutional "underlife," as Goffman, calls it, thus has fewer dark and shadowy areas in which to flourish. The greater the degree of youth involvement, therefore, the greater the identification youths will have with the organization as a whole and the more likely they will adopt as their own the official norms and values they have had some part in influencing.

None of the programs we observed was democratic in operation. One staff member at Confront articulated to me the reasons for the lack of democracy, and in doing so she expressed a view that was broadly if not explicitly shared by staff members in all programs:

> She wouldn't trust the group to make decisions that affected their future. "If they could make those decisions, they wouldn't be here." She said that a group might make decisions about learning experiences [punishments] but would not discuss whether a person should leave for a break [go to a foster home], go on second stage, etc. She said she would confer with other staff about such decisions but not formally, and she would not consult other kids.

Although staff members in all programs reserved some options for themselves, in some programs staff made opportunities available for youths to take on essential tasks and to become engaged in a set of officially devised mutual obligations. Four variables indicate the relative availability of such opportunities in the twenty-three programs, and these form the participation scale, as shown in Table 3–1 and detailed in the following text.

Two or More Community Meetings per Week. The first of these variables was the presence or absence of at least two community meetings each week at which all or most staff and all residents came together to discuss a shared problem or to participate in some collective activity. At Primal and Confront these daily meetings included a recitation of the house concept[2] as well as a variety of "pull-ups" (at Primal this meant criticisms of other house members with suggestions for changes in behavior) or "learning experiences" (at Confront this usually meant a person had to wear a sign around his neck as a punishment). In addition, house meetings could be called at any time:

> Usually there are two or three a week dealing with bad attitudes going down in the house, problems that everyone needs to think about, etc. A general meeting is different—it is called when a particular kid (or perhaps more than one) has done something outrageous, and needs to be shot down and dealt with by the whole house; a kid really gets blasted to pieces at such a meeting.

These house meetings were reinforced by frequent group sessions of high intensity (confrontation groups, primal scream therapy groups, "haircuts")[3] involving portions of the youth population. A similar pattern of community meetings and less intensive group sessions was evident at "I Belong," Shirley, and Topsfield; they also used daily community meetings for resolving the problems of group living, as well as two therapy groups that also met almost daily. Sun-

Table 3–1.   Scores on Variables Composing Participation Scale, by Program[a]

| | Participation Variables | | | | |
	Two or More Community Meetings/ Week	Regular Decision-Making Role for Youths	Youth Role as Counselor	Youth Role as Disci-pliner	Total Partici-pation Score
Institutional Programs					
Cottage 8	1	1	1	1	4
Elms	1	1	1	1	4
Westview	1	1	1	1	4
Clara Barton	1	1	1	1	4
Putnam	1	1	1	3	6
Cottage 9	1	1	1	1	4
Regiment	1	1	1	1	4
Shelter	1	1	1	1	4
Warning	1	1	1	1	4
Fatigue	1	1	1	1	4
Mother	1	1	1	1	4
Reward	1	1	1	1	4
Group Treatment Programs					
"I Belong"	3	3	3	3	12
Topsfield	3	3	3	3	12
Shirley	3	3	3	3	12
Sunset	1	3	1	3	8
Primal	3	3	3	3	12
Confront	3	3	3	3	12
Group	3	3	3	3	12
Open House	3	3	3	3	12
Open Community Programs					
Drop-in	1	1	1	1	4
Pick-up	1	1	1	1	4
Pair	1	3	1	1	6

[a]Programs with the particular characteristic received a score of 3 and those without it a score of 1. Scores of 2 were assigned to programs where the trait was partially evident (see text).

set cottage had maintained such a schedule until several months before our observation, but in the summer it had no therapy groups and only sporadic community meetings.

At Group and Open House the small-group sessions and community meetings were one and the same, since each house contained only about ten residents. They met together with most staff present (at most meetings) almost daily, and discussed problems of personal adjustment and group living ranging from relationships with parents to arrangements for cooking breakfast.

Frequent and regular meetings did not guarantee substance, however. Cottage 8 was the only one of the non-group-treatment programs to schedule frequent community meetings—they occurred as often as four times a week. The longest such meeting that our observer noted consumed seven minutes and was judged by at least one boy to be a marathon session. "The usual meeting takes about one minute to get the roll counted and one minute to find out if anybody's got anything to say." At Cottage 8 the counselor was the only staff member to attend these perfunctory sessions. For that reason, it—along with the remaining non-group-treatment programs and Sunset—were scored as having no regular community meetings.

Group meetings were not a part of the regularly organized activities in any of the other programs, and community meetings, although not unknown, were irregular if they occurred at all; when they did occur they often took either the form observed in Cottage 8—brief, routine, and staff-dominated—or were called by staff to lecture youths about some particular issue or incident of rule-breaking. At Warning, for example, irregular community meetings focused on housekeeping chores, on promulgation or rules, or on the horrors of prison life ("You think you're a piece of shit because that's the way they treat you"); the need for self-respect and communication within the program ("instead of helping your brother out the window, you should be helping him out the door"); and the possibility that Warning would be closed down "if people did not act as if they cared." In the training school cottages the irregular group meetings typically involved staff announcements—for example, about changes in the step level of privileges for the residents—although the weekly meetings at Putnam and Clara Barton gave girls considerable opportunity to gripe about staff behavior and the rules.

The regularity of such meetings cannot assure youth participation, but it is difficult to achieve collective participation without such occasions for collective involvement. The sense of continuity, of collective effort, of sharing an ongoing commitment can come from frequent meetings of a group but is much harder to' create at irregular events. Nor can the tradition of participation by youths be created or sustained at irregular or infrequent sessions.

Regular Decision-Making Role for Youths. The second indicator of organizational facilitation of youth participation, as shown in Table 3-1, was whether or not youths were regularly given opportunities during our observation to participate formally in making decisions. While offhand staff questions about whether "any of you guys would like to play basketball now" were fairly common, formal solicitations of opinions and allocation of responsibility for decisions were rarer. Group or community meetings provided a context for such official consultations. Thus all the group-treatment programs as well as one community program (Pair) gave youths at least some input into decision-making, and were so scored. These decisions included, for example, votes about accepting new members at Confront; a vote on allocating financial responsibility for a broken dishwasher at Open House; or votes about whether a member should have his "ground" removed or his level changed at Group, "I Belong," Topsfield, Shirley, and Sunset. At Shirley and Sunset, boys elected officers who ran the community meetings using something resembling parliamentary procedure; youths made and passed motions concerning cottage rules (staff voted as well but could veto results). At Shirley, particularly, this practice led to an elaborate structure of rules for everything; at one meeting, for example, debate revolved around whether there was a specific rule defining lighting firecrackers as a "nonnegotiable drop to Level One" (the lowest privilege level). Every imaginable offense apparently had a particular punishment attached.

At Primal, youth participation in decision-making was also evident, but it did not have a democratic format. Youths were given responsibility for almost every aspect of the day-to-day running of the program and were required in this capacity to make frequent decisions. Only those assigned as workers—the lowest, entry-level positions at the bottom of the formal hierarchy—had little discretion; all were ultimately responsible for their decisions to the youths in levels above them, and, ultimately, the youths serving as senior coordinators were responsible to the few staff members.

Youth Role as Counselor or Discipliner. The last two indexes of organized support for youth involvement in program operation (Table 3-1) are interrelated in our particular sample of programs and therefore will be treated together here. They indicate whether or not youths were given responsibility and opportunity to counsel and to discipline their peers. All the group-treatment programs except Sunset —that is, Topsfield, "I Belong," Shirley, Open House, Group, Confront, and Primal—provided their participants with both repeated encouragement and opportunity during group confrontations or group meetings to learn about and comment on the personal, social, and psychological problems of other residents. At Warning the staff advocated such mutual concern, consideration, and help, but provided no structured opportunities for counseling to occur. In none of the other programs was there either pressure or opportunity for youths to counsel their peers.

In addition, the group meetings in these seven group-treatment programs and the occasional community meetings at Sunset and Putnam provided a context in which the youths were encouraged, under close staff supervision, to challenge and berate one another for misdeeds within the program. At most of these programs they could also help decide on the punishments to be meted out to offending peers:

> At the house meeting Barbara [staff] asked the kids if they all thought that Sam should pay for the fixing of the dishwasher since he broke it intentionally. All decided yes—Sam accepted. The kids also talked about how things have been borrowed from rooms and broken before returned. All decided this must stop. Cynthia [resident] said that if the kids don't take better care of things at the home soon they would not have anything left to enjoy. Ned [resident] seconded it.

The staff members at Group encouraged participation in these meetings by probing members for response.

> Herb [staff]: Phil has asked that we consider his "ground." Phil?
>
> Phil: I'd like to be able to go home to visit my parents in Hometown and have my ground lifted around here. But I don't want to go into Hometown to see my friends. [He goes on about being on ground for two weeks since his thirty days were up (the standard initial ground for new residents). He says he is talking more but has not yet talked with all the staff and all the other kids.] "I've been trying to talk more."
>
> Herb: How do you feel about that guys? [Long silence.] How about you Pete?
>
> Pete: He's a good shit and nice to be around and all that shit. I can't vote because I really don't know Phil. We haven't talked or nuthin'. I don't really know him or what his goals are.

More dramatic were the confrontations at Primal and Confront during which youths were expected to challenge one another over failures to live up to the program's standards for interpersonal relationships and conduct. These confrontations often began with screamed obscenities and went on at high decibel levels as the youths criticized one another's conduct. Staff encouraged these intense interchanges by forcefully pointing out: "If you don't yell it, you must not mean it."

These meetings and confrontations enabled youths to take a visible and active part in enforcing program norms, which served to cement their own commitment to those norms. Although most youths were almost inevitably the target of staff members' and peers' attempts at control on occasion, they were far more frequently the administrators of such punishment. Social control became, therefore, a force for integration into the program rather than a wedge alienating youths from it. Such opportunities for participation were not evident in any of the other programs.

Table 3-1 indicates that the participation scores were generally high in the group-treatment cluster of programs and low elsewhere; it is participation—or at least one distinctive version of it—that defines group treatment. Yet within that cluster there was significant variation which bore on the substance of inmate subcultures. Once again we are reminded that program goals and practice are only imperfectly related.

THE SUPERVISION OF YOUTH RELATIONSHIPS

Prior to the invention of the separate-and-silent system, and since its abandonment, correctional officials have allowed—often begrudgingly —considerable interaction among the people in their charge. Humanitarian impulses have led to the gradual diminution of the last vestiges of a system that totally isolated inmates from one another, although officials still resort to twenty-four-hour lockups in times of crisis. Rules such as those requiring silence at meals, for example, are disappearing.

But the long-term decline in coercive techniques for limiting inmate interaction has left many prisons and correctional settings with few alternative methods for shaping inmate relationships and monitoring inmate behavior. The presence or absence of such techniques or their noncoercive equivalents is both theoretically and practically important. High levels of supervision can provide an approved framework to guide or limit youth interaction and relationships and, by imbuing them with legitimate organizational meaning, can add substantial official input to the way inmates view one another and the organization.

In addition, close supervision may increase the pressure for consistency between youths' behavior and official standards. By contrast, when such supervision is lacking, inmates must evolve their own relationships on their own terms and enforce their own distinctive standards of conduct. Participation in the official functions of the organization provides one way of guiding youth activity and relationships, but it may be inadequate by itself to provide such guidance or unnecessary to accomplish that end. Supervision can be developed independent of participation.

Official supervision of youth relationships was gauged by three variables in this study, as listed in Table 3-2 and considered individually below.

Frequency of Organized Group Activities. Supervision is enhanced when there are frequent organized group activities to structure and focus youth relationships on organizationally approved goals. Subscribing to the basic principle that "idle hands are the devil's tools," some programs scheduled their days so fully that only rare moments were free for youths to plan with one another about running away, or to organize a loose syndicate for smuggling in drugs. Instead, program officials took control of the content of much of the interaction among youths by creating and shifting the context and direction for their interchanges.

Programs were assigned a score of 3, 2, or 1 (Table 3-2) depending on whether they had planned group activities on at least five evenings *and* days a week; at least five evenings *or* days a week; or less frequently.[4] Fourteen of the programs we observed scheduled regular activities that ranged from guitar classes to primal scream therapy groups during either or both the day or evening hours and thus received scores of 2 or 3. At Primal and Confront, for example, youths moved through a rigorous round of housekeeping and therapeutic activities with rare moments of free time. The boys and girls in Fatigue, Regiment, and Reward were faced with almost nonstop educational and recreational activities from morning until night. At Fatigue, for instance,

> The staff organize activities to fill up virtually all the day. Kevin [head of child care] said to his counselors that they should try to take the kids out in the evenings as well as afternoons, or if they are at Fatigue, there should be something scheduled, like bingo. "It's better for us that way." Only if there is a reason such as bad weather or if the kids have been active all day and are tired should they stay around Fatigue.

At the other extreme was Cottage 9, where the morning and afternoon visits to the toilet were the only events to break the monotony of sitting, playing cards, reading magazines, or staring at the broken television. In other programs such as Open House and Pair, four or

Table 3-2. Scores on Variables Composing Supervision Scale, by Program[a]

| | *Supervision Variables* | | | |
	Frequency of Orga- nized Group Activities	*Absence of Free Refusal to Join Activities*	*Official Structure of Youth Relation- ships*	*Total Super- vision Score*
Institutional Programs				
Cottage 8	3	1	1	5
Elms	2	1	1	4
Westview	1	1	1	3
Clara Barton	2	1	1	4
Putnam	2	1	1	4
Cottage 9	1	1	1	3
Regiment	3	3	1	7
Shelter	1	1	1	3
Warning	1	1	1	3
Fatigue	2	1	1	4
Mother	2	1	1	4
Reward	3	3	1	7
Group Treatment Programs				
"I Belong"	3	3	1	7
Topsfield	3	1	1	5
Shirley	3	1	1	5
Sunset	1	1	1	3
Primal	3	3	3	9
Confront	3	3	2	8
Group	1	1	1	3
Open House	1	1	1	3
Open Community Programs				
Drop-in	1	1	1	3
Pick-up	2	1	1	4
Pair	1	1	1	3

[a]Programs with the trait received a score of 3 and those without it a score of 1. Scores of 2 were assigned to programs where the trait was partially evident (see text).

five of the youths were almost always off in the nearby communities at work or with friends, making the scheduling of group activities difficult and infrequent for the remaining three or four residents.

Absence of Free Refusal to Join Activities. The supervisory function of group activities was reduced when staff members allowed youths a free choice about taking part in them. Most programs with regularly scheduled events gave youths a choice of joining in, while several—"I Belong," Primal, Confront, Regiment, and Reward—required participation in *some* activity. Where choices were freely made, the dispersion of youths in organized activities and in their own pursuits at times forced the cancellation of an activity for lack of interest, and always reduced the ability of staff members to keep track of the widely scattered youths. For example, the observer at Mother reported:

> 6:45 p.m. to 7:45 p.m.: Softball organized by the recreation staff. Most of the kids played except Phyllis, Cynthia, and Marcelle who stayed in Phyllis' room and played the guitar. During this time Cynthia ran away with Joan who also did not play softball.

Staff decisions to treat youths like adults and give them considerable free choice in their activities thus had its costs for supervision. Some programs, such as Reward, managed to combine required participation with some element of choice by offering a variety of simultaneous activities from which youths could select. Such an approach generally required a large number of residents and staff, however, to support and sponsor multiple activities. Those programs that had regularly organized activities in which youths were required to participate received scores of 3 on this variable, while the other programs got scores of 1, as shown in Table 3-2.

Official Structure of Youth Relationships.   The last variable in the supervision scale shown in Table 3-2 was the presence or absence of a pervasive, formally organized set of relationships among youths. Rather than confining themselves to influencing youth relationships indirectly by structuring the context in which they occurred, only Primal and Confront differentiated youth positions by function and ranked them by authority. Primal's official organization chart, with slots in which the names of the residents were inserted, portrayed the most pervasive system for structuring youth relationships that we observed.

Youths at Primal were assigned to one of several departments (communication, service, expediting, kitchen, maintenance, finance, and laundry).[5] They were further divided by a hierarchy moving up from workers, to "ramrods," department heads, coordinator trainees, coordinators, and finally, senior coordinators.[6] This house structure was pervasive, dictating relationships and activities during much of the day; it was also the major indicator of prestige, for progress in the program was judged in terms of climbing the Primal ladder.

The hierarchy at Confront was less extensive (three levels in the hierarchy), less important in judging progress—people were rotated through positions rather than assigned them on the basis of merit—and, therefore, far less pervasive in the daily lives of youths. Primal was thus assigned a 3 and Confront a 2, while all other programs received scores of 1 on this variable. Although several of these other programs occasionally assigned jobs to participants or asked one or two to supervise others in a clean-up effort, none had an all-encompassing formal network of relationships for youths.

Two additional variables bearing on the degree of staff supervision were not included in the scale because of their low correlation with the other items and because of their independent significance. Their potential importance, however, is established by the weighty tradition of organizational research, which gives them a special place: size and ratio of youths to staff.[7] These two variables were included separately in analyses of variations in inmate systems.

Size may be important to organizational structure for a variety of reasons, but it particularly affects the ease with which staff members can control and supervise relationships among youths. In a program of ten residents, there are 45 possible pairings among youths at any one time, but when the number of youths grows to twenty, there are 190 possible two-person relationships. This rapid escalation of possible relationships as program size increases soon makes it impossible for staff members to keep track of and to maintain control over what is going on between each potential pair of program members. On the other hand, limited number of residents and relationships in small closed programs such as Group allowed staff to keep track of program members without a full schedule of required activities.

The ratio of youths to staff members also suggests limits on staff capability to observe and order youth relationships and behavior; the higher the ratio, the less able staff people are to supervise. These ratios are misleading, however, particularly in those programs that involved youths in staff roles and functions. Primal, for example, had both the highest youth-to-staff ratio and the most rigorous supervision, carried out in part through a force of resident "expediters" whose job it was to know everyone's whereabouts and business.

The summary of the supervision scale in Table 3–2 shows as much variation in scores within clusters as between them. Some group-treatment and institutional programs utilized high levels of supervision and others low; only the open-community programs were consistently low in supervision.

RELATIONSHIP BETWEEN
PARTICIPATION AND
SUPERVISION AND OTHER
ORGANIZATIONAL CHARACTERISTICS

The variations in organizational characteristics that have been introduced are clearly not wholly independent of one another. Their interrelationships have crucial policy and theoretical significance because they give evidence of the ways correctional goals and means may reinforce or contradict one another (see Table 3-3). The interaction among these organizational characteristics must be understood before their mutual effect on aspects of collective youth responses to the correctional regimen can be comprehended.

Participation is moderately associated with level of equality ($r = .49$) and with degree of supervision ($r = .38$). Youth participation in carrying out the basic program functions implies equality between staff and youths, and this is likely to occur where staff themselves are relatively equal—that is, where they are not assigned specialized tasks on the basis of professional competence. Thus, even more striking than the correlation is the fact that *all* the programs with high levels of participation were among the programs with the highest equality scores. Equality does not require participation, but participation necessitates equality. The relationship between participation and supervision is less tight. Many of the programs encouraging considerable participation by youths also structure activities and relationships; clearly participation in running the program provides a wide range of activities in which to keep youths busy.[8] If these activities are not available, as they were not in nonparticipatory programs such as Regiment and Reward, then recreational and educational activities must provide the major source of program structure.

Program facilitation of community contact, a major instrument for attempting to achieve the reintegration goal of correctional rehabilitation, appears inconsistent with high levels of in-program supervision ($r = -.48$). Supporting youth involvement in the community absorbs considerable staff time that might otherwise be invested in organizing group activities for program participants. Because each youth's links to his or her community are unique to that youth, forging or reforging them is a highly individualized and time consuming endeavor. Not only are the efforts of staff members directed away from the program; youths also are in and out, often on their own schedules, and are absorbed in relationships and activities outside the program. Much of their time, therefore, may be spent—whatever the investment of staff effort—away from staff

Table 3-3.   Correlations among Organizational Variables (N = 23 programs)

	Super-vision Scale	Partici-pation Scale	Commu-nity Contact Scale	Equal-ity Scale	Size	Youth-to-Staff
Supervision	—	.38	-.48	.37	.46	.37
Participation		—	-.14	.49	-.20	.05
Community Contact			—	.19	-.31	-.31
Equality				—	-.18	-.15
Size					—	.65
Youth-to-Staff Ratio						—

supervision. When youths are frequently out in the community, too few may be free at any one time for staff people to go to the trouble of arranging group activities. In addition, the variability in individual schedules makes coordination difficult.

In this sample of programs, finally, supervision seems to act as a compensatory device for handling associated increases in program size ($r =$ 0.46) and ratio of youths to staff members ($r = 0.37$) and the attendant rise in problems of supervising youth relationships. Staff members can keep track of small populations far more easily than large ones; only in the smallest programs can each staff person know all participants and keep up with all relationships among them. Equally important, small size limits staff resources for directing a range of activities and restricts the number of youths available to support or justify them. Softball games, for example, are difficult to arrange within a program of only eight or ten youths.

PARTICIPATION, SUPERVISION, AND THE CHARACTERISTICS OF YOUTH POPULATIONS

It is again necessary to examine the possibility that the characteristics of youth populations are associated with organizational traits as a consequence of self-selection and official screening of youths. Table 3-4 presents the correlations between eight population characteristics and the participation scale, supervision scale and measures of population size, and youth-staff ratio. Few of these associations are much different from zero, but several require analysis.

The .46 correlation between participation and the proportion of youths sixteen or more years of age in the program may be peculiar to the particular programs we studied, but more likely it reflects a

Table 3-4. Correlations between Remaining Organizational Variables and Population Characteristics (*N* = 23 programs)

	Partici-pation Scale	Super-vision Scale	Size	Youth-to-Staff Ratio
Percentage of youths 16 years or older	.46	-.17	-.19	-.12
Percentage of male youths	.13	-.03	-.10	-.11
Percentage of black youths	-.15	-.30	-.17	-.43
Percentage of youths from DYS	-.13	-.38	-.46	-.22
Percentage of DYS youths committing first offense before age 14	.03	.01	.32	.45
Percentage of DYS youths with previous commitment	.03	-.10	.23	.29
Percentage of DYS youths committed for crimes against persons	.07	.25	.26	.06
Percentage of DYS youths committed for juvenile status offenses	-.12	-.06	-.08	-.08

requirement for youth participation. The only two programs we observed that incorporated delinquent youths into a population of private adult and teenage clients were highly participatory—Primal and Confront; they both, therefore, had higher proportions of residents over sixteen years of age. By contrast, the difficulties of encouraging participation by youths much younger than sixteen seem great. Maturity and some sense of responsibility—characteristics associated (by no means perfectly) with age—would seem a prerequisite for staff people to be both willing and able to give up responsibility to their charges and effectively incorporate them into the program.

It may be, however, that expectations about the irresponsible nature of young people lead to self-fulfilling prophecies. Changed expectations and opportunities for showing responsibility may lead to meaningful participation by youths in their early teens. My impression, in observing youths across a range of ages, however, was that introspection and seriousness about one's own future were far more often found among older boys and girls, many of whom recognized that they soon would have to take adult responsibility for criminal actions.

The associations between program size and percentage of youths from DYS (*r* = -.46) and between youth-to-staff ratio and both the percentage of youths who were black (*r* = -.43) and the percentage of DYS youths who committed their first offenses prior to age fourteen ($r = .45$) appear to have no similar theoretical or practical importance. Instead they are probably simply peculiar to the sample of programs used in this study.

PROGRAM ORGANIZATION AND STAFF IDEOLOGY

The ways in which the twenty-three correctional programs we observed were organized and the attitudes and values of staff members in those programs were not randomly associated. Broadly speaking, the equality dimension reflects most clearly the fundamental cleavage in staff attitudes between custody and treatment orientations, a difference upon which much of the past literature on corrections has focused attention. There was, for example, a -.73 correlation between the level of equality in a program and the percentage of staff members in a program endorsing the statement: "We are putting too much faith in psychological approaches with juvenile delinquents. What we really need are stiffer laws and more vigilant law enforcement."[9]

This ideological division did not reflect the distinction between the training schools and community-based programs; instead it mirrored the division between the staff members in the relatively unreformed training school cottages (Cottages 8 and 9, Putnam, Clara Barton, Elms, and Westview) and those in the reformed institutional cottages and the community-based programs.[10] From 50 to 88 percent of staff in the former agreed with this statement, compared to 0 to 15 percent for the latter group. The responses to this item presumably reflect a broader complex of views showing in high relief the contrast between the punishment and treatment orientations. In the punishment view, youths are considered responsible for their own delinquent conduct, deserving of punishment (not necessarily harsh), and in need of strict discipline and control. The establishment of authority—and, presumably, the teaching of respect for it—are the primary concerns of staff members in day-to-day relationships with youths; clearly such a belief system is inconsistent with high equality. It is likely that the organization of such authoritarian relationships creates or reinforces such beliefs among staff.

By contrast, the treatment orientation views youths as people with problems—low self-esteem, personal psychological difficulties, family conflicts, inadequate job opportunities, pressures from criminal companions—which are themselves the ultimate if not proximate causes of delinquency or trouble. The major focus of staff relationships with youths is the solution of these problems. Depending on one's approach and particular conception of the problem, organizational equality may or may not facilitate efforts to solve it. Paternalistic (or maternalistic) or professional/client relationships may be deemed appropriate in attacking these problems; so also may more egalitarian relationships. A treatment orientation may require youths to cooperate, respect, and trust the staff, but it need not lead inevitably to equality.

It is apparent that a simple punishment versus treatment differentiation is inadequate to represent the full spectrum of variation in staff attitudes and correctional organizations. It is not surprising, therefore, that the clarity of statistical relationships between program organization and staff views begins to lose focus beyond this initial stage of analysis. For example, staff members in the thirteen community-based programs were asked to agree or disagree that "most kids who come here only need to be given a chance and some encouragement in order to operate effectively in the community." The correlation of .37 between the proportion of staff agreeing with this statement and the degree of community contact a program allows lies in the expected direction but is nonetheless quite low. The same is true for many other staff views about youths in their charge—the relationship between their views and the nature of program organization is low; shared commitment to "understanding kids" rather than to a particular conception of delinquency causation apparently tied staff members together.

Many staff members in most of the community-based programs resisted the kinds of categorical statement of views that the questionnaire required of them; many added marginal comments qualifying their answers, and some refused to answer altogether. Individualized treatment and nonstereotyped conceptions of youths' problems were clearly the major goals of these staff members, and thus staff ideology in a particular treatment program was typically quite diverse. Although a general ideological stance was crucial to the development of the varied treatment-oriented, egalitarian programs, it did nothing to distinguish them from one another. Perhaps our research instruments were not finely tuned enough to separate those clustered ideological wavelengths from one another. It is equally probable that finer reception on our part would have revealed overlapping bands of goals and beliefs rather than distinctive ideologies.

It is for these reasons that we have relied on direct measures of organizational structure rather than on portraits of staff views as the basic analytic key to unlocking the forces that create the social and cultural systems of youths in correctional programs.

SUBCULTURES AND THE INMATE CODE

Tattoos, Kool cigarettes, popular musical groups, and Bruce Lee's kung-fu movies were some of the highly valued aspects of the youthful world we observed. The age and class-based popular culture from which these cultural elements came were, however, far less important to the operation of correctional programs and the maintenance of humane living environments than were a variety of other standards. Norms about involvement with others and the passing on of information, expectations about toughness and physical violence, and knowledge and values about criminal conduct were highly variable in the twenty-three programs.

These norms were the subject of considerable staff interest because they affected the quality of life for youths, the ease of administrative control, and the apparent short-term efficacy of rehabilitation efforts. The degree to which programs encouraged youths to participate in the program as well as the degree of staff supervision over youths were the key organizational mechanisms for manipulating the nature of these subcultural dimensions which, without these significant organizational inputs, were strikingly similar.

A major theme of the research on inmate subcultures is the regularity with which rules against informing ("dime dropping," "finking," "ratting," "snitching") appear in penal institutions for men and women, boys and girls. It is not surprising, therefore, that we accumulated considerable evidence that such norms were widely shared in the programs we observed. More striking, however, was the finding that in five of the seven programs with the highest participation scores in our sample these norms had been effectively turned on their heads—in these programs informing was prescribed, not proscribed, by youths.

In those programs with low participation scores we observed or learned of incidents illustrating the normative character of the prohibitions against informing:

Finnegan is still catching some heckling [he is being called "dime-dropper"] for his nonparticipation in the "great escape" two days earlier [seventeen boys had run]; he was being reminded of his post-break comment—something like "where'd they all go? Hey, they all went out the window." I think he said whatever he did out of naivete and "lack of cool," but some of the kids seem to think he "dimed" on them. It seems, though, that he didn't say anything until after the staff had discovered the break.

Bernie tells the observer and Dale [a resident] that he, Carl, and Stuart went downtown last night and got a six-pack. "I can buy now. I've got a friend who works in a store downtown. We drank that and then found some guys who had some grass. Those reefers were big, man." He had four to five joints while Carl had only one. Stuart got really high. They then began wandering back to the school but couldn't find it until Carl finally did. When they got back around 2 a.m. Andrew, who knew they had been AWOL, apparently beat up Carl until he said where they had been. Andrew tape recorded this admission, and then this morning offered to sell it to the counselors for 50¢ while telling Bernie that he would erase it for 50¢. At this point in the conversation, Andrew came by and Dale [who had been listening to this story with me] jumped up and grabbed him by the shirt (Andrew is a foot taller) and said "You better get rid of that tape, or I'll kick your ass." Andrew said that he had already erased it.

Last night according to staff reports eight girls ganged up on Gail Sanders in her room and beat her up so that she was taken to the hospital. The girls had gotten hold of the staff report book and read that Gail had told Bernice [staff member] that some kids were bringing drugs in. [The leader of this assault was also the major drug-runner.]

In the training school cottages and three of the community programs the term dime-dropper was used regularly with reference to informers, and accusations of dime-dropping were viewed as highly uncomplimentary.

Although support for the norm against informing was substantial in all the programs with low participation scores, youths were willing to make exceptions for themselves, and occasionally for others, when self-interest dictated. A leader at Westview commented, for example, that "I wouldn't dime drop on a kid if the cottage master has a good idea of who did wrong, but if he doesn't know and he's going to take the whole cottage off smokes [group punishment], I'd tell him who did it for the cottage's sake." Similar justifications for informing were advanced by youths in the case of a hypothetical stabbing used in the interview format. Some youths urged the victim to identify the culprit to the staff as a means of self-protection—"If he doesn't tell he'll just get his butt kicked again"; others felt silence was the safest course—"If he dime drops, he'll get killed." Evidently the norm was regarded as an instrumental device in these settings, in part, one might suppose, because youths generally had few friends to protect and little sense of loyalty to uphold. The absence of compelling human bonds left the norm a somewhat hollow shell, honored out of habit, greater dislike for the staff than of peers, or because of fear of reprisal.

The norms about informing were part of a complex of subcultural standards regarding the flow of information. Heavy pressure was placed on youths by peers and staff in the most participatory programs to talk about themselves to one another, to express their feelings openly, and to probe others about their experiences and feelings.

Youths in the other programs were, by contrast, reluctant to expose themselves to others and resistant to personal queries. Where such reluctance was greatest, counseling efforts—a major staple in the rehabilitation cupboard—were presumably inhibited. The general eagerness of youths to be interviewed in the most participatory programs, for example, contrasted sharply with the frequent reticence of youths in other programs.

In five of the seven most participatory programs—"I Belong," Topsfield, Primal, Confront, and Group—the observers saw frequent occasions of informing and sensed the expectation that youths considered such behavior proper. At Group for example,

> Jim [resident] told Fred [staff] last night that he had lied and gone to visit friends instead of family on two occasions several weeks ago. Now in the evening group he asks if he will be grounded. Several staff members say they think Jim's admission is healthy. David [resident], after hearing that Jim had told Carl [resident] about his lie at the time of his visits, calls them both to task for using the "street code" [that is, don't fink on a friend].

Similarly, at Confront, Alex proudly told the observer about an incident in which he had acted as an informer and had pressured a poorly socialized peer into giving up his larcenous intentions, if not into complete respect for the truth. A staff member at Primal told our observer:

> Norman [a resident] saw Harrison [another resident] peeping and reported him. The program director was so impressed with the way Norman handled himself and the situation that he made him a student coordinator —a promotion in the elaborate formal organization at Primal.

The argot used by staff members and youths in several of these participatory programs also reflected the subcultural nature of these standards. Youths and staff members at Group talked disparagingly about the street code (with its support of antagonism to authority and its prohibition of finking) and believed that a resident who was really "in the house" would no longer use such a code as a standard of conduct. Residents of Confront spoke of "pulling a person's cover" when exposing that individual's wrongdoing, while at Primal such an action was encompassed by the idea of "dropping a slip" on a resident.[11] Interestingly, at both Primal and Confront the police-criminal argot for admitting guilt—"to cop" to a particular act—was used. Finally, participants at Primal referred with disdain to tacit agreements among residents to overlook one another's misdeeds as "contracts" or "tips."

Communicating information to staff people about one's own feelings was considered at least as important as passing on observations about others in these programs. Opening up about emotions was distinguished from "running data," that is, giving facts about one's life without really identifying the underlying problems. Staff expectations about the need for openness in these programs were clearly shared by youths, who applied sometimes brutal pressures on peers to push them into revealing their most intimate secrets and repressed problems.

> Bruce sat in front of his audience and related his experiences on the street, his time in another program and in the hospital, the reasons behind his unwillingness to change, the reasons why he is getting so much pressure now (both he and Phil are getting haircuts every 30 minutes or so), etc. After he had bared his soul for half an hour, he took questions from the group. Jerry [a resident high in the official hierarchy]: "Yes I have a question, Bruce, and the question is why are you such a sleazy, lying fuck?" (That was the first question asked and kind of set the tone . . .) Both Bruce and Phil got haircuts after the seminar for not being honest in them and for trying to "run games" on the new kids.

At "I Belong" a youth's discomfort with these expectations and pressures may have been a contributing factor in an apparent suicide attempt:

> Around 4 or 4:30, Sy quietly told Jeff that he had taken 35 aspirin. Two staff members talked with him for some time. Sy finally vomited his guts out on a glass of salt water given to him by one of the staff.
>   This, like his threat to run away last week, [appeared to be] the result of pressure from all sides at the community meeting to get Sy to open up, to talk about himself. Several kids and staff were the main speakers. Janet [staff] finally proposed the ultimatum: If Sy didn't speak up by the end of the meeting, that would be the last time he would be asked to discuss his attitude. Sy remained silent.

Even in participatory programs such as Group where the pressures were far more mild, youths shared with staff the belief that public airing of problems and feelings was best. In commenting on Ralph's request that the group remove his ground, for example, Andy (another resident) observed, "I think you're getting along good. But I think you hold things in, you know. You don't let out your feelings but hold them in for a long time. You should work on letting your feelings out."

In contrast, at Warning, Fred—a new resident who had recently been at Confront—"was being really outgoing to the point of antagonizing some of the veteran residents. When he was out of earshot, Francis and Murphy discussed the possibility of beating him up— Murphy said there was a large crowd in Fred's room last night, and they almost did it then." Youths there were far less tolerant of "relating" by their peers. "Keep to yourself" and "mind your business" were more acceptable admonitions in programs such as Warning, which had low participation levels.

Both the wide differences in norms regarding information flow and the apparent sources of their variation are made clearer by an analysis of the correlations with and multiple regressions on organizational and population characteristics of several indexes of these norms drawn from the questionnaires. An aggregate index of youth norms regarding informing was developed from several interview items describing hypothetical instances of finking.[12] Respondents were asked to give their own evaluations of the actions of the person in the story *and* to estimate how many youths in the program approved of this behavior. The latter responses were used to create a scale measuring youth perceptions of the views of their peers about informing, and programs were assigned scores corresponding to the percentage of youths with a high score on this pro-informing scale.

Zero-order correlations between this scale and the set of independent variables reveal that participation, supervision, and equality scores are positively and quite strongly associated with pro-informing sentiment (see Table 3-5). Because of the intercorrelations among these three organizational characteristics, however, inclusion of all three in a single regression is redundant. The most powerful and theoretically meaningful regression includes only the supervision and participation scales and explains 69 percent of the variance in pro-informing. No characteristic of the youth populations shows a high zero-order correlation with the anti-informing scale or adds substantially to the regression. It appears, therefore, that the combination of high participation of youths in program operation and high supervision of youths by staff—both in the context of high levels of program equality—provide the leverage needed to overturn a basic youth norm.

Participation and equality together reduce the onus of informing by clouding over the "we-they" distinction that makes finking a traitorous act. Participation enlists youths in doing therapy with their peers, and thus makes plausible and acceptable the belief that informing helps rather than hurts the target. Participation also means that official rewards are bestowed by peers and staff for informing, while high levels of supervision increase the probability that nonin-

Table 3-5. Multiple Regression on Independent Variables of Percentage of Youths with High Score on Perceived Peer Support for Informing Scale (*N* = 23 programs)[a]

Independent Variables	Zero-Order Correlation with Dependent Variable	Standardized Regression Coefficient	F Ratio
Percentage of youths 16 years or older	.25		
Percentage of male youths	.07		
Percentage of black youths	–.36		
Percentage of youths from DYS	–.31		
Percentage of DYS youths committing first offense before age 14	.14		
Percentage of DYS youths with previous commitment	–.06		
Percentage of DYS youths committed for crimes against persons	.09		
Percentage of DYS youths committed for juvenile status offenses	–.02		
Program size	.04		
Youth-to-staff ratio	.34		
Equality scale	.56		
Community-contact scale	–.25		
Participation scale	.79	0.69	25.79
Supervision scale	.53	.27	3.81[b]

[a]For the regression equation the multiple correlation = .83 (R^2 = .69), and the F ratio = 21.85 (with 2 and 20 degrees of freedom).
[b]This F ratio is significant at the 0.10 level.

formers as well as the culprits they protect will get caught and punished. Supervision, participation, and equality thus reinforce one another and focus enormous pressure on youths to accept new norms defining appropriate conduct.

While youth norms concerning informing may be particularly important for the maintenance of control within a program as well as symbolic of the degree to which youths have incorporated staff perceptions into their own world views, norms regarding the revelation of one's own emotions and personal problems have particular relevance to most conventional attempts at rehabilitation. Only youths in the thirteen community-based programs were asked questions concerning their expectations about privacy. From these items, a scale was constructed to indicate variations among these programs in norms of openness about emotions and personal problems.[13] Zero-order correlations reveal a strong correlation between participation and the antiprivacy scale (r = .74), and moderate correlations with community contact (r = −.59), supervision (r = .47), and proportion youths 16 or over (r = .57). The correlations of participation and supervision are consistent with the argument about their central role in shaping subcultures.

The final regression equation, however, uses only participation and community-contact scales as independent variables; it is summarized in Table 3-6. On the one hand, the responsibility that youths share with staff in the most participatory programs for therapy and discipline forces youths to redefine the implications of talking about themselves. On the other hand, higher levels of contact between youths and community members contribute to considerable antagonism by youths to the public expression of feelings and problems. Under such circumstances staff cannot exert as much pressure to alter youth standards about open discussion of their problems and feelings. This lack of pressure results both from the reduced leverage

Table 3-6. Multiple Regression on Independent Variables of Percentage of Youths with High Scores on Antiprivacy Scale (*N* = 13 programs)[a]

Independent Variables	Zero-Order Correlation with Dependent Variable	Standardized Regression Coefficient	F Ratio
Percentage of youths 16 or older	.57		
Percentage of male youths	−.04		
Percentage of black youths	−.30		
Percentage of youths from DYS	−.30		
Percentage of DYS youths committing first offense before age 14	.17		
Percentage of DYS youths with previous commitment	.24		
Percentage of DYS youths committed for crimes against persons	.33		
Percentage of DYS youths committed for juvenile status offenses	−.09		
Program size	.37		
Youth-to-staff ratio	.30		
Equality scale	.32		
Community-contact scale	−.59	−0.41	5.16
Participation scale	.74	.62	11.70
Supervision scale	.47		

[a]For the regression equation the multiple correlation = .84 (R^2 = .70), and the F ratio = 15.65 (with 2 and 10 degrees of freedom).

staff have with youths and from the reduced emphasis on treatment when community contact is high.

The importance of community contact here underlines the difficulties inherent in simultaneous attempts to engage youths in their communities and to get them involved in a mutual or group effort at resolving personal problems. Open House provided the clearest example of this difficulty. Although committed to the establishment of a "positive peer culture" through regular group meetings and youth participation, the staff of Open House had only partial success in molding a subculture because the youths were relatively free to come and go in the community. Intragroup relationships—the focus of much of the interaction, social pressure, and norms in other programs with similar goals and participatory organization—were simply not salient to youths at Open House; most had more freely chosen and enticing ties in the community, and their attention was thus directed outward instead of inward toward the program.

Normative pressure for or against revealing oneself in public may also affect self-conceptions, as we shall see later in this chapter, and act to inhibit youths from defining themselves as persons in need of counseling, help, or change; it may also prevent them from accepting staff attempts to "rap" with them.

Norms concerning the flow of information indicate the general sense on the part of youths about the appropriateness of their getting involved in the correctional organization. Reticence means reluctant or limited involvement in the correctional organization. A more direct measure of youths' collective judgments about the appropriateness of becoming involved in the program came from their responses to the statement included in both the 1971 and 1973 questionnaires: "When there is a problem in the program the staff should work it out without bothering the kids about it." A regression of the proportion of youths disagreeing or strongly disagreeing with this assertion reaffirms the powerful effect on subcultures of participation in the context of high program equality (see Table 3.7). It is the only variable that remains a substantial contributor to the equation after eliminating insignificant variables. By sharing official responsibilities with youths, staff people were able to foster a collective sense among them that the program was theirs as well as the staff's, and that they should take part in decision-making.

Another central aspect of youth subcultures involved the degree of tolerance of nonuniversalistic conduct. Generally the youths we observed followed the American tradition by somewhat ambivalently endorsing the standard of equal treatment and railing against apparent favoritism by staff members. Thus, one of the great value con-

Table 3-7. Multiple Regression on Independent Variables of Percentage of Youths Agreeing They Should Help Solve Problems of Their Program (N = 23 programs)[a]

Independent Variables	Zero-Order Correlation with Dependent Variable	Standardized Regression Coefficient	F Ratio
Percentage of youths 16 years or older	.31		
Percentage of male youths	-.01		
Percentage of black youths	.05		
Percentage of youths from DYS	-.06		
Percentage of DYS youths committing first offense before age 14	.02		
Percentage of DYS youths with previous commitment	.06		
Percentage of DYS youths committed for crimes against persons	-.02		
Percentage of DYS youths committed for juvenile status offenses	.00		
Program size	-.08		
Youth-to-staff ratio	.09		
Equality scale	.51		
Community-contact scale	-.21		
Participation scale	.63	0.63	13.58
Supervision scale	.10		

[a]For the regression equation the multiple correlation = .63 (R^2 = .39), and the F ratio = 13.58 (with 1 and 21 degrees of freedom).

flicts in criminal justice—between individualized treatment and uniform, equal justice—was translated into day-to-day anger or resentment among youths. Field notes at Cottage 9 record, for example, that "all of the boys are very upset about the inequities of the Board [DYS], particularly that Jeff Andrews is being released to go to Topsfield. Some kids are also angry that Fred Wilhelm is going to see his parents and may be released before he is paroled." Although youths repeatedly made requests or demands that exceptions be made for them, tolerance was low when others got a break.

"Different strokes for different folks" served as a guiding motto at Primal and Confront, and symbolized the attempt in most of the participatory group-treatment programs to get youths to join in and accept the idea of individualized treatment, a view which treatment-oriented staff strongly shared. Only in these programs did staff members reverse the expectation of youths that they should receive equal treatment. It is not surprising, therefore, that the correlation between the participation scale and the proportion of youths in each program agreeing that "each kid should receive the same discipline for breaking the same rule" is -.62; greater participation is associated with less frequent endorsement of universalistic staff conduct. The multiple regression equation explaining variations in acceptance of the universalism norm contains two variables in addition to participation (see Table 3-8). Programs with higher proportions of youths from the Department of Youth Services and with lower ratios of youths to staff are, all else being equal, likely to show stronger support for uniform treatment of youths by staff.

Although the causal linkages between the youth/staff ratio and the universalism norm are unclear, the link between the norm and population composition has at least a plausible explanation. The nature of involuntary commitment to the program, and the experience in the juvenile court leading to it, both emphasize the importance of universalistic standards; youths are likely to come to a program questioning the fairness and equity of decisions made about them in the

Table 3-8. Multiple Regression on Independent Variables of Percentage of Youths Agreeing That the Staff Should Discipline Inmates Equally (*N* = 23 programs)[a]

Independent Variables	Zero-Order Correlation with Dependent Variable	Standardized Regression Coefficient	F Ratio
Percentage of youths 16 or older	-.09		
Percentage of male youths	.08		
Percentage of black youths	.38		
Percentage of youths from DYS	.49	0.34	6.56
Percentage of DYS youths committing first offense before age 14	-.17		
Percentage of DYS youths with previous commitment	.11		
Percentage of DYS youths committed for crimes against persons	-.15		
Percentage of DYS youths committed for juvenile status offense	.04		
Program size	-.22		
Youth-to-staff ratio	-.46	-.36	7.39
Equality scale	-.49		
Community-contact scale	.31		
Participation scale	-.62	-.56	18.28
Supervision scale	-.53		

[a]For the regression equation the multiple correlation = .83 (R^2 = .68), and the F ratio = 13.58 (with 3 and 19 degrees of freedom).

past, and thus will be particularly sensitive to the problem of equal treatment. For other youths the reasons for their presence are rooted in more personal and individual circumstances, and they will be more amenable to accepting for themselves and others differentiated treatment appropriate to these individual circumstances.

SCHOOLS FOR CRIME?

"I learned to break into houses here. I also learned how to steal cars. This place doesn't help you a bit." This complaint by a boy at Sunset echoes the concern of many observers that putting youths with records of criminal behavior together in one place simply creates a school for crime. In our forays into the field, we met few youths, coming or going, who might be thought of as hardened criminals; nevertheless, in some programs observers encountered a vast store of knowledge about jimmying windows, hot-wiring cars, vandalizing pleasure boats, soliciting "johns" on the street, and the subtle differences among highs from various drugs.

When they had time on their hands and were outside the reach of staff supervision, youths looked for amusement. At times the entertainment was itself illegal—running away, smoking marijuana, stealing food or the program's van—but "war stories," were cheaper in terms of effort and staff or police reprisals, and far more common. At Warning, where such stories abounded, one boy carried a carefully folded newspaper clipping describing his last escapade, while another proudly told and retold the story of his first trial after which "he claimed, he went sort of berserk, attacking the cop who had allegedly lied, breaking the bannister and forcing the judge to retreat to chambers."

The glorification or at least acceptance of crime communicated by these actions and stories was, however, a significant aspect of the youth subcultures in only a few programs. A population with large numbers of boys with substantial records of lawbreaking was a prerequisite; girls typically were not involved in this kind of discussion, probably because few of them had the wealth of experiences to share with their peers and because the excitement, toughness, and *bravado* these exploits played up were less important values for the girls.

A repertoire of experiences in a population was not sufficient to produce these stories, however. High levels of community contact tended to remove the need to fill time with talk among program members—youths could be elsewhere doing other things; in programs such as Open House, Pair, Drop-in, and Pick-up, such discussion was minimal.

In addition, of course, youths assigned to the most open programs were generally less knowledgeable about and; one might assume, less committed to criminal activity than those in some of the more closed, higher security programs. On the other hand, closed programs that successfully shaped other aspects of youth norms also shaped this one. High participation usually combined with high supervision succeeded in vastly reducing the value of war stories, and substituted for them "relating" about one another's personal problems. At Primal, Confront, Group, "I Belong," and Topsfield— although the youths had their stories to tell (as we learned in our interviews)—such talk was not generally tolerated and was rarely heard. High levels of supervision without youth participation, as at Regiment, reduced the opportunity and the frequency but not the impulse for youths to talk about their exploits. War stories were most common, therefore, only in those programs for boys with low supervision, little community contact, and low youth participation— most of the institutional training school cottages, programs such as Warning, and to a lesser extent (because the boys had relatively few delinquent experiences) at Fatigue.

Far more widespread—not confined to particular populations or as thoroughly contained by program manipulation—was communication and reinforcement of values about drug and alcohol use. Although relatively few of the youths we met during the two summers of observation had been arrested on drug charges, a very large proportion of them had tried drugs—particularly marijuana—at some time. The use of marijuana and the consumption of alcoholic beverages were not only acceptable but expected; nonusers were "straight" while users were "cool."

The frequent discussions of drugs and drink and the wide vocabulary of synonyms for being "high" indicated the central importance of "dope" and "booze" in the lives of these young people. The strong expectation that one *should* use drugs or alcohol was evident in the conversation between two residents of Group and two young, ex-resident staff members about an upcoming Led Zeppelin concert they were all planning to attend. Getting high, they all assumed, was natural:

> Steve [staff] asks how this concert will be arranged "since you boys will want to get fucked up for it, but you better not be fucked up when you get back to the house if you go by yourselves. It would be OK if you were with a staff member." Stewart [staff] says that he may take the guys, but he is going to be straight for this concert. "I want to hear it," he says. Randy [resident] responds "I can't go to a concert straight."

One of the boys later ran from the program after being disciplined for returning intoxicated from this concert.

Although almost universally outraged by hard drugs, staff members took somewhat different positions on marijuana use within and outside the programs, and their views had differing effects depending upon the type of program. Staff members in nonresidential programs, where community contact was greatest, were the most tolerant. The director of Pick-up told me when I was arranging our observation that they "did not pay much attention if kids went off to smoke a couple of joints." Similarly, most staff members at Drop-in lamented the program director's decision that staff could never under any circumstances drink beer and smoke pot with youths as they had the previous evening.

> Lisa shared her feelings about last night. She especially was disappointed because the result of their evening had been that the kids were more open. She saw it as something kids in the neighborhood do and felt that they might as well do it together even though she was aware that families and DYS could make trouble if they found out.

In the training schools and residential programs staff members were particularly cognizant of their legal responsibilities; drug use was strictly prohibited, and users were usually punished when discovered. At several institutional training school cottages and community programs (including Warning and Regiment), staff members even engaged in periodic shakedowns to root out suspected caches of drugs. Despite this common although often ambivalent staff view, youths rarely subscribed to an in-program prohibition against drugs. Only in the most participatory group-treatment programs—Group, Confront, Primal, "I Belong," and Topsfield—did youths speak out against the use of drugs in the house.

To the degree that it was accepted, this norm against in-house drug use was clearly situational for many youths. As one boy in Group noted in explaining his answer to a story item in the interview about a boy hiding marijuana from the staff, "That's street code. While I'm here I'd disapprove. It's the house rules, and it would hurt the person breaking the rule. It's weird cause I'm all for marijuana." The Led Zeppelin concert incident indicates that some staff members tended also to draw the same distinction.

At Primal alone, with its rigid social structure and uniquely pervasive supervision of youths, however, the norms against drugs (not alcoholic beverages) shared by staff and youths were absolute and almost universally accepted. Even indirect suggestions that marijuana use might be acceptable drew a quick and tough response:

Alan told me after looking around to make sure that we couldn't be over-heard, that he had been "dealt with"—this can be a "haircut" or "blast" or anything—for repeating to some other kids a news story that he heard on the Cronkite show about marijuana laws being relaxed in some town. He had added jokingly, that the town would probably soon be flooded with kids.

It is not surprising, therefore, that Primal was the only one of the twenty-three programs in which we found no evidence that drugs were present and used by participants. This analysis provides additional confirmation that participatory programs with high levels of supervision are more effective at suppressing, at least temporarily, the appearance in their programs of subcultural elements that many of their members presumably share at entry.

ORGANIZATIONAL STRUCTURE, SUBCULTURES, AND SELF-CONCEPTIONS

Collectively shared definitions of a program situation affect the way youths behave in it; these definitions can also structure or alter youths' conceptions of themselves. The cross-sectional data presented here do not allow us to separate out direct organizational effects on self-conceptions from their indirect effects through the shaping of subcultures, but they clearly communicate evidence that self-conceptions of youths vary systematically according to the characteristics of the correctional organizations they are in.

In both 1971 and 1973, youths were asked to choose which of five statements best described them. Considerably different proportions of youths in the twenty-three programs identified themselves either as "someone with personal problems" or "someone who is trying to straighten out," rather than as "someone who got a raw deal," "who knows what the score is and how to play it cool," or "who doesn't let anyone push him around." A regression of the percentage of youths choosing one of the first two responses on the set of independent variables resulted in the equation summarized in Table 3-9. The level of equality has a large positive regression coefficient, whereas community contact has a large negative one.

Those programs in which youths were more equal to staff members were the ones in which youths tended not to view themselves as victims of the system who must fight back at it or manipulate it. Equality appeared to carry a message that "kids are to be helped here because they have problems," and that message was reflected in appropriate conceptions of self.

Table 3-9. Multiple Regression on Independent Variables of Percentage of Youths Describing Themselves as "Having Personal Problems" or "Trying to Go Straight" (*N* = 23 programs)[a]

Independent Variables	Zero-Order Correlation with Dependent Variable	Standardized Regression Coefficient	F Ratio
Percentage of youths 16 years or older	-.25		
Percentage of male youths	-.56		
Percentage of black youths	-.22		
Percentage of youths from DYS	-.24		
Percentage of DYS youths committing first offense before age 14	-.53		
Percentage of DYS youths with previous commitment	-.37		
Percentage of DYS youths committed for crimes against persons	-.53		
Percentage of DYS youths committed for juvenile status offenses	.66	0.66	49.31
Program size	-.03		
Youth-to-staff ratio	.10		
Equality scale	.45	.55	33.00
Community contact scale	-.36	-.45	21.94
Participation scale	.33		
Supervision scale	.38		

[a]For the regression equation the multiple correlation = .91 (R^2 = .83), and the F ratio = 31.96 (with 3 and 19 degrees of freedom).

The community-contact variable continues to show the tension between reintegration and rehabilitation. All else being equal, increases in contact between program youths and community members made youths more reluctant to locate the source of their problems in themselves. A program focus on altering youths' relationships with various community members—such as school teachers, police, peers, and parents—thus has clear implications for the self-conceptions of program participants. A narrow if not exclusive focus on changing youths themselves in more closed programs has very different consequences for self-conceptions.

One population variable contributes heavily to this regression and adds to our understanding of the interplay between organization and population traits. The percentage of DYS youths in the program who were committed for juvenile offenses (runaway, stubborn child, and so on) has a correlation of .66 with the dependent variable and shows a large positive regression coefficient in the final equation. Because

the juvenile offenses themselves typically represent a personal problem in the relationship between parent and child, it is not surprising
that youths in populations with higher proportions of status offenders would be amenable to view themselves in the problem frame.[14]

"I don't have to change myself so much, what I mostly need is
for people to stop hassling me and give me a chance." Only youths
in the 1973 sample were asked to "strongly agree," "agree," "disagree," or "strongly disagree" with this statement, but the differing
distribution of responses among programs both supports and adds
to the first finding on self-conceptions. The direction and strength
of the correlations between the percentage of youths agreeing or
strongly agreeing with this statement and the level of equality
($r = -.55$); participation ($r = -.78$); and community contact ($r = .44$)
sustain the argument and present the opposite side of the coin. While
community contact does not encourage conception of oneself as
having problems, equality and particularly participation in therapeutic activities promote such self-conceptions. Of these organizational
dimensions, only the participation scale remains in the regression
equation, however (see Table 3–10).

Differences in the characteristics of the youth populations also
help explain variations in the distribution of these perceptions
about the need for "a chance" rather than "self-change." The percentage of black youths in a program has a positive regression coefficient in this equation, which suggests that with all else held constant,
increases in the proportions of blacks in youth populations led to an
increase in the proportion of youths believing they need a chance.[15]
The view that one is victimized by circumstance may have better
objective justification in the social situation of blacks generally than
of whites, and may have received some ideological support from
peers in programs where blacks were more numerous. Additionally,
the rhetoric of protest has provided blacks with a socially acceptable
(and perhaps ideologically necessary) means of deflecting blame from
themselves onto racism or the power structure.

Finally, youths in both 1971 and 1973 were asked to respond to
two related statements that together provide a measure of their sense
of individual efficacy.[16] The .74 zero-order correlation and the out-
sized standardized regression coefficient of equality stand out in the
regression of the proportion of youths with high efficacy scores on
the set of independent variables (see Table 3–11). At the same time
that equality helps create some sense of personal responsibility for
one's plight, it seems also to encourage a greater sense of control over
one's life. In egalitarian programs youths are less often the victims
of the whims of arbitrary and inconsistent staff members whose

Table 3–10. Multiple Regression on Independent Variables of Percentage of Youths Agreeing They "Need a Chance" (*N* = 13 programs)

Independent Variables	Zero-Order Correlation with Dependent Variable	Standardized Regression Coefficient	F Ratio
Percentage of youths 16 years or older	-.45		
Percentage of male youths	.09		
Percentage of black youths	.52	0.34	3.65[b]
Percentage of youths from DYS	.11		
Percentage of DYS youths committing first offense before age 14	-.13		
Percentage of DYS youths with previous commitment	-.15		
Percentage of DYS youths committed for crimes against persons	.03		
Percentage of DYS youths committed for juvenile status offenses	.15		
Program size	-.11		
Youth-to-staff ratio	-.40		
Equality scale	-.56		
Community-contact scale	.44		
Participation scale	-.78	-.69	15.13
Supervision scale	-.29		

[a]For the regression equation the multiple correlation = .84 (R^2 = .71), and the *F* ratio = 12.34 (with 2 and 10 degrees of freedom).
[b]This *F* ratio is significant at the 0.10 level.

behavior is held up to, but does not meet, a rigorous standard of equal treatment. Nor are the symbolic degradations of self that are so characteristic of nonegalitarian institutions as available to crush the spirits of the participants in more egalitarian programs.

Population composition again adds a weighty variable to this regression that explains variations in the sense of individual efficacy among members of programs. The percentage of boys in the program population has a negative regression coefficient (and zero-order correlation), implying that, all else being equal, the higher the proportion of boys in a program, the lower the sense of individual effectiveness of the program members.[17] The reason for this relationship is obscure, although it may be that sex-role pressures for success are greater for boys, and the sense of failure and of ineffectiveness resulting from incarceration looms larger for them than for girls. Whatever the causal relationship in this instance, however, the sex composition of the population clearly had other ramifications

Table 3–11. Multiple Regression on Independent Variables of the Percentage of Youths with High Individual Efficacy Scores (N = 23 programs)[a]

Independent Variables	Zero-Order Correlation with Dependent Variable	Standardized Regression Coefficient	F Ratio
Percentage of youths 16 years or older	-.10		
Percentage of male youths	-.39	-0.45	6.65
Percentage of black youths	-.19		
Percentage of youths from DYS	-.19		
Percentage of DYS youths committing first offense before age 14	-.43		
Percentage of DYS youths with previous commitment	-.40		
Percentage of DYS youths committed for crimes against persons	-.19		
Percentage of DYS youths committed for juvenile status offenses	.25		
Program size	-.11		
Youth-to-staff ratio	-.11		
Equality scale	.74	.78	49.20
Community-contact scale	.01		
Participation scale	.39		
Supervision scale	.22		

[a]For the regression equation the multiple correlation = .87 (R^2 = .76), and the F ratio = 30.89 (with 2 and 20 degrees of freedom).

for the character of youth subcultures and quality of life within programs.

SEX AND SUBCULTURE

There were substantial differences among programs in sex-related expectations concerning youth relationships and behavior. Traditional notions of masculinity were evident in the all-male programs —in both the community programs and in the training schools— although they were somewhat moderated in the two more participatory group-treatment programs for boys—Group and "I Belong." The expectations about appropriate masculine behavior were clearest in all but one of the institutional programs for boys—that is, in Cottages 8 and 9, Elms, Westview, Warning, and Fatigue—and in two less participatory group-treatment programs—Sunset and Shirley. In these, values and argot reflected concern with toughness and dominance. Youths talked about "bogarting" one another (pushing someone around), "blanket parties" (gang beatings of an individual who is incapacitated by throwing a blanket over him), "putting the fizzies on" (fighting), and "being cold" (unemotionally brutal). The boys loved the fights on TV programs and frequently joined in with shouts of encouragement; if they had the opportunity, they chose gangster, Kung Fu, or James Bond movies because of their intense action and violence. In addition, particularly in programs with youths older than fourteen or fifteen, the boys bragged about their sexual exploits and were rather contemptuous of the restrictions marriage imposed on a man's freedom. (A youth noticed an observer's wedding ring and asked, "Are you married?" The observer said yes. The youth replied, "I thought you were cooler than that.") The favorite put-down of other boys was "faggot," emphasizing the premium placed on heterosexuality.

The most significant variation on these themes in all-male programs occurred in Group and "I Belong" where, as we have seen, boys were pressed hard to open up and express their positive and negative feelings toward one another and to talk about their problems. The recurrent public airing of private feelings made an emphasis on toughness less appropriate, as did the prohibition by staff of any physical violence or horseplay. During the meetings at Group, perhaps inevitably, for example, two of the boys spoke with great tenderness about their girlfriends and their hopes to be married. In such a context the public expectation of masculine exploitation of women was also downplayed. The differences between Group and "I Belong" and the other all-male programs reflected the familiar combination of differences in staff philosophy and program organization.

While the staff members at Group and "I Belong" actively campaigned against some elements of the conventional male subculture, those at the all-male training school cottages and at Warning, Fatigue, and even in Pick-up entered into horseplay with the boys and appeared to share and support many of their conceptions of masculinity. For example, in Fatigue, which served younger boys, staff requests or commands often drew a relatively good-natured show of defiance, and the child-care workers responded with threats of force until the mock confrontation became a playful/serious physical tussle leading to the inevitable staff victory. Youthful capitulation to superior force was a face-saving way of conforming to the staff, but it also encouraged physical aggressiveness among the residents. This ritualistic exchange was, of course, not so evident with older and stronger boys, in part because staff victory was not so certain. Masters at the more traditional training school cottages were as likely to ignore fights as to break them up, and in so doing subtly supported the validity of expectations about toughness. Staff also gave more direct encouragement: "Why do you think those kids are picking on you? Because you don't do anything. You're getting hit anyhow so you better make it cost them."

The staff members at Regiment, by contrast, neither encouraged aggressiveness—fighting and horseplay were prohibited—nor exerted pressures toward a changed perspective. As a consequence the boys there "talked the same game" as they did at Pick-up, Fatigue, Warning, and the training school cottages, but rarely had the opportunity to turn their talk into action.

In the five all-girls' programs, some subcultural elements often stereotypically associated with females were apparent. First, romantic interest in boys was a major preoccupation. Girls spent considerable time writing letters to boyfriends and talking about them with peers. Sexual techniques and abilities often entered into these discussions, and the argot, particularly at Clara Barton and Putnam cottages, was replete with sexual references.

Second, moodiness and strong outbursts of emotions appeared to be acceptable if not expected behavior in the girls' programs. For example, one girl at Mother

> stormed out to her room and slammed the door. Karen [the counselor] went over to the window to look and see if Ginny [the girl] was leaving by the fire escape. Then we heard the crash of broken glass and things being thrown against the wall. Karen went to the door and told Ginny to stop. She then called Charles [another staff member] downstairs saying, "Ginny is having a nutty." Ginny kept screaming that she "didn't care," that "it didn't matter." Charles ran up, went into the room, and grabbed the girl who wrenched herself away from him screaming obscenities. He screamed back at her and she "broke" and cried.

Third, and most significantly, girls were intensely interested in the character of their relationships with one another; popularity, not toughness or coolness was the major dimension along which girls evaluated one another. Although, as will be shown in the next chapter, the web of social relationships among girls we observed in no way approached the complexity of the quasifamily systems described by Giallombardo and Carter, girls kept track carefully of shifting relationships among their peers and openly discussed their own friends and enemies.[18]

Barbara Carter's description of an earlier family system at the Lancaster School for Girls (where Putnam and Clara Barton were located) was evidenced by continued existence in 1971 of bits and pieces of the extensive secretive argot associated with such a system; "Holland," for example, meant "hope our love lasts and never dies," while "Italy" stood for "I truly always love you" in the notes and whispered communications of the girls. While these carryovers were unique to the Lancaster cottages, in all the girls' programs the residents directly, repeatedly, and openly evaluated their changing relationships with and feelings toward one another. "I like her" or "I hate her" were with many variations the theme of much interaction among girls; frequently, negative comments were made directly and openly, leaving girls little doubt about their standing with others.

This preoccupation with intimate relationships between peers may well underlie the development of quasifamilies in many institutions for girls and women. Such families provide some order (based on a model most consistent with the conventional female role) to these relationships that are the major focus of group life. The longer confinement (lower turnover of members) and greater isolation from people in the community (particularly from boys and men) that is typical of women's prisons and institutions for girls may be required for the development of such complex systems; however, the greater openness in the community programs and shorter sentences—averaging about three months at the training school cottages and several weeks at Shelter (a detention center)—seem to have reduced the intensity and complexity of relationships among girls.

Just as openness to community contact and short-term placement may have worked against the emergence of full-blown male or female subcultures, so also did coeducation. Unfortunately for research purposes, the coeducational programs we observed were also either very high in community contact (Drop-in, Pair, Open House) or highly participatory (Topsfield, Primal, Confront), factors that of themselves appear to have decreased the salience of in-program relationships or to have dampened the expression of sex-related subcultural elements carried into the program by youths.

It is difficult, therefore, to separate out the unique effects of bringing boys and girls together in the same program. Theoretically, at least, the effect of coeducation by itself should be to reduce the need of individuals to affirm masculinity or femininity through somewhat exaggerated allegiance to sex subcultures and rules. Since sexual identity receives crucial affirmation through interaction with people of the other sex, these identities should be somewhat more secure in coeducation programs, and rely less on stereotypical sex-role behavior. In addition, of course, the presence of both sexes in a program is likely to call forth sex-role standards about how to deal with members of the other sex; the definitions of situation selected under such conditions will then draw upon these guides for behavior rather than those appropriate to interaction with other males or other females.

The programs that brought males and females together definitely showed this expected moderation of sex subcultures, and we are convinced that the cause at least in part was their sex composition. A comparison, for example, of two highly participatory group-treatment programs—Group (all male) and Confront (male and female)—supports this conclusion. Although staff did little to reinforce it and effectively countered much of its outward manifestation, elements of the traditional male subculture clearly remained at Group. Play- or slap-fighting and taunting one another half-jokingly about being "faggots" were common there, but virtually nonexistent at Confront. High participation and the group-treatment ideology did not set these programs apart; but sex composition did.

FAILURES IN SUBCULTURE CHANGE: THE LESSONS OF SHIRLEY AND OPEN HOUSE

Not all participatory programs in the group-treatment cluster succeeded in substantially shaping youth subcultures. Shirley Cottage and Open House provide case studies of failure that further clarify the manner in which program provisions for youth participation can make manipulation of subcultures feasible. At Shirley, for example, boys dime-dropped for instrumental reasons, as they did in the less participatory programs, but few youths accepted informing as a principle. "The staff say that's not dime-dropping, it's being responsible," observed one youth. But, he went on, "the other kids don't like it—all the kids, not just the ones who get dimed on."

The lack of total success in shaping youth subculture evident in this and other observations can be attributed in large part to a fundamental inconsistency in Shirley's organization and to a failure in staff supervision of youths. Caught in the transition between the traditional institutions and Commissioner Miller's pressure to develop therapeutic communities, the Shirley staff included, on the one hand, traditional cottage parents whose task was largely the maintenance of order and, on the other, a coterie of young, therapy-oriented staff from the Industrial School. Staff conflicts abounded. "There is general complaining by all the staff about the laxity of supervision by other staff members," observed one counselor, reflecting the views of many.

The inconsistencies that the staff structure created were reinforced by the lack of clear guidance provided to youths by staff members in the community meetings. Rather than becoming engaged in the process of applying (and perhaps slightly modifying) a set of rules based on clearly articulated values, youths at Shirley became the creators and administrators of a burdensome set of rules, often suggested by staff members but officially enacted by "democratic vote" of youths and staff members at each meeting. Complained one youth, "The rules, the goddamned rules in this place, if they wrote those rules down, they'd cover every goddamned brick in here, and like Edwards [staff], if there isn't a rule, he'll make one up." Twice compromised and confused by an inconsistent staff structure and by the failure to articulate a clear set of general standards and values, staff influence over the shape of youth values and norms was only slight at Shirley.

These inconsistencies combined with a failure to supervise youths, either through fully programmed days or zealous enforcement of rules. "Two staff members in particular," reported an observer, "complain about their having to act as heavies because other staffers won't call certain kids on their derelictions." One consequence of this failure in supervision was repeated outbreaks of fighting among boys as retribution for staff-induced informing. "There is a rule that kids can't assault one another for dime-dropping during the community meeting. But, in fact, most of the fights in the cottage arise from just such finking."

A rule against violence, diligently enforced, is essential to staff attempts to shape subcultures. Without protection, youths' self-interests may dictate conformity to the wishes of the physically strong rather than the morally correct (in the view of staff). The response to violence at programs such as Primal and Group that more effectively altered youth subcultures makes clear the difference. At Group even the throwing of an ice cube in anger during a group meeting was treated as a major offense, evoking staff outrage and considerable attention in subsequent meetings. When a boy later tried to fight with a staff member after sniffing paint remover he was immediately evicted from the program after DYS was advised to make hurried arrangements for temporary quarters for him. This move was justified largely as a way of protecting both youths and staff. Hints of physical violence at Primal could have brought the perpetrator into the boxing ring, where several of the larger program members, equipped with well-padded boxing gloves, thoroughly pummeled the youth to provide "a taste of his or her own medicine." During our observations the ring had to be used only once, when an inept youth slammed a door on another resident's hands and arms.

Open House's lack of complete success in its attempts to create the intended positive peer subculture resulted from different causes, for there youths faced few restrictions and were able to move about the surrounding urban area. In Open House the intensity of mutual contact among youths was not nearly so great as in the more closed programs. As a consequence, though liking the program and the freedom it provided, youths had little reason to heed staff demands and, as a result, staff leverage over youths' attitudes and values was dramatically reduced. The inability of the able staff at Open House to capture youths' attention and control their subculture must be balanced against their apparent success in linking youths to schools and jobs in the city.

The warring impulses between the goals of integration or reintegration into the community and therapy and value change were ever present; the staff at Open House, perhaps more than any other program we observed, gave these conflicting goals even weight. In programs at each extreme of emphasis, however, the pressures of opposing goals and methods were also perceived. At Primal, for example, with its terrific intensity and isolation,

> Andrea [staff] told me that the director was discussing plans to allow kids who had been residents for four or five months to have free evenings out in a nearby city. This can only be done now by higher status kids and re-entry people—usually kids who have been around for eight months or so. The change is contemplated because there have been several problems with kids who had kind of a culture shock when they went out and tried to work and relate in society, after having been sheltered in a therapeutic community for so long.

Nevertheless the director and staff members were convinced that youths had to learn a new set of values and fundamentally alter their conceptions of themselves first if they were to develop into productive, law-abiding citizens.

At the other end of the spectrum, in Drop-in—a nonresidential program with a strong advocacy component—the director noted with some pride that in the past the program staff had been very helpful in representing youths in court, yet he also feared that such an advocacy service could lead youths to see the staff simply "as a group of people who were willing to break their necks for them in court," and, he concluded wistfully, "that's not too therapeutic." The temptation to act as therapist rather than agent for social change was an attractive one, but it was inconsistent with the heavy demands on staff of the advocacy program. Neither the director nor his colleagues at Drop-in and other programs with high levels of community contact, however, were convinced that youths had to alter their values substantially in order to be successful in the free community. Rather, they felt in general that youths had to learn to cope with the temptations of life in the context of a system of values and norms in the community to which they would continue to be exposed.

Although some blending of a reintegration strategy with one directed toward a therapeutic value change occurred in all the programs, there was considerable tension between the two, as illustrated particularly in the case of Open House. One should not, of course, conclude that these two approaches are inevitably mutually exclusive; the tensions between them are real, however, and making the approaches compatible requires organizational innovations not observed in any of the programs in our sample.

While there is tension between community contact and participation, there is mutual reinforcement between participation and supervision. The limited failure at Shirley to shape subcultures arose particularly from a breakdown of this supervisory capacity resulting from an awkward mix of staff roles; the inconsistency in staff conduct and the related absence of a clear guiding ideology seriously compromised the effectiveness of democratic youth participation. Greater supervision would have increased the impact on the youth subculture of the limited participation evident at Shirley Cottage.

SUBCULTURE DEVELOPMENT AND POPULATION COMPOSITION AND CHANGE

Even in those programs where success in shaping subcultures was great, a constant battle had to be waged to sustain the staff-endowed subculture. The observer at Topsfield saw, for example, that "a reluctance to confront one another appeared around the beginning of August. The staff responded by setting up The Book in which kids were supposed to record grievances about other kids. But that didn't work."

The constant shifts in population were a major cause of these fluctuations in the acceptance of staff definitions of the situation. The replacement of socialized youths by raw recruits continually jeopardized the balance. Particularly important agents for continuity and for allegiance to staff values in the community-based programs were the private clients with whom DYS youths were mixed in Primal and Confront. Privately referred and typically middle class, they embraced program philosophies more easily than the involuntary, typically lower-class, arrivals from DYS. Staff members at both programs claimed that the private referrals "didn't have as far to go" or "were smarter and could grasp the concept better" than the DYS youths.

Administrators of both programs also described the problems they had experienced when, in their view, too large a proportion of the population was composed of DYS youths; the programs lost their intensity, and resistance of residents to staff views was much more common. Such a problem was particularly the case when DYS youths came in together and could sustain one another's resistance. It is probable, therefore, that the development of the youth subcultures at Primal and Confront was facilitated by the receptivity of the private segment of their populations. Such a system of integrating the population and diluting potential resistance had its limits as well as advantages, however. In Confront many of the private clients were considerably older (in their mid-twenties) than the DYS youths and, more important, had come to the program because they were experiencing marital problems. DYS youths had a far more difficult time relating to them than the youths at Primal had in identifying with the private clients there, who typically were in their late teens and often faced the threat of criminal punishment for drug abuse or criminal activity.

Another population characteristic that may have been important in attaining and maintaining a staff-defined subculture was one that staff people would have been reluctant to control openly or consciously. The population of the five most participatory programs were predominately or exclusively white (ranging from four blacks at Topsfield to none at Group). While this predominance of whites was not characteristic only of the populations of these programs, it is possible that it was an important factor in making possible the relatively successful integration of youths into the participatory programs. Black youths may be more resistant to integration into a participatory program when they constitute a visible and sizable minority. The tendency for blacks to be somewhat more cohesive than whites (to be discussed in the next chapter) could increase their ability and motivation to resist involvement in a participatory pro-

gram, at least one promoting an ideology viewed by some as irrelevant at best and adverse at worst to their needs as individuals and as
Afro-Americans.

CONCLUSIONS AND SUMMARY:
IMPLICATIONS FOR THEORY
AND POLICY

The theoretical debate about the origins of inmate subcultures has
revolved around whether they develop in response to the conditions
of imprisonment or are carried by inmates into correctional environments from the outside. Sykes and Messinger and Goffman, despite
their identification as the foremost proponents of the former view,
made clear that the latter approach is not in fact inconsistent with
theirs. Whereas Sykes and Messinger left the question of importation an open one in concluding their seminal article, Goffman argued
more assertively that "total institutions do not substitute their own
unique culture for something already formed."[19] The data analyzed
in this chapter provide strong support for both views; under some
organizational conditions inmate subcultures reflect—either intensified
or not—some values and norms flourishing in certain segments of free
society, while under other conditions a new set of values prompted
by staff ideology come to be shared by youths.[20]

   Importation occurs when the norms and values appropriate to
adaptation in the outside world—particularly to the street life of
low-income neighborhoods—also prove to aid adaptation to correctional settings. Where equality is low, inmates face the problem of
responding both to authorities and to a group of potentially dangerous peers, a situation not unlike that confronted by many youths
in schools and on the street. Segregation of males and females in correctional programs highlights even further the problem of peer relationships and emphasizes the utility of subcultural elements that
guide male-male or female-female relationships and reinforce gender
identity. Finally, in nonegalitarian settings, staff members often
knowingly or unknowingly give support to imported norms and
values that serve to divide inmates and prevent them from organizing
resistance to the coercive regime.

   The introduction of equality into a program does not by itself
alter the problem of defining and responding to peer relationships; it
does change the relationship between staff members and inmates,
however, and provides both groups with opportunity and incentives

for more positive mutual attitudes. Without the additional introduction of participation and supervision, however, youths are left to
evolve and, typically, import their own standards for relationships
with one another. Where equality exists by itself in a closed setting,
intensification of imported values defining peer relationships occurs
much as it does in a nonegalitarian institution. If high levels of
equality and community contact are joined, however, imported
values are not intensified through a closed circle of interaction, but
neither are staff members able to counter them strongly. In contrast,
supervision when combined with equality suppresses the expression
of imported values and prevents their intensification, but it provides
no alternative set of standards to guide peer relationships.

The appearance of significant participation in an egalitarian program (particularly when it is combined with high supervision)
changes the rules of the game entirely by providing rewards for particular kinds of relationships among youths and by monitoring and
punishing behavior deemed appropriate with reference to street
values. People rarely persist in holding beliefs and behaving in ways
that are punished or that go unrewarded either by authorities or by
their peers. When organizations systematically attack imported values
and practices and offer and enforce attractive substitutes for them,
they may effectively accomplish at least limited resocialization.

These data thus suggest that Sykes and Messinger's emphasis on
the pains of imprisonment as *the* organizational source of inmate
subcultures should be modified, although the data make it clear that
inmate subcultures are responsive to organizational conditions. Not
all privations are equally important, however, and other aspects of
organizations, such as rewards and opportunities, are influential in
the formation of inmate subcultures. In the most restrictive organizational setting we observed (Primal), for example, the loss of
privacy was particularly evident, but it reinforced staff control over
youths' attitudes and values rather than undermined it.

The crucial privations in the programs we observed were those that
had to do with inmate relationships to staff members—measured in
this study by the inequality-equality dimension. Where equality is
low, youths will be driven together, or at least away from the staff,
and are likely to interpret harsh conditions as deprivations imposed
upon them. Where equality is high, however, staff members may
effectively use some organizationally imposed privations to shape
youth subcultures and to guide collective interpretations of living
conditions; privations do not necessarily come to be viewed as
deprivations. Nor do inmates react merely to what is withheld from
them. They also respond to rewards and opportunities provided

by staff members and peers both in egalitarian and nonegalitarian settings. The organizational structure, broadly conceived—but particularly as represented in the equality, community-contact, participation, and supervision dimensions—is crucial to understanding inmate subculture development.

In concluding that organizational structure has a significant impact on inmate subcultures, it has been necessary to assume that youths entering the most participatory programs initially shared values and norms similar to those of youths in other programs. Otherwise one could argue that subcultural differences were a product of differences in imported subcultures. Because of the cross-sectional character of the data, this explanation is particularly difficult to refute. We have no systematic longitudinal evidence with which to test rigorously this assumption that some subcultural differences were products of organizational rather than population differences; we do have, however, numerous shreds of data to suggest that assumption's validity.

As the data on previous program experience and criminal activity attest, the DYS youths who entered the most participatory programs appear comparable to their counterparts in the least participatory programs in the seriousness of their crimes and in the apparent previous lack of success DYS had had in working with them. In addition, although population characteristics were sometimes important in both the regression analyses and the qualitative analyses, they were never sufficient by themselves to explain all the variations in subcultural elements; thus the imperfections in the equivalency of program populations were not enough to explain differences in subcultures.

More relevant are our observations of DYS youths entering the most participatory programs. Universally, these youths were withdrawn and suspicious of staff members and other youths (we must infer this from their reluctance to talk to either), and only gradually did they become acclimated to the programs' expectations of them. At several programs, for example, some youths continued to reject these expectations with "It's bad to be a dime-dropper" or "I'm no fink," suggesting that such norms were not unknown to the residents. We also have the testimony of youths such as David of Group that "I've really changed since I've been here" and that he had renounced "the street code" he once shared. At Primal the necessity of such "conversions" was recognized in the program argot. New residents were expected, as several youths said in their interviews, "to act 'as if' at first; then it [Primal's philosophy and norms] becomes a part of you." It is thus apparent that, at least for the DYS youths involved, the initial selection of participants was not sufficient to explain subcultural differences between less and more participatory programs.

Just as striking are the implications of the evidence from nonresidential and open residential programs where institutionally imposed privations were slight, as was staff influence over youth subcultures. These subcultures differed only slightly from those in the more closed and least participatory institutional cottages. Expectations concerning passing information, belief in the principle of equal treatment, and manifestations of male, female, and youth subcultures were amazingly alike in these very different settings. Such general broadly shared values, norms, and orientations are brought by youths to correctional settings. These values are likely to receive collective youth support ultimately unless staff members interpose their own differing definitions of appropriate behavior through organizational strategies combining participation and supervision with equality in the context of strictly limited community contact.

The common content as well as the variations in subcultures in diverse organizations show that most of the subcultural elements originate in sources far broader than a "criminal subculture." A fairly open program such as Fatigue was composed primarily of working- and lower-class boys with no official record of delinquency, but with family conditions requiring at least temporary residential placement. Yet many of their conceptions of appropriate behavior—if not their knowledge of criminal techniques—differed little from those of boys with long criminal records living in fairly closed settings. Equivalence or similarity of inmate populations on these more general variables thus insured a basic likeness in the broad outlines of experience and values youths brought with them to varied correctional organizations.

Although our cross-sectional data give us some hints that value change or resocialization, not population selection alone, accounted for many of the subcultural differences between participatory and other programs, they do not resolve a second question about the permanency of the values changes that did occur. These changes were achieved through the force of heavy peer pressure, and whether or not they persisted when these pressures were withdrawn and others substituted for them is unclear. Many participatory programs resolved this problem by maintaining pressures on graduates either by taking them on as staff members or by locating them in a nearby community (rather than their home neighborhood) where they could keep close touch with the program and its values. How well such techniques worked and what happened in their absence is a key question for future research.[21]

Our data thus make clear that substantial staff control over the shape of youth subcultures can occur under certain organizational conditions. What conditions if any make possible similar levels of control over youth social structures and behavior? Unlike subcultures, social structures must evolve within the correctional setting because youths are unlikely to have established relationships with one another prior to entry; similarly, behavior is situational depending on personalities, norms, and opportunities, rewards, and punishments. The variability of these phenomena should thus be amenable to organizational influence, the subject of the next chapter.

NOTES

1. For a rare example of the massive importation of social networks into a prison, see James Jacobs, "Street Gangs Behind Bars," *Social Problems* 21 (Winter 1974): 395–409; he reports the presence of large numbers of gang members in an Illinois prison. Under such unusual conditions any attempt to influence subcultures is likely to fail. The presence of cohesive inmate groups or groups whose members are initially hostile to staff will reduce the ability of correctional staff to overcome initial inmate hostility and suspicion. *A low level of mutual attraction among inmates may be a precondition to staff success at overcoming initial hostility and suspicion on the part of inmates and at redirecting inmate attitudes and beliefs toward support of organizational goals.* For further discussion of this issue, see Chapter 4.

2. For example, following are excerpts from the Primal philosophy: "With eagerness of spirit, we shall find ourselves through knowing others. / We shall no longer be driven by our guilt and fears, but by our trust and convictions. / . . . . / . . . . / Seeing ourselves in the eyes of others, we shall demand change. / . . . . / No longer able to delay, we must now accept responsibility for ourselves and others. / . . . . / We must first attack the principles upon which all our former opinions were founded, and put them in their proper perspective."

3. "Haircuts" were given to people who had broken a rule or been negligent, inefficient, or incompetent in their duties. The offender would enter a room after knocking at the door and being invited in. Then he would face a loud and concentrated stream of verbal criticism and abuse from several of his superiors in the house administrative hierarchy.

4. The two nonresidential community programs could not easily be scored in this fashion. Drop-in and Pick-up differed substantially, however, in the extent of programming; whereas youths in the former program spent much of their time hanging around, talking, and shooting pool, those at the latter were picked up only when a specific activity such as a boat trip, fishing, or bicycle building had been planned. Drop-in was therefore assigned a score of 1 and Pick-up a 2.

5. The expediters were, in effect, an internal security force. Expediters roamed about checking where people were and where they should be.

6. Ramrods essentially were foremen or first-level supervisors.

7. The measurement of program size and staff-youth ratios posed some-

thing of a problem, particularly in the training school cottages. Whether the populations of the cottages alone or of the whole institutions should be counted and whether the ratio should be computed from totals of cottage staff or institutional staff was unclear, particularly in the case of cottages still integrated into the institutional regime. Because they are the basic units of analysis in this study, the cottage populations and staffs were used for calculation of these figures. Rather than use the raw population figures, which were somewhat unstable because of runs, transfers, and releases, however, each program was classified into one of six categories based on its highest population level (1 = 0–10, 2 = 11–20, 3 = 21–30, 4 = 31–40, 5 = 41–50, 6 = 51+) in order to provide a measure of size; the category numbers were then used as scores in the data analysis.

8. Many traditional penal institutions have adopted a strategy superficially similar to this one, of course, both to keep inmates busy and to reduce operating costs; many critics point out that trades programs in training schools and vocational training in prisons often serve to maintain the institutions rather than prepare inmates for jobs. But forcing labor from an inferior caste of inmates (that is, in the context of low equality) is quite different from engaging youths as near equals in a collective process of decision-making and program operation.

9. In the 1973 staff interview I used the phrase "kids in trouble" rather than "juvenile delinquents" because of the general resistance to the use of the latter term in the community-based programs.

10. There were not enough staff members (only two) at Putnam cottage responding to this item to include them here, though presumably their responses would have been similar to those of staff at the other institutional cottages.

11. This expression meant literally to place in a box a slip of paper identifying a resident or residents whom the "slip-dropper" wished to confront in a group about some short-coming or unacceptable behavior. Coordinators then arranged groups where these confrontations could occur.

12. Youth evaluations of the actions of imaginary inmates described in three brief stories were included in the scale. Briefly, those stories involved the actions of Dooley, who refused to tell the staff the name of another program member who cut him with a knife; of Long, who hid some marijuana from the staff at the request of his friend Smith; and a counselor who officially reported a theft that his counselee inadvertently admitted in a counseling session. Youths were asked after each of these three stories whether they thought "all," "most," "50-50" (volunteered), "few," or "none" of the youths in the program would agree with the actions of Dooley, Long, and the counselor. (In Feld's questionnaire the alternatives were "almost all," "over half," "50-50" (volunteered), "less than half," and "very few," which were scored in an equivalent fashion). Responses to the Dooley and Long stories were scored 1, 2, 3, 4, and 5, respectively, and responses to the counselor story were scored 5, 4, 3, 2, and 1, respectively. The average correlation between variables in this scale is .36. These scores were then summed. The cutting point between high and low scale scores was the midpoint of the possible scale values.

13. The privacy scale was constructed from the following items in the 1973 youth questionnaires: "It's better if you don't let other people know what your feelings are"; "In life people should try to go it alone and not have to depend on

others"; "Other kids have no business knowing what my personal problems are"; "The best way to get along here is to pretend that you're trying to change yourself"; and a story question in which an imaginary Henderson withdraws from group activities and tells the staff he/she would rather be alone. The "strongly agree," "agree," "50–50" (volunteered), "disagree," and "strongly disagree" responses to the first four items and the "strongly approve," "approve," "50–50" (volunteered), "disapprove," and "strongly disapprove" responses to Henderson's behavior in the story question were scored, respectively, 5, 4, 3, 2, 1. The average correlation between variables in this scale is .27. These scores were summed. The cutting point between high and low scale scores was the midpoint of possible scale values.

14. The relationship between offense and self-conception also exists at the individual level of analysis; only 64 percent of youths charged with a criminal offense compared to 78 percent of those accused of a status offense viewed themselves as "having personal problems" or "trying to go straight."

15. The relationship between race and the belief that one "needs a chance" holds at the individual level; 75 percent of the black respondents compared to 52 percent of white respondents "agreed" or "strongly agreed" with this item.

16. Youths were asked to "strongly agree," "agree," "50–50" (volunteered), "disagree," or "strongly disagree" with these statements: "If you try to change things very much, you usually make them worse" and "I'd want to know that something would really work before I'd be willing to take a chance on it." The correlation between responses to these items is .28; these responses (scored 1, 2, 3, 4, and 5, respectively) were summed to create the scale score. The cutting point between high and low scale scores was the midpoint of possible scale values.

17. The relationship between sex and sense of personal efficacy holds at the individual level; 21 percent of the boys compared to 37 percent of the girls had high efficacy scores.

18. Rose Giallombardo, *The Social World of Imprisoned Girls: A Comparative Study of Institutions for Juvenile Delinquents* (New York: Wiley, 1974); Rose Giallombardo, *Society of Women: A Study of a Women's Prison* (New York: Wiley, 1966); and Barbara Carter, "Reform School Families," *Society* 11 (November/December 1973): 36–43.

19. Erving Goffman, "On the Characteristics of Total Institutions," in *Asylums: Essays on the Social Situation of Mental Patients and Other Inmates* (Garden City, N.Y.: Doubleday, Anchor, 1961), p. 22.

20. It may be more accurate to say that these values are latent in the inmate population rather than wholly new to it. The role of the organization thus may be to reinforce these values rather than other more dominant imported values.

21. Some attention is given to this question in the longitudinal study of DYS youths reported in Robert Coates, Alden Miller, and Lloyd Ohlin, *Diversity in a Youth Correctional System: Handling Delinquents in Massachusetts*, in this series.

Chapter 4

Bogarting and Relating: Patterns of
Youth Social Structure and Behavior

The toughest part of being here is getting along with the other kids without getting your head kicked in.

You don't get in fights or anything [here]. It's a good place. Kids don't pick on you.

For the first time I have a group of friends who I can relate to.

"How many kids are up here?" asked the skinny fourteen year old as he slouched down in a chair and faced his admissions interview with a detention center counselor. This boy's question dramatizes the high priority commonly assigned by youths in correctional programs to their relationships with peers. Whether these relationships are threatening and difficult or gratifying and supportive makes an enormous difference in the life of a participant in a correctional program. Variations in organizational structure promote impressive differences in the importance youths place on interaction with their peers within the program, in the general tenor of these relationships, and in patterns of youth behavior. This chapter will explore the nature of and reasons for these differences.

Argot roles such as "gorillas" or "politicians" among men and "butches" or "femmes" among women have traditionally attracted the most attention in discussions of inmate social structure, and they may be of particular importance to inmates. They should not, however, be conceived as an exhaustive catalog of inmate social positions. The social structure of inmate systems includes at least five kinds of social relationships that must be conceptually and empirically distinguished. First, there are subgroups of inmates based on race,

age, criminal career, locale of residence, or other salient characteristics.[1] Second, there are the informal primary groupings of
friends or comrades. Third, there may be networks of instrumental
or secondary relationships revolving around production or supply
of illicit goods and services. Fourth, there are inmate leadership
hierarchies (which may involve distinct dimensions of coercive
and persuasive power). Fifth, there are official positions allocated by
correctional administrators—for example, metal shop supervisor or
honor unit member. The links between these sets of relationships as
well as the extent of development and nature of each are highly
variable.

Staff direction of the structure of youth relationships and patterns
of behavior requires fewer far-reaching organizational pressures than
does staff control over the nature of youth subcultures. It is a basic
tenet of the research on individual and social change that people's
values and groups' cultures are less amenable to change or influence
than is individual behavior. Although it may take fewer organizational resources to shape them, youth social structures and behavior
patterns are also far more diverse, fluid, and situational than are subcultures. Program subcultures show considerable continuity either
with official values and expectations or with values and norms held
by major segments of the free population, but social differentiation,
although based in part on subcultural elements, must typically be
created without benefit of previously established social ties among
youths. Social differentiation emerges *de novo* in each correctional
setting. Similarly, the behavior of youths in a correctional program,
although patterned, depends on situational contingencies that include youth and staff prescriptions for and proscriptions of particular activities, the effectiveness of enforcement mechanisms, and
personal needs, as well as on the values and norms of inmate subcultures.

As a consequence, the nature of social structures and of patterns
of youthful behavior depend heavily on the organizational factors
that create and limit opportunities and rewards for interaction
and activity and on the composition of the youth population. They
also depend heavily, however, on circumstances usually beyond
the control of correctional administrators (and beyond the measurement of this study). Shifts in youth population, for example, or
community events ranging from ghetto riots to nearby rock concerts,
apparently minor occurrences within the program, and even climatic
conditions can indirectly or directly, temporarily or fundamentally,
alter patterns of relationships and behavior. Individual personalities
in particular may be important in small programs; a hell-raiser, a

skilled manipulator, a bully, a dedicated drug-user may provide the impetus for restructuring relationships, attitudes, and behavior. In a closed program, especially, changes feed on themselves and one another with the result that small events can have major and unanticipated consequences. Many correctional administrators, therefore, live and work on an hour-by-hour basis trying to keep the lid on.

Three factors should act in vastly differing ways to defuse this kind of tension and reduce the high degree of uncertainty about future events in correctional settings. First, high levels of participation (in the context of high equality) can effectively shape the subculture of youths, and thus can insulate against the onslaught of circumstance by monitoring and directing the way in which youths will interpret and act upon events. Second, substantial amounts of supervision (also in the context of high equality) effectively direct, or at least suppress, youth relationships and activities that are unplanned or unintended by staff members. Third, high levels of community contact reduce the intensity of internal program dynamics by directing attention and relationships outward, thus defusing the possibly explosive effects of population changes and other events.

We now turn to a more detailed examination of the direct and indirect effects of these organizational traits and the composition of youth populations on the nature of youth relationships and behavior.

YOUTH COHESION AND SOLIDARITY

Social differentiation occurs in the context of and contributes to the general level of solidarity or cohesion among youths. In the development of the functional and importation theories of inmate systems particularly, attention was directed toward examining and explaining the "solidary opposition" of inmates to prison staff. To focus on the extent of solidary opposition of inmates is, in fact, to raise questions about the degree of social integration at two different levels within correctional organizations. On one level (solidarity), there is interest in the degree of social integration within the inmate group, and on the other level (opposition) there is interest in the extent to which inmates are integrated into the official organization of the correctional facility and share its ideology. Confusion about the meaning of solidarity or social integration may cloud our understanding of the issues and data.

Solidarity, cohesion, and social integration are terms that are used almost interchangeably in sociological writing to indicate a concern with the question of how groups are bound together.[2] A number of factors have been identified as the means of achieving social solidarity at the societal level: the sharing of norms and values; widespread behavioral conformity to these norms; functional interdependence; and great population heterogeneity.[3] In smaller groups, mutual liking, the gratifications of interaction, and the provision of identity are viewed as sources of cohesion.

Coercion by a powerful elite is also a method of binding a large or small group together, but it is a technique not usually included in discussions of social integration.[4] Nevertheless, a study of prisons or other correctional alternatives would not make sense without taking into account both the power and limits of coercion by authorities as a mechanism for holding inmate populations together. Inmates typically do not choose one another as companions; the state makes this choice for them and forces that companionship on them. Coercion clearly acts as the boundary-maintaining force, at least initially, for most inmate groups.[5] Within the external boundaries so created, however, the question remains: To what degree are inmates bound together internally, and if so by what mechanisms?

The previous two chapters examined the cultural components of solidarity, and thus of "opposition"—the sharing of norms and values by youths. Cohesion and solidarity will be studied in this chapter in terms of the patterns of mutual attraction and social differentiation. Just as youths are likely to be initially suspicious of staff members when they enter a new correctional setting, they are also going to be extremely wary of one another. Delinquents may have little faith in the law or in those who uphold it, but they are probably more likely to expect staff to behave toward them according to a set of rules than they would their peers. Thrust into a place with at least a few youths who have been set apart for their aggressiveness, uncontrollable behavior, or maladjustment, inmates must be on guard to pick their companions carefully and critically.

Such care in choosing companions is not necessarily inconsistent with the assertion of Eugene Debs and others who have experienced prison life that "the inmates of prisons are not the irretrievable, vicious, depraved element they are commonly believed to be, but upon the average they are like ourselves. . . ."[6] To the degree that this is true of the average inmate, it is not true or likely to be thought true of *all* inmates. The small percentage of dangerous persons that almost all correctional administrators admit exists in their institutions must be identified by inmates for self-protection, and the fear of *them* is likely to expand to suspicion toward all. The emergence of social relationships among youths thus necessarily involves a stage of testing that must be repeated for each new entrant. To the degree that youths find peer behavior predictable and nonthreatening, they will develop more positive assessments of their fellow inmates. The characteristics of the correctional organization that influence this behavior and relationships among youths should thus be crucial in differentiating programs.

The initial mutual suspicion among youths is crucial to the existence of organizational control. On the one hand, in the battle to convince initially hostile or uncertain youths to trust the staff, mutual distrust among youths is almost a prerequisite. The presence in a correctional organization of cohesive groups of youths whose members are hostile to staff members reduces the opportunity for staff to overcome their resistance; a cohesive group of youths is better able to prevent tentative alignments between their members and staff people. On the other hand, more coercive organizations also rely on initial and continued hostility among youths to prevent them from becoming an organized force capable of wresting power from the staff. But only in rare circumstances such as those reported by Jacobs are there previously established bonds among youths that create initial high levels of youth cohesion.[7]

Evidence concerning the initial orientation of youths toward one another was scanty in our subculture studies, although the data included consistent observations that newcomers quietly watched their peers in the same way that they "checked out" the staff members. In another study, Bartollas and his colleagues reported that "in over two years of interviewing boys on their first day [at an Ohio training school], every youth was found to be fearful—not surprising considering the rumors."[8] We did not see outright fear so much as uncertainty and mutual suspicion.

An index of the general level of cohesion (the degree to which associating with other youths is attractive) within a program was constructed from several correlated responses to items in the youth interview.[9] The final regression of this cohesion scale on the set of independent variables uses two of these variables—program equality and the percentage of black program members (see Table 4-1)— and explains 61 percent of the variance in cohesion levels among programs.

High levels of program equality contribute to greater cohesion among youths for a variety of reasons. Equality within a program promotes a positive view of relationships generally; in Chapter 2 we saw that youths' views of staff were also far more positive in programs with higher levels of equality. The egalitarian model provides a far more positive design for relationships among peers than does the hierarchical model so prominent in the least egalitarian programs. In addition, by making strides toward integrating youths and staff into the same social network, high program equality enables

Table 4-1. Multiple Regression on Independent Variables of Percentage of
Youths with High Peer Cohesion Scores (*N* = 23 programs)

Independent Variables	Zero-Order Correlation with Dependent Variable	Standardized Regression Coefficient	F Ratio
Percentage of youths 16 years or older	.06		
Percentage of male youths	-.15		
Percentage of black youths	-.43	-0.37	6.96
Percentage of youths from DYS	-.16		
Percentage of DYS youths committing first offense before age 14	-.14		
Percentage of DYS youths with previous commitment	-.38		
Percentage of DYS youths committed for crimes against persons	-.01		
Percentage of DYS youths committed for juvenile status offenses	.00		
Program size	-.06		
Youth-to-staff ratio	-.04		
Equality scale	.68	.64	20.52
Community-contact scale	-.08		
Participation scale	.58		
Supervision scale	.45		

[a]For the regression equation the multiple correlation = .77 (R^2 = .60), and the
F ratio = 14.95 (with 2 and 20 degrees of freedom).

staff members to keep a closer watch on youth relationships than if
youths were separated into a social world of their own. Participation
furthers this integration, and with it the control that staff can exert
over exploitative relationships. Although participation is not included in the regression (its zero-order correlation to cohesion level
is .58), the six most participatory programs are among the ten programs in which half or more of the youths had high cohesion scores.

The inclusion of the proportion of blacks in the equation requires
further exploration. It is unclear from the aggregate measures
whether blacks are less likely than whites to perceive cohesiveness
among their peers or whether the presence of large proportions of
blacks in a population is itself a divisive factor.

That 44 percent of blacks compared to 46 percent of whites had
high cohesion scores suggests the association is not a result of perceptions of low cohesiveness on the part of minority individuals;
blacks were as likely as whites to have high cohesion scores. Instead
Table 4-2 indicates that both blacks and whites perceived less general

Table 4-2.   Youths with High and Low Cohesion Scores, by Race and Racial Composition of Program (percentages)

Cohesion Level	Programs with above 30% Minority Population (5 programs)		Programs with 1 to 29% Minority Population (14 programs)		Programs with All-White Population (4 programs)	
	Blacks	Whites	Blacks	Whites	Blacks	Whites
High	36%	35%	51%	44%	—	74%
Low	64	65	49	56	—	26
	100%	100%	100%	100%		100%
	(N = 33)	(N = 57)	(N = 37)	(N = 216)		(N = 39)

cohesiveness as the proportion of minority youths in the population increased. Racial divisions—but little racial conflict—existed in programs with minority-group members, and became more evident as their proportion increased; two social structures rather than one tended to develop, thus cutting considerably program-wide cohesion.

The four programs that had high levels of cohesion but relatively low participation are worthy of individual analysis because they suggest a number of important principles about organizational influences on youth relationships. Drop-in, where 85 percent of the youths had high cohesion scores, was the only program we studied whose members (at least most of them) were already acquainted with each other. Drop-in was, in fact, a true community program, located in an area where the residents had a strong sense of identity and pride. Relationships within the community and a general sense of loyalty to other community members were carried over into the program. This unique case illustrates the importance of examining the initial characteristics of youth populations; in some rare situations the assumption that youths (inmates) are initially suspicious of another is not justified.

Regiment and Reward, two of the most tightly structured programs we observed and the only closely supervised ones that were not also highly participatory, were also relatively high in cohesion. That 50 percent of the boys at Regiment had high cohesion scores was particularly striking given the high turnover in the population there (the average stay was about two weeks). The high levels of cohesion in both programs may have developed in part because of the high levels of staff supervision. In most of the programs that were not well supervised the potential and reality of fights and intimidation (particularly by larger boys of smaller ones and by groups of girls of loners) reinforced the presumably high levels of initial mutual mistrust. Regiment's heavy structuring of activities and high supervision over youth interaction, by contrast, enabled the boys to overcome, at least in part, their initial mistrust of one another. Boys at Regiment commented that it was a safe place to be, unlike several other detention facilities. In addition to engaging in the full schedule of daily activities, youths were required to live in single rooms and severely restricted in the number of boys allowed in one room at one time. It was rare at Regiment for boys to congregate out of the range of staff supervision. Similarly, cohesion was encouraged among girls at Reward by the strict watch kept over the residents and their relationships with one another; conflicts were soon discovered and attempts made to resolve them:

> Mrs. Gallant started tickling Cynthia to make her stop using swear words when they were watching the foot races together; she also stopped Nan from bothering Louise, saying "You can't tease Louise, she's in a bad mood."

The relatively high levels of cohesion among the girls at Reward and also at Shelter reflect another intriguing pattern. In contrast to the argument by Giallombardo that the traditional female subculture fosters jealousy and conflict among girls and women, our data showed boys' programs to be generally less cohesive than those for girls.[10] In comparing all but the six most participatory programs (which included two boys' and four coeducation programs), an average of 29 percent of the youths in the all-boys programs had high cohesion scores, in contrast to 49 percent in all-girls programs. This finding is consistent with the interpretation of the contrast between the male and female subcultures; the latter places far greater emphasis on popularity with one's peers while the former emphasizes aggressiveness and toughness, certainly divisive forces in affecting peer relationships.[11]

The effect of community contact on level of cohesion in a program cannot be precisely gauged from our data because nowhere did we gather direct measures of the salience of in-program relationships to youths. There is indirect evidence, however, that the intensity and importance of relationships among program peers was reduced by community contact. In the thirteen community-based programs youths were asked a number of questions that have been combined to create a scale measuring youths' evaluations of the programs they were in.[12] In general, when cohesion was high, youths judged their programs positively, but when it was low they typically did not. Youths did not like to be in programs where their relationships with peers were not appealing. In programs where community contact was especially high, however, youths evaluated programs positively regardless of the level of cohesion. The unattractiveness of peer relations was less relevant to assessments by youths than the allure of the programs themselves. The freedom or the activities outweighed the absence of a generally congenial group of fellow participants; the freedom in particular allowed youths to choose or maintain companions outside the program and thus made the uncongeniality of their peers far less important.

A key characteristic of most of the programs that fostered more cohesion among youths was the staff's willingness to remove particularly troublesome members. Just as short-term value changes could occur only where a no-violence rule was strictly enforced, cohesion among youths developed where bullies and troublemakers were either removed in closed programs by transfer elsewhere or made nearly irrelevant by the reduced social density in open programs. In small programs especially, one or two particularly uncontrollable youths could force their peers to withdraw into themselves for fear of offending or provoking an attack. In programs with low cohesion scores, such as Cottages 9 and 8, Warning, Fatigue, and Mother, observers noted that considerable intimidation by a few boys or girls appeared to have a considerable effect on social intercourse. Frequently these offenders remained in the programs. One or two of a group of girls who beat up an informer at Mother were only temporarily removed from the program; a powerful boy who struck fear in the hearts of both the boys and the staff at Fatigue remained there for several months after having severely beaten a fellow resident.

By contrast, closed programs with high cohesion scores, such as Primal, Confront, and Group, would promptly rid themselves, much to the relief of their residents, of youths who showed their inability to adapt to the program. When Lee was transferred from Group the day after he had sniffed paint-remover and attempted to fight with two staff members, one boy noted that Lee's departure would "make it more comfortable for me," while another youth commented that Lee scared him and had made adjustment to the house difficult. Staff supervision over youth relationships and staff decisiveness in responding to problem-causing youths, as well as equality and racial homogeneity in the inmate population, thus contribute substantially to the development of program cohesiveness.

FRIENDSHIP PATTERNS

The same forces that divide group members and make them generally mistrustful and hostile will also serve to reduce the likelihood that members of a program will find close friends within it. Similarly, the forces that build widespread mutual trust and respect among individuals in a group also act to increase the chance that members will form close friendships within that group. In the latter instances, staff members supervise and control interaction among youths in a manner that enables them ultimately to overcome their initial suspicion of one another and to come to know most of their peers. In the former cases, the absence of staff control encourages mutual exploitation among youths and leads to a reinforcement of initial distrust and hostility.

Group cohesion and close friendships are not identical, however. One can have close friends within a group and mistrust most other group members; one can also be generally attracted to other members of a group without having any close friends among them. In the interviews, youths were asked to indicate how many close friendships they had developed since they had been in the program ("more than 5," "3-5," "1 or 2," "none"). Aggregated responses to this question roughly indicate the ease with which friendships were made within a program.

The proportion of youths who indicated they had two or more close friends in the program was regressed on the full set of program and population characteristics, but only one variable emerged as significant (see Table 4-3)—the program score on the participation scale (r = .45) was the only substantial predictor of the frequency of friendship formation, recalling the importance of participation in facilitating cohesion. By encouraging and supervising interaction among youths and protecting them from violence, the participatory programs provided a more fertile ground for friendships.

Unmeasured variability in program and population characteristics must account for much of the large proportion of variation left unexplained by the level of participation. Primal and Confront, for example, though highly participatory, discouraged close, exclusive friendships; instead youths were expected to divide their time evenly among all co-residents. Cottage 9, Regiment, and Shelter all were relatively short-term placements with high population turnover, minimizing the chances for friendships to form. Similarly important was the unmeasured variations in the mix of program participants, the particular blend of personalities so important to friendship formation and so variable in small programs where there are severe limits on the availability of possible friends.

Two interesting but hardly conclusive observations suggest that, at least within highly participatory programs, high levels even of controlled community contact on the part of some members tend to separate them from the group and thus make them liable for

Table 4-3. Multiple Regression on Independent Variables of Percentage of Youths Indicating They Have Two or More Close Friends in the Program (*N* = 23 programs)[a]

Independent Variables	Zero-Order Correlation with Dependent Variable	Standardized Regression Coefficient	F Ratio
Percentage of youths 16 years or older	.22		
Percentage of male youths	.26		
Percentage of black youths	−.24		
Percentage of youths from DYS	.05		
Percentage of DYS youths committing first offense before age 14	.05		
Percentage of DYS youths with previous commitment	.01		
Percentage of DYS youths committed for crimes against persons	.21		
Percentage of DYS youths committed for juvenile status offenses	−.37		
Program size	−.10		
Youth-to-staff ratio	.12		
Equality scale	.35		
Community-contact scale	.18		
Participation scale	.45	0.45	5.26
Supervision scale	.25		

[a]For the regression equation the multiple correlation = .45 (R^2 = .20), and the F ratio = 5.26 (with 1 and 21 degrees of freedom).

exclusion from friendships cliques. At Group, for example, the one boy who had a full-time job and a local girlfriend was the only resident not chosen by any peers as a friend in a series of sociometric questions in the interview. In addition, he did not enter into the few group meetings he attended except for occasional sarcastic comments. Similarly, at Confront the one boy who was on "second stage" and worked full time expressed resentment "at all the shit he had been getting [from other residents] since he started work."

SISTERS AND SOUL BROTHERS: PATTERNS OF ASSOCIATION AMONG YOUTHS

An important characteristic of the social structures in all but the most participatory programs, according to our theory, is differentiation among program members on the basis of what Walter Miller has called status class characteristics such as sex, age, social class, occupation, and race.[13] Associating with people of the same social class, race, and age generally tends to be more rewarding then associating with dissimilar people, because those of like status class tend to share experiences, interests, symbols, and perspectives that facilitate interaction. In addition, association along status-class lines can serve both as a protective device for individuals who do not know what to expect from their peers and as a means of affirming identities that may be jeopardized by isolation from social supports in the community.

In the most highly participatory programs, by contrast, such differentiation should pale to insignificance alongside organizationally mandated social structure: the experiences within the program are of greatest significance in participatory programs, and other diverse traits should be accorded less importance by youths. Unfortunately, the populations of the twenty-three programs we studied did not have equivalent distributions of the various status-class characteristics. Nevertheless, some revealing comparisons are possible.

In the programs we studied that had a relatively large proportion or number of blacks, intraracial interaction was far more frequent than interracial contact. These patterns stand out in observed patterns of association and in the sociograms constructed from the responses to a question asking youths to identify the three people with whom they most often "hung around."[14] Distinct clusters of blacks and whites were evident in each of these programs.[15]

These patterns of association had different meanings for blacks and whites. For black youths, especially boys, intraracial interaction carried with it a sense of solidarity (fragile though it was) and racial identity that was lacking for whites. The three blacks at Pair identified one another as friends in the sociogram, thus forming a close-knit group. In larger programs the bonds were less tangible but nevertheless significant. Blacks shared subcultural symbols—slapping of hands, raising of a clenched fist, calling one another brother—which bound them together in their own eyes and in the eyes of whites.[16] At Elms, for example,

> Jackson was singing "Say it Loud. I'm Black and I'm Proud," and Olivetti [a white leader] turned around and looked at him, but Jackson kept on singing. Olivetti said, "Say it quick. I'm white and I'm slick." Jackson made fun of "being white and slick"; he said that he'd rather be black and proud because it sounds better.

Even in jest the trappings of black power unified blacks and excluded whites:

Jessie went into a hilarious soul preacher routine for the benefit of the poolroom crowd, exhorting them to break their chains, to rise up and kill every last white racist. With a raised clenched fist, and a "follow me, Brothers," he marched toward the TV room, turning at the last moment to discover that his brothers were still around the pool table, laughing.

No equivalent symbols unified white youths.

In the other programs where blacks were present in small proportions or numbers, they tended to be integrated with whites into a single structure of relationships. Nevertheless, we observed at programs such as Confront, Open House, and Mother that black entrants to these programs quickly gravitated toward the minority residents already there. The one exception to this rule was at Primal where the three blacks (one new arrival during our observation) were very much separated in the official hierarchy and in informal relationships.

One of the clear consequences of the relatively higher level of black solidarity was the emergence of a limited degree of dominance by blacks (even where they were in the minority, as they almost always were) in programs with even modest numbers of black participants. Whereas 65 percent of black program members received two or more choices as "leader" in a sociometric item in the youth interview, only 26 percent of whites were similarly chosen. Both blacks and whites often answered the question (in programs for boys only) by volunteering leaders for "the blacks" and "the whites," and the black leaders were typically the most dominant of these two sets.

Racial divisions were not nearly as distinctive among girls. Although black girls were more likely to choose other blacks as friends than whites, they were generally integrated into the program social structure and often at the center of it. At Putnam, for example, the girl who was for a time the single black resident was an acknowledged leader. One resident attributed the relatively limited degree of division along racial lines among girls to the "fact" that white girls "go with blacks on the outs"—it was not uncommon to find that white girls had posters of black rock musicians and political figures on their walls, and some white girls had black boy friends in the community.

The most vivid instance of differential association based on status-class characteristics other than race occurred at one of the two most participatory group-treatment programs, Confront. There the division between the privately supported, middle-class adults (mostly women facing marital problems) and the DYS-supported, lower-class teenagers was clearly evident in our sociograms. Although the two sets of people were brought together in groups and in work on assigned jobs around the house, they tended not to associate with one another informally. Adults, who were paying their own bills, generally believed that the DYS youths were "slowing them down" because they were not really committed to the program and to the house concept, while DYS youths thought the adults were "know-it-alls."

Somewhat similar class and age differences were present at Primal, but no parallel variations were evident in patterns of association; DYS youths were distributed throughout the official house hierarchy, despite the fact that DYS youths as a class were denounced as untrustworthy by the program director on several occasions after a run had occurred. Problems had arisen at Primal, however, when the proportion of DYS residents in the total population was—in the view of the director—too high. These youths had, the director reported, stuck together and successfully resisted inculcation into the program subculture. Primal's relative success in preventing the emergence of status-class-based networks of association thus may have been a consequence of the controlled composition of its population as well as of the integrative effects of its official social structure.

Sex differences, unlike age and race differences, did not act as a barrier to association among youths. In all six of the coeducational programs, youths were about as likely to indicate that they associated with peers of the same sex as with those of the other sex, although all-boy and all-girl cliques were occasionally apparent. Nevertheless, in Topsfield and Primal, girls had separate community meetings on occasion to decide how to handle some outrageous conduct by a male resident. The showing of a solidarity among girls was not duplicated by boys. As was the case for blacks, social movements in the larger society may well have awakened a sense of status-class identity among girls; white males, however, were the major targets of both movements and had no cause around which to organize.

YOUTH LEADERSHIP

From the point of view of staff people and youths alike, the character of youth leadership in a program closely reflected the effective degree of official control and the extent of comfort in day-to-day living. The structure of the correctional program along with the content of the youth subculture ultimately dictated the nature of this leadership. Two direct measures of leadership structure came from the youth interviews: a sociometric question asking youths to name three persons who "have the most influence with other kids," and a series of seven statements about leaders to which youths reacted with "strongly agree," "agree," "50–50" (volunteered), "disagree," or "strongly disagree." These latter responses were scored and summed to create a scale measuring youth perception of staff-supportive leadership.

The percentage of youths in each program having high scale scores was regressed on the set of fourteen variables indicating program and population characteristics. After nonsignificant variables were eliminated from the equation, two remained: the level of program equality and the level of youth participation together explained 69 percent of the variance in staff-supportive leadership (see Table 4–4).

By breaking down barriers between youths and staff, program equality allows interpenetration of social bonds between these two groups and makes staff influence over the direction of youth relationships more feasible. Equality also makes it more likely that

Table 4–4. Multiple Regression on Independent Variables of Percentage of Youths with High Scores on Perceived Staff-Supportive Youth Leaders Scale (N = 23 programs)[a]

Independent Variables	Zero-Order Correlation with Dependent Variable	Standardized Regression Coefficient	F Ratio
Percentage of youths 16 years or older	−.01		
Percentage of male youths	−.09		
Percentage of black youths	−.17		
Percentage of youths from DYS	−.16		
Percentage of DYS youths committing first offense before age 14	−.24		
Percentage of DYS youths with previous commitment	−.37		
Percentage of DYS youths committed for crimes against persons	.06		
Percentage of DYS youths committed for juvenile status offenses	.08		
Program size	−.09		
Youth-to-staff ratio	.05		
Equality scale	.78	0.63	19.50
Community-contact scale	−.18		
Participation scale	.63	.32	5.14
Supervision scale	.47		

[a]For the regression equation the multiple correlation = .83 (R^2 = .69), and the F ratio = 22.47 (with 2 and 20 degrees of freedom).

166 Designing Correctional Organizations for Youths

leaders, like their peers, will have favorable perceptions of staff, perceptions that will be reflected in the nature of their leadership. Participation further integrates youths into an official network of relationships, helping to ensure that persons officially promoted as leaders are so perceived by their peers.

An examination of youths' sociometric choices of the most influential peers and observations of them in action reveal even more about the joint influence of organizational structure and youth subcultures on the character of youth leadership. The interpretation of the preceding regression suggests that the youths chosen by their peers as leaders in participatory programs will also have been assigned to official leadership positions by staff members; in the programs with lower equality and participation, however, peer leaders will be persons who embody or who advance the cause of the separate subcultural standards shared by youths. Strong empirical support for this view comes from a comparison of the field note descriptions of the individuals identified as leaders in the twenty-three programs.

Of the programs at the participatory end of the scale, Primal was the only one to have created for youths an elaborate official hierarchy of positions. "Climbing the Primal ladder" was the major sign of progress in the program, while being "shot down" (demoted) was a consequence of mistakes or uncooperativeness. It is not surprising then that the five youths most often named as leaders by their peers at Primal were all on the top rungs of the ladder in positions as coordinators, coordinator trainees, and department heads. This perfect correspondence between official and unofficial leadership was not duplicated in any of the other programs we studied, largely because official hierarchies were either nonexistent or poorly defined elsewhere.

The importance of such official structuring of leadership is made more vivid in the contrast between leadership at Primal and at Confront; Confront was the program most closely resembling Primal in philosophy and organization. Youths at Confront were assigned to positions in a three-level hierarchy on a rotating basis rather than as a reflection of progress in the program.[18]

Although ramrods and department heads at Confront had considerable authority in assigning and supervising work around the house, they did not rise to their posts through achievement. Youths, then, looked elsewhere for leaders and selected peers who were "cool," outgoing, and fun to be with; all six leaders were also among those youths most frequently chosen as friends in other sociometric items. Of these six, three were less than fully committed to the program, and, at times, the fun they initiated meant trouble.[19] One of the leaders, for example, led the theft and subsequent use of drugs from a locked cabinet. Absence of a clear, staff-defined leadership hierarchy among youths thus opened the way for popular or forceful individuals to assume leadership roles regardless of the degree of their conformity to the program philosophy and rules.

In a number of other programs, staff people found ways to endorse or recognize officially the informal emergence of some youths as leaders. At Open House and Drop-in, for example, a program participant had been chosen to serve in a semiofficial capacity as a junior counselor. Both of these youths were also named as leaders by peers; however, it appeared that instead of inspiring these choices, the staff appointments reflected them.[20] In both these programs, however, youths other than those designated by staff were pointed to by members as leaders, as well. In several of the institutional training school cottages, youths who—through their personal qualities or physical strength—were viewed as leaders by their peers, sometimes received special privileges from staff. At Elms, for instance, two of the strongest whites were houseboys, a role that allowed them access to the food supply, which they used to further reinforce their leadership positions. As in many correctional institutions, then, staff members tried (and succeeded) in using these co-opted leaders to maintain a semblance of order among their prisoners.

Staff members generally had minimal success in imposing leadership based on criteria different from those used informally by youths themselves. In programs other than Primal, where official standards were the guiding factor, the people identified as leaders appear to have assumed that role because of the particular match between their personal qualities and the traits emphasized by the informal subcultures in their programs. In the coeducational programs, as we have noted, sex-based subcultures tended to be blunted, so those youths who were leaders in Topsfield, Open House, Pair, and Confront were characterized by generally valued attributes: some degree of emotional stability, personability, and "cool" behavior. The one obvious exception to this rule was the belligerent, aggressive boy at Open House who was identified as a leader by his peers because of his pushiness.

The qualities of leadership in most single-sex programs were—like the subcultures in them—more distinctive than those in coeducational programs. In Cottages 9 and 8, Sunset, Westview, and Elms, and in Warning, Fatigue, and—to a lesser extent—in Pick-up and Regiment, the boys identified as leaders were with few exceptions among the biggest and strongest (often the oldest) and the most willing and able to use that strength to coerce their fellow residents.[21] Generally they exerted themselves in order to make their own lives and those of their closest followers more comfortable. Two common examples of the ways in which this power was used by the leaders come from Warning and Cottage 9:

> During the Three Stooges in the TV room where there was a large crowd, Smitty noticed something wrong with the sound—he was seated on a couch in the rear. He mumbled, "Hey, somebody fix the fuckin' thing, man." Peterson, seated very close to the set, got up and adjusted it. Earlier, all the comfortable TV room chairs were occupied. Spencer came in and motioned with his head for Metzger to vacate such a chair; Metzger moved to one of the metal chairs.
>
> Downie and Cross are doing a crossword puzzle. Topman sits down and says "Give it to me." Cross replies "We were doing it"; Topman asks, "You want me to smack your fuckin' head?" Cross insists "We were doing it." Topman says "I'll give you three to give it to me, or I'll smash your fuckin' head." Cross gives him the puzzle.

Staff members at Group, the only highly participatory program for boys, did manage to prevent the emergence of muscle-based leadership, but did so by diluting the strength of male subcultural values while maintaining an absolute ban on violence; neither of the two toughest and most aggressive boys there was identified as a leader. Without much structured activity, however, informal leaders did emerge, but, as at Confront, their leadership was based on likability which was, in one case, combined with mischievousness. Both leaders were generally committed to the house, however, and felt bound—within the program—by its expectations.

The same degree of variation in subcultural emphasis and in organizational structure did not exist among the five girls' programs. Thus, leaders were evident in all five programs, and they shared rather similar traits. Girls identified as leaders at Clara Barton and Putnam cottages, and at Reward, Mother, and Shelter, were generally in control of their emotions—"cooler" and more mature—and extraordinarily able to manipulate the emotions of their peers. In particular these skills enabled them to provoke other girls to taunt lower-status residents, a common activity in all five programs.[22] At the same time, each leader seemed to have "adopted" a lower status girl whom she protected and mothered:

> Then Lisa [leader] answered a query intended for Joan about why she was walking bow-legged. Lisa said "Cause she's got cunt rot!" Mary [leader] added from across the room, "No she don't, it's the syph." Joan responded while staring at the table, "It is not; it's a chafing. It is

not syph." Fran [leader] kept telling Mary to leave Joan alone: "If you'd quit pickin' on her, she'd be better." Mary responded, "I don't care; she's acting like a fuckin' asshole." Joan ran out into the hall screaming and crying, "They won't leave me alone."

In addition, leaders were often attractive and thoroughly experienced with men and with drugs—all highly valued traits in the subculture shared by the girls.

A number of variables reduced the social density of programs— that is, the intensity of in-program interaction—and thus stunted the growth of youth hierarchies. In some programs agreement among youths about the identity of leaders was much lower than in others. The 20 percent of program members receiving the most choices as leaders drew from 30 percent to 94 percent of the total choices for leaders in the twenty-three programs: the lower the percentage, the less clear the leadership structure.[23]

The five programs with the lowest percentages (30 to 40 percent)—Pick-up, Drop-in, Pair, Shelter and Regiment—showed several contrasting characteristics that all contributed to radically reduced intensity of interaction.[24] Pick-up, Drop-in, and Pair had the highest levels of community contact—and thus the lowest frequency of in-program interaction—of any programs we observed. Shelter and Regiment, on the other hand, although almost completely closed, were both detention centers with the highest population turnover rates of the twenty-three programs. Despite opportunities for the development of informal social organization, there was not enough stability of detainee population to sustain clear role differentiation. In Reward, which also had a relatively unclear leadership structure (48 percent of choices), leaders were given little chance to lead since virtually every minute was spent in closely supervised activities arranged by the staff. As at Regiment, where even during the rare periods of free time no more than three boys could be in one room together without supervision, at Reward girls spent their free time in groups closely watched by their group mother.

When these restrictions were combined with an absolute prohibition against physical force, they effectively prevented the emergence of strong and aggressive leaders or any clear leadership structure. Despite low levels of youth participation at Regiment and Reward, close supervision and varied group activity, combined with significant staff-youth equality, effectively prevented (at least with a population with rapid turnover at Regiment) the development of informal youth hierarchies and their manifestation in physical and verbal intimidation. This was done at Regiment in the face of a male subculture which, though suppressed by limited opportunities for interaction among youths, nevertheless endorsed the same notions of aggressive masculinity found, for example, at Cottage 9, Fatigue, and Warning.

In summary, it appears that egalitarian and participatory organizations have an impact on youth leadership patterns in at least two ways. First, to the degree that they impose a pervasive structure of their own on youth relationships, the most participatory programs themselves define who their youth leaders are. The extensive structure required to do this, however, is found in few programs (only Primal in our sample). Second, such organizations direct youth subcultures, and in this way control to some degree the terms under which youth leadership develops on its own. Such subcultural modifications occurred in the most participatory programs we observed, as noted in the previous chapter. It is also true that subcultures were somewhat similarly moderated in less participatory but coeducational programs.

Short of promoting full participation in their programs, staff members can control youth leadership by preventing its clear emergence. Very high levels of community contact reduce the frequency and salience of in-program relationships sufficiently to prevent youth leaders from becoming clearly differentiated. The same result follows where population turnover is high and length of residence is brief, or where there is a combination of strict supervision and a heavy regimen of varied and enjoyable activities. In programs where neither participation nor supervision is extensive, youth leaders emerge, and their characteristics reflect the sex or adolescent subcultures that flourish in such settings.

BOGARTING, GETTING HIGH, AND SPLITTING: VARIATIONS IN TROUBLESOME BEHAVIOR

The analysis of variations in subcultures and social structure sets the stage for an examination of some differences in youth behavior that are especially important to program maintenance and success, as well as to the quality of life experienced by detained youths. Drug use and running away particularly threatened staff control and jeopardized programs by exposing them to adverse publicity and administrative pressures from DYS. During our observations, for example, two boys ran way from Regiment and were killed when their stolen car collided with another during a high-speed chase. At Warning the escape one night of seventeen boys (half the residents) through a jimmied window screen led to a small crime wave in the neighborhood and embarrassing newspaper reports. Although periodic instances of sniffing everything imaginable (glue, Right Guard, Pam, and Strip-eze, among other substances), smoking marijuana and consuming alcohol, along with more infrequent cases of hard-drug use, rarely received newspaper attention, they were a constant concern to staff members who wished to avoid threatening publicity and, of course, to prevent what most regarded as negative behavior. Fighting was viewed as negatively as was drug use in the group-treatment programs, while it was expected, at least in moderation, in some of the institutional and community programs; in all settings, however, its occurrence threatened the safety of the participants themselves, and was therefore an especially important component of behavior. In this section, we shall make some rough comparisons of the nature and frequency of these kinds of behavior, which were entered as "troublesome" in our observational reports of the twenty-three programs.

Although their nature varied somewhat from place to place, most troublesome incidents that we observed took place in the institutional training school cottages plus Sunset and Shirley, and in four of the institutional community programs—Warning, Fatigue, Mother, and Shelter. Both the reasons for the variations among these programs and the factors that set them apart from the remaining programs are important to understand.

During our observation there were about thirty runs from Warning, twenty-five from Mother, fourteen from Westview, and ten from Shirley, while only two occurred at Fatigue and Cottage 8, one at Shelter, and none at Cottage 9. Serious fights as well as semiplayful ones were almost daily events at Warning, Cottages 9 and 8, Elms, and Westview, while the latter only were frequent at Fatigue. "Bogarting," however, was common in all of the institutional boys' programs as older, stronger youths pressured their smaller peers for seats in cars, for cigarettes, and so on, almost endlessly. Marijuana was, to our knowledge, smoked on several occasions by youths on the premises of each of the programs, and youths often returned from outings (and at Mother from runs), smelling of liquor or stoned on drugs.

Drug abuse was clearly most frequent at Mother, where several girls frequently brought back supplies either from weekends home or runs into parties in a nearby town. A cache of beer and hard liquor was discovered by the staff in the basement at Shelter. Even without these resources, youths would attempt to get high on an amazing variety of products.

Petty larcenies were common at most programs, as was vandalism at Fatigue and Cottages 9 and 8. The girls at Mother, Clara Barton, and Putnam were particularly prone to throwing "nutties"—wild emotional outburst—while girls at Shelter exhibited their own milder moodiness. Physical attacks were relatively infrequent among girls, but were observed at Clara Barton, Putnam, and Mother. The enterprising residents at Shelter also used a Polaroid camera to take obscene pictures of one another to show to some workmen next door. The backdrop of all these events was an almost constant petty bickering and verbal abuse among youths and between youths and staff members.

Before comparing the level of troublesome events in these programs with their frequency and kind in other programs, let us probe the reasons for the variations among programs within this set. Many of the differences are attributable to the differing compositions of the youth populations. In each program, as discussed in Chapter 3, there flourished the version for the appropriate sex of a street subculture. Differential incidence of drug use, tantrums, or "nutties" (higher for girls), and fighting and "bogarting" (higher for boys) is explicable largely in terms of these subcultural differences.

The fact that the frequency of real fights in some boys' programs was vastly higher than it was at others can be explained in a number of ways. Most obviously, the boys at Warning and Cottage 9 where fights were most common had more serious records of criminal behavior—including crimes of personal violence—or of misconduct within other cottages or programs than their counterparts at Fatigue, most of whom had never been arrested. It is intriguing, however, to speculate that the higher social density at Warning and Cottage 9 contributed to the frequency of violence there: at Warning from twenty to thirty boys were frequently locked out of the wings where their rooms were and confined together in the TV room, pool room, and at times, the group-meeting room. In Cottage 9 they milled around an even more limited area with less to do. This summertime concentration of hot and bored boys in a small area was explosive, and it contrasted sharply with the situation at the other boys' cottages and at Fatigue, where the residents roamed about more freely and had more sponsored activity to direct them away from one another.

The difference in run rates is also striking, but more difficult to explain. Although one might attribute the low rate at Shelter to the high attraction girls expressed for the program, for their peers, and for the staff, it is difficult if not impossible to explain the low rate at Fatigue and Cottage 9 in a similar fashion. These were the only programs we observed where condemnation of the program was clearly part of the youth subculture. When asked what they liked about these places, the boys typically replied, "Nothing." Nevertheless, despite Fatigue's openness almost no one ran. Quite literally, though, the boys had nowhere else to go, and few had enough experience on the streets (unlike the boys at Warning) to make it on their own. In contrast, the heavily guarded boys at Cottage 9 were effectively contained by coercion. The girls at Mother had more experience as runners (often that was the offense they were committed for), but they typically ran away only for an evening or night on the town and returned afterwards.

The absence of observed drug use at Cottage 9 and Clara Barton and its infrequency at Cottage 8 and Putnam may have reflected the greater isolation of youths in these programs. Drugs typically came into programs by way of visitors or after forays by youths into the community; the infrequency of these opportunities may have effectively prevented access to drugs and thus their use. In addition, prohibitions or restrictions on the use of a more socially acceptable addiction—cigarettes—in these programs may have turned youths' attention from the luxury of drug-induced highs to the "necessity" of day-to-day use of cigarettes. Thus, many of the rule violations in these four programs revolved around stealing cigarettes or around possession of contraband cigarettes and matches.

The contrasts between behavior in these programs and that evident at two community institutions—Reward and Regiment—are striking and must largely be explained in terms of organizational differences between the two sets of programs; the combination of high equality and supervision at Reward and Regiment impeded rule violations by giving staff members access to the inmate underlife while at the same time limiting its emergence. In five weeks of observation at Regiment we learned of only one fight between boys there, and few instances of "bogarting"; six runs occurred during this time, and in one instance a staff member recognized the aroma of marijuana smoke in a bathroom. The next most significant problems were the theft of a deck of cards, the breaking of a radio antenna off a resident's radio, and an outbreak of lice in the long hair of several boys. Complaints were few and bickering infrequent.

Except for this last observation, life at Reward was similarly serene. One girl of the twelve in the unit we studied ran (while on a weekend home), and another girl stole and used some drugs brought from home by the resident of another unit. Other trouble was rather tame compared to that at the other girls' programs: for example a resident outraged the sensibilities of the group mother by pursuing her peers for a definition of "fart." Some harrassment, bickering, and moodiness were evident among the girls, but it went on at a much lower pitch than at Mother.

For the excitement-hungry observer, the four programs most open to youth-community contact—Pair, Drop-in, Pick-up, and Open House—would also have been a disappointment. Curfew violations, arguments over household responsibilities, an overnight visit by a boyfriend (with an ensuing pregnancy), two runs from Open House and one from Pair, and one instance of drug use at Pair and of drunkenness at Open House were the most exciting events during five weeks in the two open residential programs. In the nonresidential programs, illegal swimming near a Navy installation, yelling obscenities to passers-by while riding in a car, some occasional bullying, the temporary theft of a napkin holder at a lunch counter, and the joint participation of staff and youths in a quiet evening of beer-drinking and marijuana-smoking were the most troublesome events during our period of observation.

Finally, the five most participatory group-treatment programs also exhibited relatively infrequent and generally innocuous troublesome incidents. One boy ran at Group during our observation, while six youths fled Confront, two ran from Primal, none left "I Belong," and six (in one day) ran from Topsfield.[25] In addition, there were two instances of drug use (sniffing Right Guard and stealing pills) at Confront, one instance of sniffing at Group, and just prior to the runs, eight youths took amphetamines at Topsfield. A single one-punch fight at Group was the only event of the sort in any of these programs. At Group, minor arguments arose quite frequently because of housekeeping chores (at breakfast or lunch when the boys were competing with one another for scarce kitchen space while making their meals), periodically at "I Belong," Topsfield, and Confront (few of these hostilities were expressed "on the floor"; they came out in group confrontation sessions) and rarely at Primal (all arguments were aired in official group confrontations). In the most bizarre but indicative of the reported troublesome incidents, a new resident at Primal left nearly $1,000 in cash and some prescription barbiturates out on her bed in an open dormitory for several hours; nothing was taken, but the two resident guides who were responsible for her were given "haircuts" for their carelessness.

Three familiar factors are important in explaining the similarities and differences in levels of troublesome behavior among the programs: program organization, openness to community contact, and population composition. Those programs with most frequent trouble included the least egalitarian programs. The organizational variables this dimension summarizes had some indirect effects on behavior through their previously discussed impact on subculture and social structure, and several additional organizational characteristics had a direct effect on patterns of youth behavior as well.

Moderately to highly structured activities characterized Topsfield, "I Belong," Reward, Regiment, Confront, and Primal; youths in these programs had little time or opportunity to get into trouble. The youths at Group had little programmed activity to keep them busy, but the smallness of their numbers and the continuous presence of two or more staff members around the house partly made up for the absence of structured activity. Reward and Regiment had success in controlling trouble equal to that of the group-treatment programs despite the fact that their subcultures were similar to those shared by male and female street people, while the subcultures in the group-treatment programs were defined and transmitted by the program staff. In contrast, structured activity was far less common and free time was more copious in the institutional training school cottages and at Warning, Fatigue, Mother, and Shelter; youths frequently made mischievous use of this freedom in ways shaped by the values of their respective subcultures.

Equally or more important, staff members in these latter programs were often inconsistent in responding to misbehavior and had few sanctions to apply when they did. They generally relied on the imposition of restrictions such as "a five-day ground," reduction in "level of freedom" or some equivalent in points (Warning, Fatigue, and Mother used point systems that allowed youths various privileges if they accumulated sufficient points by attending activities and behaving well in them). The commission of several infractions, however, quickly made the sanctions meaningless (what was another day of "ground" when you already had twenty-one?), and staff members were often forced to retract some of the restrictions. In addition, many rule violations were ignored. This inconsistent application of relatively puny sanctions contrasted vividly with the situation at "I Belong," Topsfield, Reward, Regiment, Group, Confront, and Primal.

Fighting, for example, which was expected in the institutional cottages and at Warning and Fatigue, drew minimal response there from staff (beyond sometimes belated intervention). At Primal, by contrast, any physical violence (such as slamming a door as a prank and hurting the hand of someone knocking on it) put the offender in the boxing ring with several strong fellow residents wearing boxing gloves who ably demonstrated to him the futility of fighting. At Group, a person was grounded merely for throwing an ice cube at a fellow resident, and at Group and Regiment fighters were removed from the program.

Drug use was also tolerated in Warning, Fatigue (in both of which we observed staff studiously ignore instances of marijuana smoking), Mother, and Shelter. Offenders might be grounded for a few days. The one Strip-eze sniffer at Group was summarily dismissed from the program, while the "pill-poppers" at Confront had their hair shaved off and were made to wear signs around their necks. Staff members thus appeared to take rule violations much more seriously in Reward, Regiment, Group, Confront, and Primal, and responded to them with more authority than did staff in the institutional cottages and programs—Sunset, Shirley, Warning, Fatigue, Mother, and Shelter.[26]

Youths who ran away from Topsfield, "I Belong," Reward, Regiment, Group, Confront, and Primal were not automatically welcomed back into the program. Residents at Confront voted on the question of allowing a runner to return, and they imposed "learning experiences" on those who were readmitted. Program directors at Regiment and Primal refused reentry (only temporarily in the latter) to escapees. In contrast, the records held by several youths at Mother and Warning of over twenty runs each suggest the level of tolerance in these programs. The proportion of youths in a program who claimed, in response to an interview item, not to have run from it provides a more systematic measure of this aspect of misbehavior. When these percentages were regressed on the fourteen independent variables, only the level of equality ultimately remained significant (see Table 4–5).

The moderate contribution made by a program's equality score to the explanation of variation in the index of the frequency of runaways reinforces the conclusion that the combination of equality and participation generally helps to increase staff control rather than to decrease it. The full integration of youths into a program can offset the attractions of the free community. The presence of guards, locks, and fences, however, makes captivity a constant issue and constantly reinforces the involuntary character of a program. Open, more equalitarian programs exert pressures on youths to accept their own presence and, in fact, to show commitment to a program. It is more difficult to explain to oneself or to others why one is still around if there are no physical constraints keeping one in. For example, at Topsfield,

> Gene, after hearing the first "escape" story in the questionnaire said, "I was thinkin' of Lyman [training school] when I answered that 'cuz that just wouldn't happen here. No one "escapes" from this place; you

Table 4-5. Multiple Regression on Independent Variables of Percentage of Youths *Not* Having Run Away from Their Current Program (*N* = 23 programs)[a]

Independent Variables	Zero-Order Correlation with Dependent Variable	Standardized Regression Coefficient	F Ratio
Percentage of youths 16 or older	-.16		
Percentage of male youths	.08		
Percentage of black youths	.17		
Percentage of youths from DYS	-.34		
Percentage of DYS youths committing first offense before age 14	-.03		
Percentage of DYS youths with previous commitment	-.47		
Percentage of DYS youths committed for crimes against persons	-.02		
Percentage of DYS youths committed for juvenile status offenses	-.19		
Program size	-.28		
Youth-to-staff ratio	-.02		
Equality scale	.61	0.61	12.42
Community-contact scale	.12		
Participation scale	.25		
Supervision scale	.23		

[a]For the regression equation the multiple correlation = .61 (R^2 = .37) and the F ratio = 12.42 (with 1 and 21 degrees of freedom).

can just walk out. When I first saw this place it blew my mind. Anywhere else, if a kid told a staff member to fuck off he'd get his head busted open. This place is a dream. . . . In a way it's harder to get along here than at a place like Shirley or Lyman [training schools]."

In the background of many egalitarian programs, however, there also lurks the possibility of coercion; where running away may physically be very easy, it cannot be tolerated. Youths who leave may not be allowed back; instead when recaptured they are often assigned to less attractive programs. Even the less immediate legal threats of commitment to another program if one runs away served to enforce some degree of commitment to the organization. To accept those legal threats is to say that the current program is preferable to some other unknown or known alternative, and such a statement of preference involves at least a minimal amount of commitment to the program. In this subtle fashion youths were drawn into egalitarian programs rather than set against them. A youth's awareness of a program's openness, combined with a recognition of the highly predictable consequence of running, can act as a far more secure barrier than fences and locked doors and screened windows.

The level of community contact and the composition of the youth populations also were clearly relevant, as the contrasts between the programs with most frequent troubles and Pick-up, Drop-in, Open House, and Pair attest. Despite the relative lack of impact by staff on subcultures and social structures in the programs with high community contact, troublesome behavior was relatively infrequent. Youths in these programs were in less intense interaction with one another because of the smaller size and the openness of the programs. The lower intensity of interaction reduced the likelihood of interpersonal tension and conflict. In addition, of course, the community provided a wide arena for youths to "mess around" in, and channeled some trouble out of the program. Our data also suggest, however (see Table 1-2) that youths who entered programs with high levels of youth-community contact were in less serious and repeated trouble with the law than their counterparts in some other programs, and were perhaps less troublesome generally.

CONCLUSIONS AND SUMMARY: IMPLICATIONS FOR THEORY AND POLICY

This examination of the impact of organizational and population variables on views of staff and on informal subcultures, social structure, and behavior patterns of youthful inmates has made clear the necessity of viewing inmate systems, not as monolithic entities, but rather as the sum of separable, although related, elements. Different aspects of correctional organization and of population characteristics are implicated as causes of the variations in these diverse elements. At Regiment and Reward among the institutional programs, for example, many of the subcultural elements found in training school cottages for boys and girls were evident, but both staff members and inmates viewed one another more positively, and the behavior of youths was more rule-governed because of the greater levels of equality and of supervision in these institutions. It appears possible, therefore, to exert considerable control over the tenor of inmate relationships and behavior without making substantial alterations in youth value systems.

This finding further expands and complicates the proposition that organizational and population characteristics work together in producing inmate systems. Where given free reign, imported elements play the strongest part in youths' collective definition of the terms of their imprisonment; where equality and participation is low, the experiences, values, and beliefs of the dominant segment of the inmate population will be adopted and will constitute the inmate subculture. Equality by itself can overcome individual inmate suspicion and collective condemnation of staff, but it cannot alone counter other key norms guiding relationships among youths. Further, high participation, particularly when combined with high supervision (and low community contact), can act to alter some of the values and norms youths hold, at least temporarily and in the context of the program.

Organizational elements can also directly influence patterns of social relationships and behavior that are, of necessity, indigenous to the organization. The data examined in this chapter direct attention particularly to the way community contact reduces social density, diminishes the importance and clarity of in-program relationships, and lowers the frequency of much in-program rule-breaking. Supervision directly and participation indirectly, through the value changes they promote, each help keep behavior in line with staff expectations, and by doing so increase the confidence and trust youths have in one another. Without such supervision, participation, or community contact, the imported and intensified subcultures guide youths' behavior; staff members remain either cut off from inmate underlife by inequality or weakened in influencing its direction by equality.

The policy implications of such findings are very important. To a limited degree, one can select the targets for change or direction in inmate systems. The full array of group-treatment techniques employed by a concept house is not the only alternative to coercive, bureaucratic institutions. Change along each of the organizational dimensions leads to some alteration of one aspect or another of informal inmate systems. Chapter 5 provides a review and analysis of what changes in each dimension do imply about aspects of inmate systems and correctional policy.

NOTES

1. The works of John Irwin, *The Felon* (Englewood Cliffs, N.J.: Prentice-Hall, 1970), and of Leo Carroll, *Hacks, Blacks, and Cons* (Lexington, Mass.: D.C. Heath 1975) place considerable emphasis on these kinds of patterns of association.

2. Talcott Parsons, of course, has identified this as "the Hobbesian problem

of order." See *The Structure of Social Action*, (New York: McGraw-Hill, 1937), 1: 89-94. Gresham Sykes and Sheldon Messinger, "The Inmate Social System," *Theoretical Studies in Social Organization of the Prison*, ed. Richard Cloward et al. (New York: Social Science Research Council, 1960), p. 16, poses the problem in similar terms by invoking Hobbes's image of "a war of all against all" as the extreme, compared to which inmate social systems appear relatively ordered.

3. See, for example, Emile Durkheim, *The Division of Labor in Society*, trans. George Simpson (New York: Macmillan, 1933); Werner Landecker, "Types of Integration and Their Measurement," *American Journal of Sociology* 56 (January 1951): 332-40; Robert Angell, "Integration: Social Integration," *International Encyclopedia of the Social Sciences* (1968 ed.), 7: 380-86; and Stanley Schachter, "Cohesion, Social," ibid., 2: 542-46.

4. Ralf Dahrendorf, *Class and Class Conflict in Industrial Society* (Stanford, Calif.: Stanford University Press, 1959). Dahrendorf, of course, proposes his conflict theory as an alternative to what he terms the integration model of society.

5. To the degree that youths or inmates are allowed to choose which of several alternative programs they wish to enter (as occurs ideally for many DYS youths), and to the degree that programs allow current members to accept or reject potential entrants (as occurred at several programs we observed), individual choices arising from attraction to programs and people become key forces in maintaining the boundaries of group membership.

6. Quoted in Jessica Mitford, *Kind and Usual Punishment: The Prison Business* (New York: Knopf, 1973), p. 7.

7. James Jacobs, "Street Gangs Behind Bars," *Social Problems* 21 (Winter 1974): 395-409.

8. Clemens Bartollas, Simon Dinitz, and Stuart Miller, *Juvenile Victimization: The Institutional Paradox* (New York: Wiley, 1977), p. 53.

9. The youth cohesion scale was constructed from the following three items: "Most of the kids here are not loyal to each other when the going gets tough"—"strongly agree," "agree," "50-50" (volunteered), "disagree," "strongly disagree"; "Would you say that kids here: "usually help each other," "50-50" (volunteered), "usually look out for themselves?"; and "Do you think most of the kids here can be trusted?"—"yes," "50-50" (volunteered), "no." The responses to the first item were scored 1, 2, 3, 4, and 5, and the responses to the second two items were scored 5, 3, and 1, respectively. The average inter-item correlation is .35. The scores on these items were summed. The cutting point between high and low scores on this scale was the midpoint of the possible scale values.

10. Rose Giallombardo, *The Social World of Imprisoned Girls: A Comparative Study of Institutions for Juvenile Delinquents* (New York: Wiley, 1974), pp. 3-4.

11. This relationship is even more striking considering that all the girls' programs were institutional programs where cohesion was relatively low, and two of the boys' programs were designed as group-treatment programs where cohesion was supposed to be high. The inability to control for program characteristics would seem, in this case, not to weaken the interpretation.

12. The program preference scale was constructed from the following items: "There are really more things I enjoy doing around here than at home"; "This place isn't nearly as bad as I thought it would be"; "For right now, I'd rather be here than home with my family." The "strongly agree," "agree," "50–50" (volunteered), "disagree," and "strongly disagree" responses to these items were scored 5, 4, 3, 2, and 1, respectively. The average interitem correlation is .30. The scores on these items were summed. The cutting point between high and low scores on this scale was the midpoint of possible scale values.

13. Walter B. Miller, "Subculture, Social Reform, and the 'Culture of Poverty,'" *Human Organization* 30 (Summer 1971): 111–25.

14. We utilized Whyte's technique of "positional mapmaking" on occasion; see William F. Whyte, *Street Corner Society: The Social Structure of an Italian Slum* (Chicago: University of Chicago Press, 1955), p. 333.

15. At Fatigue, however, three blacks—none of whom was "streetwise"—were integrated into the friendship networks of their white peers.

16. Interestingly, a modified version of the black-power handshake had been taken over by white boys in most of the programs we observed. Such subcultural diffusion bespeaks the unspoken admiration for black solidarity held by many whites.

17. These statements were: (1) "Most of the leaders are ready to fight other kids almost any time"; (2) "They have little or nothing to do with the adults here"; (3) "They keep the other kids from getting into trouble; (4) "They try to straighten out and get something good out of the place"; (5) "They are able to help other kids with their personal problems"; (6) "They get along well with the staff"; and (7) "They goof-off and don't care about changing their ways." The responses were scored 1, 2, 3, 4, and 5, respectively, for statements (1), (2), and (7), and 5, 4, 3, 2, and 1, respectively, for the remaining statements. The interitem correlations average .35. The scores on these items were summed. A high scale score was defined as one above the midpoint of possible scale scores.

18. Demotions did occur on occasion but appeared to be the exception rather than the rule. For example, one boy who was giving staff members a difficult time because of their refusal to allow him to go home to his grandmother's funeral, "was taken off ramrod because of 'his image.'"

19. An indication of their lack of commitment is the fact that they were among the few Confront youths who still clung to the antifinking norm of the street code.

20. Most of the youths at Drop-in could not or would not identify any leaders at all; the lack of clarity of leadership in a nonresidential program is consistent with my argument that in-program relationships have less salience in programs with high levels of youth-community contact.

21. One exception, for example, was a spindly but bright and articulate thirteen year old, whose heroes were prohibition-era gangsters. He had been the organizer of an extortion ring at Fatigue until the staff broke it up. He remained an effective manipulator of some of his larger peers, however.

22. Lower-status residents—"square," slow, or "dumb" youths—were often simply ignored in boys' programs, but the girls frequently went out of their way to harrass such youngsters. In all programs they were known simply as "assholes."

23. Since few programs had populations numbered in multiples of five, extrapolation was used to estimate the proportion of leadership choices received by exactly 20 percent of the participants in each program.

24. The range of percentages for these five programs compares to 44-94 percent for the remaining ones.

25. The reason for the relatively high frequency of runs at Confront was quite apparent. The limited nature of the official youth hierarchy there and its lack of any relationship to in-program progress prevented it from tying youths to the organization as the more extensive hierarchy did at Primal. The ties at Group were more personal, based on close staff-youth bonds. At Topsfield the periodic flaring up of staff conflict may have contributed to lowered morale and this major breakout by youths.

26. Another important feature of the five most participatory group-treatment programs was their use of group meetings to expose interpersonal conflicts to public scrutiny and to provide legitimate methods for their resolution. In this manner they helped release the tensions arising from intense interaction in a relatively closed setting. No comparable mechanisms were available in any other program, although, as we have noted, the staff members at Regiment curtailed the amount of interaction among youths, and those at Reward kept close tabs on interaction.

✳ *Chapter 5*

Restructuring Correctional Organizations: Alternatives and Dilemmas

In the introduction to this book it was claimed that training schools and prisons have been double failures because they have not been able to achieve the goals of either long-term rehabilitation or short-term management and humane care. Some believe that these failures are inevitable in any penal system. The analysis in the preceding chapters shows otherwise, at least with respect to the achievement of these short-term goals in juvenile corrections.[1]

The variation in inmate life in several cottages of the partially reorganized training schools in Massachusetts and in a number of community programs that later replaced these institutions makes evident that there can be success in shaping or directing the development of informal inmate systems. That success is of varying kinds, however, and depends largely upon the structure (and ultimately the goals) of correctional organizations. Those concerned with guiding inmate systems for the purposes of administrative effectiveness and humane care, or in the hope of long-term rehabilitation, would do well to consider seriously the possibilities and implications of organizational innovation. This chapter focuses on each of the dimensions of organizational variation around which the data analysis has revolved.

Combining generalizations and hypotheses from the Massachusetts data, the advantages and disadvantages of moving correctional organizations from one pole of each dimension to the other will be examined. The implications of inmate population composition for correctional organization are outlined, and the implications for correctional systems of introducing more egalitarian programs are assessed. Although research and policy concerning adult corrections are cited on occasion to highlight the issues in the following sections, the policy analysis itself is focused on juvenile corrections. The limitations of extending both the empirical generalizations and the policy conclusions to adult corrections are, however, examined briefly.

EQUALITY: THE KEY TO ORGANIZATIONAL CHANGE

Any effort to direct the development of inmate systems within a correctional program must begin with the establishment of relatively high levels of staff and staff-offender equality, as defined in Chapters 1 and 2. The relationships between prisoners and line staff members are, by all accounts, the most important aspect of any correctional setting. The New York State Special Commission on Attica, for example, observed that "the relationship between officer and inmate was the central dynamic of life at Attica, as it must be in every prison," and Sykes claimed, in his classic study of New Jersey State Prison, that the guard is "the pivotal figure on which the custodial bureaucracy turns."[2]

The position of the guards or cottage parents vis-à-vis correctional administrators and professional staff and with respect to the youths or inmates they interact with fundamentally defines a correctional organization. Bureaucratic and authoritarian organizations that officially prohibit fraternization between inmates and guards or invest guards and the edifices they staff with the symbols of official power, control, and remoteness inevitably encourage the development of inmate systems growing out of the sex, social class, ethnic, and criminal experiences of the inmate population.[3] These semi-autonomous social, cultural, and behavioral systems foster mutual exploitation and distrust among inmates, tension between inmates and staff, and perpetual problems of control for authorities.

By contrast, lowering barriers through high equality promotes trust and communication between staff members and inmates and serves as an opening wedge—but only that—in directing the development or controlling some aspects of informal inmate systems. The data suggest that a high level of equality is a necessary but not sufficient condition for altering other organizational dimensions. Community contact or high levels of participation and supervision must also be present, in order to alter significant aspects of informal life among offenders—their degree of trust in one another, their beliefs and values, and the character of their informal social organization and behavior.

Given such a stark contrast in outcomes, one might well ask why anyone would choose a nonegalitarian correctional organization. There are, of course, risks in undoing some of the coercive aspects of correctional organizations, and these motivate the arguments offered against greater equality. These fears are overstated, however, and at times misconceived. In addition to the heavy weight of tradition, four related concerns about an egalitarian style of organization help sustain the essentially coercive and bureaucratic practices in training schools and prisons.

First, equalizing relationships between inmates and staff (and, crucially, among staff) may be viewed by some as a sacrifice of order and discipline and a turning over of control from lawfully empowered officials to officially adjudged lawbreakers. Such an argument assumes that traditional bureaucratic regimes effectively control their prisoners. Yet from the earliest sociological portraits of inmate life to the data from the institutional training school cottages of this study—Cottages 9 and 8, Westview, Elms, Clara Barton, and Putnam—there is clear documentation that inmate underlife is a force virtually coequal with official rules, if not dominant, in guiding the lives of inmates and day-to-day institutional practice. As Sykes has noted, administrators and guards unofficially concede considerable amounts of their authority and power to inmates to make the system work.[4]

In both training schools and prisons for males, guards and administrators regularly trade favors with the men or boys who are inmate leaders—for example, a supply of illicit goods in return for control by these leaders over the behavior of fellow prisoners. The manipulation of unofficially created opportunities plays a central part in traditional institutions.[5] Brutal coercion by guards thus can frequently be avoided, but it is often replaced by inmate controls that are constrained neither by due process requirements nor by reformers' standards of humane treatment. By means of the inmate code, correctional officers and inmate leaders encourage inmates to remain isolated from one another, making control by the organized few—staff and inmate leaders—easier.

In women's and girls' prisons the family systems that typically evolve tend to diffuse organized resistance to staff and to direct the attention of women and girls to their relationships with one another rather than toward their living conditions and relationships with staff members. Giallombardo points out that "the kinship network which integrates the inmates by intimate social bonds and serves to maintain the internal equilibrium of the inmate social system is the very structure which also functions to keep the inmates forever divided into small family units."[6] Implicitly, staff people seem to tolerate such a system and encourage its existence by reinforcing the general attitudes toward the family and sex roles that help sustain it.[7]

Although the informal social and cultural systems of inmates receive unofficial support from staff as a mechanism for holding a lid on the inmate population, the order and control that are achieved through these mechanisms are limited and tenuous at best. Inmates continue to steal property from each other and the institution, and to assault other inmates and staff; disobedience of staff orders by inmates is common. No one is certain when grievances and conflicts may break to the surface in large-scale conflict. Every day staff members must carry on their daily business while paying close attention to the structure of inmate life.

To suggest that greater equality in correctional settings would necessarily decrease staff authority and control over inmates is therefore absurd; such authority is already extremely limited in most coercive institutions. Increased equality would substantially alter, however, the context in which authority is now shared, and would encourage an increase in the use of the control mechanisms that work best even in large, coercive, bureaucratic institutions. Evidence about the way effective control over inmates is achieved by correctional officers shows that in practice it is not their official power and authority that give them success with prisoners, but rather their interpersonal skills, their noncondescending friendliness, honesty, and fairness.[8] These characteristics are officially discouraged in bureaucratic prisons where the trappings of authority and formality keep inmates and staff at a safe distance from one another. In an egalitarian organization the aspects of guard conduct that effectively but illicitly cement their authority in coercive and bureaucratic institutions are encouraged and made official components of the staff members' roles.

In thinking about traditional training schools and prisons, we view them perhaps too often in terms of their ideal (if that term may be used) rather than real form. Order and discipline might well be produced by a punitive, bureaucratic regime, but in the United States today there are neither the resources nor the will to impose total power. As Gibbons points out, two major constraints limit staff-imposed control in most prisons. First, personnel is limited. Ratios of one correctional officer (guard or house parent) in direct contact with inmates for every thirty or more prisoners are not uncommon. Second, very real limits are placed on staff actions in U.S. training schools and prisons today by humanitarian values and the emerging prisoners' rights movement, which have increasingly checked arbitrary and brutal administrative action:

> Autocratic rule over hostile and uncooperative inmates could theoretically be obtained at a price. Prisoners could be isolated, physically abused and coerced, and put under continual and pervasive surveillance. . . . However, these possibilities do not actually exist, for prison officials are expected to deal with their charges in a humane fashion. They are obligated to minimize the physical and social isolation of inmates, rather than maximize it, and are forbidden to abuse physically or coerce prisoners.[9]

While scanty resources are a stumbling block in any system, the legal and humanitarian pressures increase even further the defects of limited official authority and should make even more attractive an alternative organizational style that is more likely to enhance internal order and reduce tension than to make a bad situation worse.

A second plausible reservation some people express about introducing greater equality into correctional organizations is that it would deprive the institution of many of the controls that restrain inmates from escape. As is clear from the equality scale, the design of the physical structure itself—particularly the level of physical security and the nature of living arrangements—communicates information about and creates pressures for either egalitarian or bureaucratic/coercive relationships. At the price of considerable hostility, suspicion, and violence, one may purchase an uncertain degree of perimeter security in a prison or training school with walls, barbed wire, locks, screened or barred windows, electronic devices, and guards. In adult prisons inmate escapes are relatively infrequent but certainly not unknown, and the flow of illicit goods (such as drugs) into such secure institutions is common. In even the most secure juvenile institutions, security arrangements are generally loose enough that escapes can occur with moderate ease; as a matter of policy we have usually refrained from building the same gun-towered fortresses to contain fifteen year olds that we construct for twenty year olds. But punishment facilities like Cottage 9 do exist in juvenile corrections, and they contain their captives at the cost of harsh social conditions.

Security can be enhanced rather than sacrificed, however, by creating more egalitarian organizational environments. Only in such

settings can staff members and offenders officially and fully penetrate one another's social networks, and thus keep closer touch
with and control over one another's activities. Rather than patrolling
the boundaries of a hostile and internally divided group and using
informers and illicit rewards to keep in partial touch with its internal
workings, staff members in egalitarian programs are likely to be in
close informal contact with many members of a relatively nonhostile
group. The relative attractiveness and openness of such programs
decreases both the desirability and the challenge of escape.

The development of high levels of participation and supervision
can provide additional increments of security and control. Although
some egalitarian programs we observed did have difficulty with
runaways, problems of security are not inherent in such programs.
Egalitarian conditions thus are not inconsistent with attempts to
achieve the important goal of security. It is not impossible to make
steps toward more egalitarian correctional organizations in massive
concrete and steel prisons or in the less imposing frame and brick
cottages of the conventional U.S. training schools (and often in
women's prisons), but most effective movement in that direction will
require different if not newly constructed buildings.[10] The decision
about equality in organizational structure should ideally precede and
guide plans for the physical structure of correctional facilities.[11]

A third objection to more egalitarian correctional programs is
the "country club" fear: if correctional programs are made more
attractive and comfortable, people will not fear incarceration and
the result will be to reduce its capacity for special and general
deterrence. Although proponents of correctional reform often con-
veniently ignore the issue of deterrence, it is a key political (and
theoretical/empirical) issue requiring attention.

The assumption that more humane prison conditions will decrease
deterrence rests on a serious underestimation of the punitive effect
of the loss or limitation of freedom and the stigma of criminal
conviction. In addition, it could be argued that the current lack of
correctional variety and the starkness of the choice between nominal
supervision through probation and incarceration in a training school
or prison pressures judges to choose more frequently than they
would like what amounts to nonintervention—that is, probation. As a
consequence, the capacity of our current system for general deterrence is reduced because of the low likelihood of being incarcerated
for a crime. That is one of the costs of coercive institutions and long
sentences.

By significantly decreasing the harshness and invariability of incarceration (*and* the length of sentences), legislatures can make

correctional programs more acceptable alternatives for judges to choose.[12] A more differentiated correctional system, because it involves stronger intervention (and consequent limitation of freedom) than conventional probation, would increase the likelihood of moderate state intervention upon conviction of a crime, with a resultant increase in deterrence.[13] This expansion of the deterrent capacity will make up for whatever capacity is lost by mitigating the harshness of the penalities and the correctional experience of those who would have received correctional treatment prior to correctional reform.

The high probability that any correctional system will absorb as many people as it has room for (or more) should make us cautious, however, about increasing the availability of correctional alternatives. Whatever programs are made available will almost certainly be filled. Clearly, too great an expansion of state intervention beyond the level of probation might increase the costs (social and psychological for the offenders, and monetary for the state) far beyond the benefits in deterrence that could accrue from such a venture. This possible expansion of correctional intervention is one of the potential costs of a reorganized system, but the price can be reduced with an assurance that new correctional organizations *replace* rather than supplement existing ones.[14]

A fourth potential argument against increasing the level of equality within correctional programs is that such a change would encounter too much opposition among correctional officers and cottage masters and matrons who already perceive their authority as being undermined. That such resistance occurs is borne out by the Massachusetts experience; early attempts by DYS Commissioner Miller to change the training schools met resistance and sabotage as well as support. Some resistance is inevitable in an agency undergoing bureaucratic change from the top down. As Fogel makes clear, "two groups of people have historically been neglected in prison decision making—the guard and the convict, and it is the guards who can most effectively undermine organizational change."[15]

Our data demonstrate, however, that the equalization of staff and inmate roles and responsibilities is highly correlated with the intragroup equalization of staff responsibilities and roles; low-level staff empowerment, so to speak, goes hand in hand with equalization with inmates. Although equalization with inmates need not imply inmate decision-making, staff equalization is likely to lead to greater sharing of decision-making among staff members.[16] Other advantages should also accrue to staff with equalization: greater job satisfaction arising from their eased relationships with inmates, and fewer role conflicts. The involvement of line personnel in planning the process of change, in a way that did not occur in Massachusetts, might also help reduce staff resistance.

If such resistance occurs or persists, administrators must choose between retaining staff members and reaching a worthwhile correctional objective. It may be that only rare individuals can maintain through years of experience in a civil-service bureaucracy the depth and sincerity of commitment and concern for youths or inmates that we encountered in the more egalitarian programs. This observed but unmeasured quality gave deep meaning to the egalitarianism of these programs. In more than one community program, for example, staff members worked unpaid for weeks during early operation while the disordered system of payments by the state was slowly brought under control. The use of young, dedicated employees embarking on relatively short careers in corrections may be an essential part of an egalitarian system.

Restructuring the organization of staff-staff and staff-inmate relations thus may not be enough to alter staff members' conceptions of their roles and inmate views of the staff; changes in recruitment and career patterns of correctional employees may have to occur as well. But clearly these latter changes cannot have much effect on prison routine without fundamental alterations in organizational structure. The more selective recruitment and improved training of correctional officers advocated by Hawkins among others can only partially alter the key relationships between guards and those guarded; the organizational rules and structure certainly dictate guard conduct and inmate perceptions of guards at least as much as do the individual dispositions and backgrounds of the men and women who fill these roles.[17]

In fact, if James Q. Wilson's study of police departments has any applicability in other realms of the criminal justice system, it is probable that better educated and trained (more middle-class) correctional officers in a *bureaucratic* organization would behave more legalistically, imposing a harsher regime on inmates, and widening rather than closing the gap between staff members and prisoners.[18] Personnel changes *may* be needed for organizational change to succeed, but without the redefinition of staff roles and relationships, these changes will have little positive effect on informal inmate systems.

Despite the telling arguments for more egalitarian programs within a correctional system, there are real problems as well as significant benefits associated with such an organizational change. Among the most important of these problems is the high probability that not all prisoners will adjust to the egalitarian program and that some may use its freedoms (as they would use the informal inmate system in traditional coercive institutions) to exploit their fellows, to violate rules, or even to escape. What is to be done with these presumed few? Certainly, one should not design a whole correctional system in order to coerce a relatively small proportion of intractable inmates—and then discover that the coercive system gives them virtually free reign! Whatever the proportion who require secure care, the general reduction or elimination of those features that emphasize the inequality of staff and inmates makes considerable administrative sense and advances humanitarian goals for the vast majority of inmates who do not require such treatment. An answer to the question of what should happen to recalcitrants will be deferred until the end of this chapter when the system-wide implications of changes in correctional organization are considered.

Not only is egalitarianism likely to be unsuited to all inmates, but it also is likely to be an inadequate measure by itself. Increases in equality without accompanying rises in community contact or in supervision and participation may leave one with a program where the inmate system is pretty much intact, but staff authority is not—where youths like and trust staff members but still deceive them, use drugs, fight and bully one another, and reinforce street values. The examples of Warning, Fatigue, and Mother stand out particularly. Equality is not the whole answer to the problem of directing the development of inmate systems. It is, however, a first and necessary step toward improving staff-inmate relationships, toward making possible more positive ties among inmates, and toward a less tense and better controlled daily existence for staff people and inmates alike.

The possible second steps beyond equality can take programs in nearly opposite directions. If one chooses to abandon the bureaucratic, coercive model of corrections in a particular program or institution, a successful pursuit of egalitarian organization is unlikely to be sufficient by itself to defuse the more explosive and disruptive aspects of inmate systems. To oversimplify, one is left with the choice of whether: (1) to defuse inmate systems by diverting attention from them and reducing their salience through community contact; (2) to undermine the value systems upon which they are based and eliminate inmate systems altogether through participation (perhaps combined with supervision; or (3) to subdue their expression through supervision.

These further choices must be made on the basis of several criteria: ideological, theoretical, or practical judgments about the causes of crime and the most probably successful rehabilitation strategy; the specific functions of a particular institution (that is, short-term pretrial detention or court-mandated punishment); the nature of the inmate population; the available personnel and resources; and the risks one is willing to take and costs one is willing to pay. Rather than advocate one approach or another, the advantages and limitations of each organizational choice will be summarized below.

Summary of Empirical Propositions Concerning Equality

1. The organizational capability to alter conventional inmate systems depends on high levels of equality within the institution/program; other fundamental changes in correctional organization affecting inmate systems can be achieved only in the context of relatively high levels of equality.
2. By themselves, increases in equality coincide with increases in mutual respect between staff members and youths. Even where other elements of inmate systems remain unaffected, positive assessments of staff members by inmates increase with equality.
3. Increases in equality alone alter the nature of staff authority and may weaken or strengthen it depending upon other aspects of the organization.

COMMUNITY CONTACT

One path that egalitarian corrections might take leads into the community. Advocates of community-based programs want to normalize the prisoners' correctional experience, and in this way presumably make it easier to integrate or reintegrate offenders into the free community. The community-based movement has created a new set of choices for practitioners to make about their institutions and programs and about their inmates—the extent and kind of contact between community members and inmates, and what proportion, if any, of their prisoners they will allow to have such contact. These decisions will have significant effects not only on the nature of inmate life, but also on other organizational dimensions and on the likelihood of achieving other correctional goals.

Before examining the implications of community contact for inmate systems, the reader must be cautioned once again not to generalize too broadly from this analysis. The nature of community contact and the ways of organizing programs to encourage it vary substantially, and the programs we observed and our measure of community contact provide a highly limited sample of both variations. While all programs in our sample that opened up youth contacts with the community also engaged youths in activities with one another, some other programs relied largely on individual casework with youths living at home or in foster care. In such programs participants have no contact with one another, and as a result, no inmate groups or subcultures develop. The discussion of community contact here, of course, does not apply to these latter programs since our concern is only with its impact on inmate systems.

Similarly, the kind of contact a group experiences in a community may differ substantially from that discussed and measured in the equality scale. Group recreational activity (such as a program softball team playing against a local team), group work activity (for example, program members working collectively on clearing land), or group public relations activity (program members speaking at schools or showing visitors around, for instance) are not counted *here* as community contact. They are not because: (1) they do not involve contact with the specific members in the community with whom a program member is likely to associate upon release; and (2) they all occur in the context of program membership and should serve to reinforce rather than attenuate youth identification with the program. Remembering the narrow view of community contact adopted here and the purposefully limited sample of community programs, then, let us examine the implications of following this track of the egalitarian road.[19]

The primary effect within a program of increased levels of community contact is a sharply declining social density and program salience among participating youths or adults. No longer restricted in their choice of relationships to the people who share or secure their confinement, inmates can look outside to community members for much that is meaningful in their lives. The consequences for inmate systems of such a shift in orientation are enormous. It reduces the necessity for tight internal supervision by decreasing the frequency and relative importance of social contacts among program participants, and therefore limits the development of tension and conflict that build on themselves in closed settings. The decreased tension and conflict, in turn, make it less crucial for inmates to define clearly their relationships with one another. The inmate social structure (hierarchy, cliques, division of labor) is less clearly differentiated and plays a much reduced role in the lives of program participants.

At the same time, however, that a significant level of community contact brings under control some of the most debilitating aspects of inmate life, it creates new problems of controlling internal security and external relationships. Small doses of largely unsupervised contact between program and community members (such as weekends home) open the program to on-premises use of illegal goods such as drugs and alcohol. As the ratio of time spent with fellow program members to time spent with community members gets smaller and smaller, however, the chance that time outside will be used to promote deviance inside appears to decline; youths will share their drugs and alcohol with their friends in the community rather than with their peers in the programs. In either case, however, staff are likely to be concerned about controlling contacts that facilitate deviance within or outside of the program. The basic task of supervision shifts from security and the control of violence and exploitation to influencing the kinds of people in the community with whom program members associate.

As the major focus of control efforts shifts from internal to external relationships with increases in the level of community contact, the typical approaches to and definitions of rehabilitation must also change. Inducing individual delinquents or criminals to change their ways as a result of a change in values or resolution of psychological problems through direct staff efforts must generally become secondary goals at most. Staff members necessarily compromise over values and norms with their clients in order to offer relationships that can compete with those available in the free community. Without a captive audience, the staff members have to appeal to the offenders' interests and meet them on their own terms. This need to appeal to youths elevates the level of equality within a program and fosters positive, if not close, staff-youth relationships. High levels of community contact are typically accompanied by a program ideology supporting such compromises; the ideology emphasizes that youths or adults must handle the real world on their own eventually, and should be aided in adapting to it in a law-abiding fashion rather than pressured to adopt a new set of values unsuited to the environment they will have to negotiate upon release.

These ideological adjustments are important because in practice the key levers for significantly changing the values of offenders—program participation, and with it supervision—are broken by the weight of community contact. At the same time that social density and the concomitant problems of aggression and exploitation decline, so also does loyalty to and interest in one's peers. The cohesive and controlling aspects of peer pressures and relationships disappear along with the divisive components.

Staff members are also affected by the turning outward of attention and interest that high levels of community contact create among offenders. Ultimately, attempts to provide close individual planning and supervision of the relationships between young and adult offenders and members of the community divert staff attention from supervising the group of clients and coping with internal problems. It may also prevent staff from counseling each client individually; rather, attention and energy must be devoted to recruiting, cajoling, counseling, and supervising the community members who themselves ideally serve as the forces of control and change for the offender.

Not only is a high level of community contact inconsistent with sharp changes in individual and shared values, but it also appears to promote or reinforce a sense among participants that social conditions and opportunities—not themselves—are to blame for their plights. More participatory programs with relatively low levels of community contact are more effective, by contrast, in the promotion of a sense of personal responsibility for one's problems.

In the programs we observed the choice of community contact rather than other egalitarian organizational approaches had two implications. First, it meant virtually no change in the substance of inmate systems but substantial reduction in their intensity and importance to participants; youths could still like a program very much even if they distrusted and disliked other program members. In that sense, and in others as well—particularly the reduction in punishment (that is, loss of freedom)—these programs appeared far more humane than the closed institutions.

Second, the selection of high levels of community contact meant just that—significant amounts of interaction between program members and community residents. The theoretical rationale for such interaction suggests its potential effectiveness as a method of rehabilitation.[20] Community contact by itself, of course, is not enough; successful reintegration should hypothetically be linked more closely to the quality and character of interaction with community members than merely to the quantity of such contact. Our data do not bear directly on the issue of quality or on the rehabilitative efficacy of community contact, but they suggest that the management of groups of youths experiencing high community contact makes it very difficult to succeed simultaneously in group supervision, individual counseling, and careful monitoring of community interaction. The particular costs of a community-contact strategy—reduced leverage over youth values and decreased internal program control—must be balanced against these possible advantages in humane treatment and potential reintegration.[21]

Not all costs associated with community contact in the programs we observed are inevitable. Our observations hint that some of the problems of internal control in group-living programs with high levels of community contact can be reduced by the use of punishments such as brief incarceration in a detention center or more isolated program, or by permanent removal from the program. Such coercion acts as a relatively effective control in response to moderate recalcitrance or serious rule violations.[22] By using these coercive devices one can exert closer control over behavior and relationships, although not over values and beliefs. Use of a backup system of coercive controls, however, depends on the continuing existence of highly unattractive alternatives (in the eyes of youths) to community programs; only if youths fear or dislike the possibility of removal to another program can transfer or removal be an effective control. Those who choose to eliminate unattractive facilities altogether are left to channel resistant youths through a series of programs of increasing intensity (higher participation or supervision) until control is achieved.

One lesson of the analysis of community contact may be that it can most effectively be used to achieve reintegration goals by means of one-to-one programs, where there is little or no interaction among offenders. By using intensive one-to-one contacts between counselors or advocates and youths who live at home or in foster facilities, one avoids in-program groups and inmate systems altogether.[23] At the same time attention can be directed to the planning and establishment of quality contacts in the community—with full youth participation on an individual level that is difficult to achieve on a collective level.[24]

As the theory and practice of community corrections develop, so also may new methods of organizing correctional programs to provide an opportunity for community contact. Closed correctional settings will still remain with us, however. Let us therefore turn back from this path, which takes offenders progressively away from confinement and the intense inmate systems it often fosters, and explore the paths to egalitarian organization available to more closed programs.

Summary of Empirical Propositions Concerning Community Contact

1. The greater the community contact in a program, the higher the level of equality.

2. The greater the community contact in a program aimed at groups of individuals, the more difficult the establishment of high levels of participation and supervision.
3. The greater the community contact, the lower the staff ability to alter youth values and subcultures.
4. The greater the community contact, the more difficult it is for staff to impose their standards and limits on youth behavior.
5. The greater the community contact, the less intense the interaction among program members and the less well-defined the youth social structure.
6. The greater the community contact, the less likely troublesome behavior will occur within the program (that is, when youths and staff are together).

PARTICIPATION

Where significant levels of community contact are viewed as undesirable or unattainable in a program, promotion of inmate participation is a possible complement to the creation of an egalitarian organization. The frequency of interaction among members and the high proportion of time spent in a relatively closed program make it plausible that inmates will be willing to participate in collective decisions and activities. Inmates who are substantially integrated into the official organization, partly responsible for making and enforcing its rules, and involved in planning and carrying out its daily affairs, are ideally no longer faced with the individual and collective problem of adapting *to* the organization—they *are* the organization. The underlife disappears altogether as inmates become full participants in the program and are viewed as near social equals of the staff. Although the inmates along with the staff are—at least temporarily—the organization, the program's traditions and values should outweigh the effects of the disparate views of its members. Their absorption into the organization as participants thus changes the offenders—shapes or reshapes their values, structures their relationships, and guides their behavior—more than the inmates alter the organization. The organizational culture and social system is at one with that of the prisoners.

Few of the group-treatment programs we observed achieved this near complete control over inmate adaptations that can potentially result from high levels of participation, particularly when it occurs with high supervision. Nonetheless it was clearly those programs with the highest levels of participation that had the greatest impact on youth values and self-conceptions and, somewhat less frequently, on structuring the pattern of youth relationships. In general these programs also successfully controlled the behavior of their members within the program and kept their members from running away, despite the absence of physical security.

These real achievements of the participatory programs should, however, be balanced against the costs of successfully molding such an organization. As the last section made clear, community contact must be held at a minimum to gain and then sustain the members' single-minded commitment to the program. Although many intensive group-treatment programs include reentry or second-stage components, these in effect are new or different programs; the few who enter them leave the social structure and often the physical setting of the old program while presumably maintaining its values. More telling, their reentry is rarely into the world they left (neighborhood or family), but into a new locale near the program site. To the degree one believes that the maintenance of ties with community members is crucial to successful reintegration, and to the extent one's clientele will, in fact, eventually return to their home communities, then the loss of community contact is a heavy price to pay for partially (and perhaps temporarily) altered individual value systems and self-conceptions and for the absence of an inmate underlife.

At times there is also question about the humanity of the techniques used in the most intensive of these group-treatment settings, particularly in those settings known as concept houses. The obvious parallels between participation in these programs and brainwashing techniques underlines such criticisms.[25] Criticism of these programs today comes particularly from the inmates' and patients' rights movements, which demand the right to choose whether or not to be treated and to be free from cruel and unusual treatment. But what is anathema to some is acceptable to others, and it is not surprising that soon after our observation at Primal one state that had been placing their most difficult delinquents there removed them after a visit by an evaluation team, while several other states endorsed the program's methods and effectiveness.[26]

Another criticism is broadly and particularly applicable to all of the group-treatment programs, whether they use strong or mild techniques to alter inmate values. Hawkins has summarized this view, which is also articulated by both A.R.N. Cross and the American Friends Service Committee. According to Hawkins, the AFSC argues that "'as part of treatment and rehabilitation, cultural assimilation is forced upon' offenders. In other words, attempts are made 'to impose a middle class life-style' and 'the increasingly outmoded Protestant work ethic' on them. . . . Cross is equally critical of the belief in 'the merits of inculcating middle-class values' in offend-ers "[27]

While the advocates of the group-treatment programs we ob-served might disagree that the values they teach are in fact as widely shared in middle-class society as they should be, their preferences for verbalizing emotions and for introspection appear to be more in tune with American upper-middle-class values. In the view of critics, forced assimilation is likely to be maladaptive for offenders and decrease their interest in defining their delinquent or criminal actions in political terms. People who return to low-income communities may find that the values they learn in such programs do not fit well with those of their neighbors and are inappropriate for the opportun-ity structures they encounter. By turning individuals inward to accept responsibility for their own delinquent or criminal acts and condition, these programs reduce their readiness to voice social criticism and take radical social action.

The characteristics pointed to by these criticisms of some or all of the particular models of participatory programs we examined are not, however, inherent in the nature of participatory organization. The eight programs in the group-treatment cluster differed substan-tially in their use of participation, and in theory it is an element of organization that could promote any one of a variety of ideologies. The programs in our sample—not coincidentally—tended to share a particular treatment ideology, although they differed in the scope of the world view they attempted to inculcate in their members. Primal and Confront each had a concept that was essentially a general philosophy of life, whereas the other programs imposed more limited normative systems that presumably aided the treatment process. The modest variability in the ideologies of these programs hints at the po-tentially wider range of participatory ideologies.

The only other ideology to be officially associated with participa-tion in correctional work is a democratic one, and many analysts ap-pear to believe it has proved itself incompatible with prison life, despite apparent short-term success.[28] Early in this century, for example, Thomas Osborne introduced into two New York State pri-sons (Auburn, and later at Ossining), the limited practice of inmate self-government. A major goal of this system was to involve the in-mates in disciplining their fellow prisoners.[29] Haynes credits inmate democracy with drastically reducing the incidence of fighting and disciplinary infractions.[30] A few years later Howard Gill began a short-lived experiment in self-government at the Norfolk Prison Colony in Massachusetts in the hope of creating a positive com-munity among the inmates.[31] More recently Kohlberg and his colleagues have experimented with an essentially egalitarian and participatory unit at two correctional facilities in Connecticut.[32] Although Kohlberg's moral-development ideology undergirds that system, whatever effectiveness it has in shaping inmate systems may be due less to the moral development of inmates than to the democratic principles and participatory structure of the program. Democratic ideology appears less alien in a time when therapeutic approaches are under attack; it might thus serve as an attractive alternative model to concept houses and group-treatment programs for organizing inmate participation.

To do so, however, the idea of inmate democracy must live down the bad reputation it has gained among correctional administrators.[33] The inmate democracies that died lacked three key characteristics of the most successful participatory programs we observed—small size, staff equality, and sufficient supervision. If prison democracies included these traits they would succeed more fully and encounter less resistance than earlier experiments.

The programs we saw were small enough—up to seventy residents—to allow (or require) full participation of *every* group member in program activities and collective decisions. By contrast, other inmate democracies have been *representative* rather than participatory because of their location in large centralized institutions. Full participation helps prevent dominance and ultimate corruption of the system by a few inmate opportunists.

The early inmate democracies did not include line staff as co-equals—their exclusion inevitably created an unofficial struggle for power between prisoners and guards rather than a joint effort to solve problems and resolve conflicts.

The level of staff supervision of inmates in the early experiments was never great enough to eliminate as much violence and intimidation among prisoners as was possible. No participatory programs can operate successfully without sufficient levels of supervision to ensure that informal peer pressures are not brought to bear to keep people from fully and freely expressing themselves. Similarly, informal punishment of inmates by staff members must be prevented through careful coordination and supervision of staff. Nearly complete suppression of violence and physical intimidation is a prerequisite for the success of any participatory program; without it, informal coercion—rather than public group pressure and decision—tends to be the major controlling force in a democratic as well as in a coercive prison. These problems could be avoided by creating small, relatively autonomous correctional units (even in one large but decentralized facility), which are organized in egalitarian fashion with high levels of supervision.

It is clear that participation and resultant value change can only occur where some ideology is developed and clearly articulated. Such an ideology provides the alternative value system into which inmates are socialized. It is not coincidental that both concept houses and the briefly successful early inmate democracies seemed to rely on the charismatic leadership of persons who articulated and embodied such ideologies. That they rested on explicit values and at times did, through intensive pressures, achieve some measure of resocialization (at least in the short run) is both the triumph and the sore point of participatory programs. Ultimately in our society many may question the appropriateness of any program ideology and of the attempt to alter the beliefs of a captive audience. The content of these ideologies, however, should be thought of separately from participatory organization itself.[34] The organization of participation in combination with equality and supervision is a potent force in preventing altogether the emergence of an informal inmate system and in resocializing prisoners. But it is an organizational tool to be used with caution and conscience.

Summary of Empirical Propositions Concerning Participation

1. High levels of program participation are unlikely to be achieved in the context of a significant degree of community contact.
2. High levels of participation promote at least temporary changes in some individual values and self-conceptions and give staff substantial control over the content of the youth subculture (which is no longer part of an autonomous informal inmate underlife).
3. High levels of participation, particularly when combined with high supervision, can structure the social relationships and direct the behavior of youths in accordance with staff wishes.

SUPERVISION

Close supervision over relationships among offenders within a program helps create humane and orderly living environments in programs that are completely or mostly closed to community contact. As defined in this study supervision has meant something other than the watchful eye of a guard over inmates in the yard or of a cottage master over a roomful of television viewers, pool players, and magazine readers. It means the participation of offenders in an intense, organized round of activities involving program staff members.

Inmates of prisons and training schools often complain bitterly about inactivity. Left without officially sponsored activity, inmates may improvise individually or collectively their own illicit activities or experience frustration. Both responses may lead to trouble for officials and other inmates. In contrast, a full schedule of attractive activities in which all prisoners engage leaves little time or room for informal organization or conspiracy. The impact of such supervision is not on individual values or subcultures (except when used in concert with participation), but rather on social structure and behavior.

Most important, supervision insures that inmates will not abuse and exploit one another, as they often do when staff concentrate only on controlling the perimeter of an institution and not on protecting prisoners within it. A major consequence of the reduction in abuse is decreasing mutual fear and distrust among inmates.

Unfortunately, supervision is costly and particularly difficult to achieve in small groups (fewer than twelve to fifteen people), with insufficient numbers of participants to support an array of activities.[35] It requires a fairly large number of staff members unless inmates take on staff roles as they typically do in participatory organizations. On the other hand, supervision is likely to break down in a large organization (over eighty to one hundred residents) where it becomes far less likely that staff members will know or be able to keep track of each member. Expensive in terms of staff and requiring an optimum size of between perhaps twenty and eighty inmates, supervision is not an easy aspect of organization to achieve. Some clustering of otherwise autonomous small units in a larger institution would, however, allow the sharing of personnel and activities necessary to overcome these difficulties.

A high level of supervision has nonmonetary costs as well: it tends to reduce the privacy of individuals and limit some aspects of free choice. The penetration of staff members into inmate activities and relationships means that two or three persons cannot easily disappear together to talk. Similarly, once program activities are planned—ideally perhaps through some collective decision-making (participation)—individuals must have only limited freedom not to take part. The value of group activity as a control device is that it keeps inmates together in officially sponsored and monitored activity. Free nonparticipation removes individuals from staff supervision, and undercuts any attempts at democratic participation; if individuals can choose not to pay the price of their collective decisions, then participation in decisions is shallow.

Finally, high levels of in-program supervision are difficult to achieve when high levels of community contact are supported by the organization. Nonetheless, close monitoring of relationships between offenders and community members is possible. Such monitoring does not mean following an offender through the daily round of activities; it does mean making careful arrangements with the offender and community members—family, employers, school officials, friends—about the ground rules for external contact and periodic checks to see that these rules are followed.

Such arrangements are made necessary in part to insure that community residents do not harm program members by providing them with opportunities for troublesome behavior. In the programs we observed, the near certainty of finding illegal drugs and alcohol at local parties and teenage gathering spots such as beaches and rock concerts forced staff to place some areas of the community off-limits to the youths in their programs.

Careful monitoring of relationships outside the programs is enormously time-consuming and tends to preclude in-program supervision, however. Only one of the residential programs we observed (Group) devoted the staff time necessary to work on overseeing community ties for the two or three (out of ten) residents who had community-contact privileges. A major reason for the infrequency of close oversight of community contact in the programs we observed may well have been the group nature of the programs selected for study. Individual counseling relationships are more appropriate to the monitoring of community contacts and would eliminate any need for in-program supervision.

In programs closed to the community, supervision serves to subdue the expression of inmate subcultures and to control relationships and behavior. Obviously such results might also be achieved by a system of solitary confinement or enforced silence, but these controls are unlikely to appear under any other coercive arrangements. Equality between inmates and staff and the development of varied, meaningful, and attractive activities are essential both to the success of supervision and to keep it from being merely dictatorial repression—despite tendencies in that direction.

Summary of Empirical Propositions
Concerning Supervision

1. In-program supervision is more difficult to achieve the greater the level of community contact.
2. The greater the supervision, the more attenuated is the inmate social structure.
3. The greater the supervision, the lower is the frequency of rule

violations within the program, particularly physical violence and escapes.

POPULATION COMPOSITION

Correctional administrators have little or no power to control who enters their system. The characteristics of the people who are ultimately subject to correctional supervision are highly significant, however, for—as the data analysis indicates—they influence the nature of inmate subcultures and may limit the degree and manner in which equality, community contact, participation, and supervision can be effectively developed. Although homogeneous in the sense that they come largely from the lower classes of our society, prisoners differ in simple but fundamentally important ways—in sex, age, race or ethnicity, and criminal experience and commitment. These variables contribute in roughly that order to variations in inmate systems. Our data are limited, of course, to programs for adolescents and to a state where the minority population is relatively low; in this section, therefore, only a brief review and analysis of what problems, limitations, or opportunities population composition creates for those concerned with directing the development of inmate systems will be undertaken. Some cautions about the extent to which this analysis applies beyond Massachusetts and beyond youth corrections will, however, be suggested.

Sex Composition

Although far from conclusive, the Massachusetts DYS data provide evidence that carefully supervised coeducational programs have advantages over single-sex programs because they dilute the sex-related subcultures and reduce the disruptive and debilitating behavior associated with them. These sex-related subcultures tended to emerge in varying degrees in all the noncoeducational programs we observed, and led to troublesome behavior in all but those programs with the highest levels of participation or supervision.

Obviously the vast overrepresentation of males in adult and juvenile correctional settings (females constituted about 3 percent of the adult prison population and 23 percent of the juvenile correctional population in 1974) will prevent changes in the sex composition of most correctional programs.[36] Community contact may, however, serve as a substitute to in-house coeducation when it gives youths or adults regular opportunities for interaction with members of the other sex. Significant increases in contact with mothers, wives, and female friends, for example, might have moderating effects on inmate systems of men and boys. Since the intensification of the sex-based subcultures causes problems for staff and inmates alike, changes in sex composition alone might ease some of the burdens created by inmate systems.

Sex composition also appears to have some special effects on self-perceptions and inmates' conceptions of staff. Youths in programs with high proportions of males generally have a lower sense of personal efficacy and are more likely to perceive the staff as rule-oriented than do youths in programs with low proportions of males. The loss of freedom at a time when adolescents are striving for independence and self-reliance—qualities that are part of the traditional masculine sex role—appears to strike boys especially hard. It may be, therefore, that males will respond with special eagerness to chances to participate in decision-making and to demonstrate their adulthood. The more programs can sponsor such affirmation of adult roles—for boys especially—the less likely it may be that they will seek to prove it through violence and defiant rule violations.[37]

Age Composition

Given the lack of substantial variation in the ages of the youths we observed, it is not surprising that age composition contributed little to our quantitative analyses of variations in inmate systems. Age composition did, however, affect the way staff members saw their abilities to handle their populations. Older populations tended to be viewed as more difficult to work with, as "tougher kids." The field observations, however, provide unsystematic evidence that even the minor differences in age composition we observed had some impact on the success of implementing one mode of egalitarian organization rather than another.

The observations suggest that participation will prove easier to establish with an older population, and supervision with a younger one. The degree of responsibility, the sense of and concern with self, the introspection and social sensitivity that are called upon and cultivated to one degree or another in participatory organizations of varying ideologies are probably more often found in fifteen to eighteen year olds than in twelve to fourteen year olds. It is possible, however, that even some of the youngest offenders would be able to take on greater responsibilities if they were offered.

On the other hand, younger teenagers may be more easily satisfied by a vigorous round of recreational and educational activities (about which they have little say); they may still be more absorbed by games and activity and less resentful of the rigor and egalitarian regimentation imposed upon them in a heavily supervised program such as Regiment or Reward. These hypotheses about the consequences of the age composition of youth populations suggest possible difficulties (but not impossibilities) in implementing certain kinds of organizational changes for particular kinds of inmate populations.

Beyond the implications of the variations in the ages of the youths we studied, there remains a crucial age-related question about the degree to which the findings and policy analyses in this book apply to adult as well as to youth corrections. While apparently the same general analysis will hold for adults as for youths, the extension must be cautious. In particular the adult nature of an inmate population is likely to limit or alter the implementation of some combinations of these four organizational dimensions.

It will likely first affect both the nature of staff-inmate equality and the willingness of administration and staff to move toward more egalitarian relationships. Movement away from authoritarian relationships between staff and inmates is far easier with youth than adult populations because age differences between staff and youths and the accompanying differences in experience, size, and strength continue to provide staff with a measure of authority and power despite the absence of guns, uniforms, keys, and terms of respectful address. Complete equality between youths and staff members thus is never achieved, although youths—because of the contrast to their low status with respect to most adults in the free community—are likely to perceive moderate levels of equality as substantial gains. For adult offenders and staff members, no such age and size differences exist to sustain authority when official symbols of it and supports for it are removed.

Without alternative sources of authority, staff members in adult correctional settings are thus particularly likely to resist attempts to take away the external trappings of power and authority. Such resistance, however, is premised on the very tenuous nature of their official authority in the face of inmate resistance and hostility. As we have seen, the uniforms and military titles are hollow symbols, indeed, and the correctional officers who are most respected and powerful are those who build personal relationships with inmates over the boundaries of the inmate and staff roles.

The actual basis of staff authority in adult prisons is, therefore, the kind of personal authority and mutual trust that egalitarian relationships tend to promote. Rather than undermining guard authority, staff-inmate equality should help remove the real and symbolic sources of division and antagonism and bring to the surface the source of authority and control that operates most effectively even in the authoritarian and bureaucratic prison setting.

Whether or not an inmate population is composed of adults may also affect the kinds of participation that offenders perceive as meaningful, just as it may affect their ability to engage in it effectively. As Fogel observes in discussing the responsibilities of a staff-inmate council, it must not merely "be involved at the level of choosing the school colors."[38] Adult offenders are likely to demand a substantially greater role in decision-making and more significant responsibilities than juvenile offenders, who may be satisfied with more superficial involvement in program affairs.

Finally, adults are unlikely to accept the kind of supervision that youths do without significant levels of participation. Egalitarian supervision probably can occur with youths because, in a sense, the unusual equality with adult staff members compensates for the rigorous schedule imposed on them; for adults equality would be meaningless without significant participation, although the protection provided by supervision would be appreciated by most adult offenders as much as by youths. For adults, equality, participation, and supervision would probably, of necessity, have to come as a package in closed facilities, whereas equality and individualized participation in planning community contact would have to be combined in a program open to the community.

Racial and Ethnic Composition

The Massachusetts DYS data analyzed here—as well as the data reported by others such as Carroll and Davidson[39]—indicate that blacks and other minorities have a somewhat greater sense of group solidarity than do whites in correctional settings.[40] This sense of group identification and support could create barriers to correctional change by sustaining inmate resistance to staff efforts to be egalitarian and to penetrate prisoner groups by establishing positive relationships with their members. In contrast, the typical lack of cohesion and loyalty among inmates makes the staff task of fostering social bonds in an egalitarian organization much easier.

The presence of larger numbers of minority-group members would seem to require several special adaptations not found in or generally necessary in Massachusetts. The first, of course, is to vastly increase the number of correctional personnel who share minority status with youth or adult offenders. Second, it seems essential to legitimate rather than repress the expression of political views and ideologies that have in recent years been articulated, particularly by some minority-group members. Staff suppression of political views would make attempts to attain equality impossible, while recognition of political views through opportunities for public expression and debate would hold that possibility open. Third, one must accept the likelihood that if some freedom of choice is allowed offenders about their living situation, considerable self-segregation by race and ethnicity might result. The implications of racial composition for how one organizes a program are considerable, it appears, but unfortunately our limited data (and the limited research in this area) make hypothesizing difficult.

Criminal History

One of the fascinating characteristics of the deinstitutionalized DYS system is its mixing of court-committed delinquent youths with other young people who come to programs from social agencies and through private referrals. Commitment to DYS by the courts is not a certain sign of a serious criminal career, however, nor is lack of a commitment an indication of inexperience with crime. Perhaps as a consequence this mixture of delinquents and nondelinquents was less significant for the character of inmate life than one might have supposed; "percentage DYS" was almost never among the significant predictors of aspects of inmate systems in the quantitative analysis.

For youths, among whom variations in development of criminal careers may not be so great as among adults, this finding should not be surprising. What the youths have in common—age-, sex-, social class-related experiences and beliefs—are far greater than the differences in experience with delinquency that may separate them. When criminal history served, however, as an indicator of differences on some of these more fundamental variables, it was related, at least indirectly, to the character of inmate systems.

In closed programs using the group-treatment model, this mix of DYS youths with others was particularly important. Our observations at Primal and Confront show that the crucial aspect of the mixture was not only the difference in criminal experience but the concomitant differences in social class, education, and therapeutic experience. Privately referred youths (and adults) were far more disposed toward and experienced in the emotional expression; verbalization, and self-analysis required in these concept houses, and they were therefore crucial to maintaining these values against the initial resistance of a largely lower- or working-class DYS clientle with little therapeutic experience.

Self-conceptions of individuals also varied with the nature of their offenses. Our data, for example, show that youth populations with higher proportions of status offenders were more likely to have higher proportions of youths who viewed themselves as "having problems" or "trying to go straight." As individual and normative group conceptions of self vary, so also will the willingness of inmates to accept particular treatment ideologies and to engage in particular kinds of programs. The nature of the offenses people commit thus may be an important indicator of the extent to which an individual or group is oriented toward a particular correctional philosophy and organization.

Differences in the criminal experience or history of the inmate populations are thus probably less important than the distribution of other associated characteristics, such as self-conception or education and social class, for the character of inmate systems. Given greater variation on this variable, however, as in adult prison populations, it might become more important to the differential development of inmate systems and the implementation of varying organizational strategies.

Although subject only to limited control by correctional officials, the characteristics of inmate populations create limits and opportunities for organizational innovation and help shape the ultimate response of prisoners to their correctional experience. Correctional planning and organization cannot sensibly be undertaken without an awareness of the potential for differences in response from varying inmate populations. Nor should the limited possibilities that do exist for controlling population composition—particularly in a decentralized correctional system with many small and varied programs—be ignored in the planning process. Despite their significance, however, variations in the composition of inmate populations did not contribute nearly as much to differences in most aspects of inmate systems as did the variations in organizational structure. It is clearly with adjustments in the latter variables that most of the hope lies for directing the development of inmate systems.

Summary of Empirical Propositions Concerning Inmate Population Composition

1. The lower the levels of participation and supervision, the greater the impact of population composition on the character of inmate systems.
2. A program population composed of males and females leads to substantial moderations of the sex-based subcultures otherwise evident.

RESTRUCTURING CORRECTIONAL SYSTEMS: PUTTING VARIED ORGANIZATIONS TOGETHER

Although this study has focused on designing individual correctional organizations in order to direct or control the development of the inmate systems in them, it has significant implications for the organization of whole correctional systems. Among the most important lessons of this analysis of program organization is that not all correctional goals can be achieved in a single program; they may, however, be more nearly achieved in a system of many semiautonomous, small programs with varied organizational structures. Each of these programs can be organized to prevent the development of destructive and disruptive inmate systems and thus contribute to the humanity and order of the correctional process.

Diversifying the programs in the system will not only reinforce the achievement of this goal but, by opening up the possibility of new system-wide strategies, will take the edge off the inevitable failures of individual programs to achieve some correctional goals. Where individual programs may fail, the system can succeed. In contrast, the current reliance of most states on a few large institutions that vary only in security level or sex composition simply compounds the individual deficiencies of similar organizations into system-wide failures.[41]

Introducing significant *variation* into the organization of programs in a correctional system first allows greater individualization of placement of persons with vastly differing needs and wishes and, with this personalization, greater voluntarism in the placement process. By giving convicted offenders a meaningful and informed role in the initial placement process and, perhaps, in later petitioning for transfers to other programs, several problems may be overcome.[42] Such a system would replace either uninformed or often paternalistic clinical decisions made by a team of classification experts with some degree of individual choice by most offenders. The inherent shortcomings of coerced cures may thus be avoided and the effectiveness of rehabilitation programs increased through the limited self-selection of clientele.

In addition, the costs of a particular kind of correctional organization may be decreased through the mechanism of *free choice*. Someone who agrees to enter a program where certain rights or privileges are denied (for example, in a concept house) must implicitly accept that loss as the price of possible and desired rehabilitation. The trade-off between high levels of community contact and humane treatment on the one hand and intensive psychological treatment on the other becomes less troublesome when the decision about entering a program is, in part, the inmate's. The availability of diverse programs may further dull the sharpness of the division between community contact and participation/supervision. Individuals within a system, if not a single program, might move from one kind of program to another, presumably increasing the level of community contact as they move through the system. What one program cannot by itself do might be done in sequence through two or more programs.

Finally, the combination of diverse programs and some degree of choice in entering them should increase the degree of control egalitarian programs can exert over their members. Diversity allows the inclusion in the system of a limited number of more coercive programs—physically secure and heavily supervised—to back up more egalitarian ones and to handle those people who demonstrate that they cannot refrain from theft, violence, or running away. The restrained and rule-governed use of such coercive facilities should enhance control particularly when offenders help choose their initial placement. The contrast in attractiveness between the chosen program and the back-up facilities should improve the likelihood that inmates will abide by rules, as will the implicit social contract they enter, which entails a promise to obey the rules in return for admission to the program. Diversity of programs and a degree of offender choice in placement in a correctional system thus should enhance the effectiveness of individual egalitarian organizations.

In addition to diversity and choice, our data suggest that a correctional system should contain programs of *limited size*. The implementation of some organizational strategies appears to depend in part on program size, and size alone in our research—even given its small range of variation—had a direct effect on some aspects of youth-staff relationships. Greater size was associated with youth perceptions of low staff consistency, an indication that developing more cohesive, consistent, and nonbureaucratic programs in corrections would be much easier in small units. Similarly size, in the sense of higher ratios of youths to staff members, decreased the likelihood of more than one close personal relationship between youths and staff. In addition, the full participation of inmates or close supervision of them, as well as the arrangement of community contacts for them, grow significantly more difficult as program size expands. Although we observed one extremely successful concept house with nearly eighty residents, it appears that a size of from roughly ten to thirty-five participants is ideally suited to the variations in egalitarian organization.

It may not be enough, therefore, for a few innovative programs to be inserted into existing systems of training schools or prisons. For correctional systems to achieve the goal of orderly and humane punishment through control over the development of inmate under-life, the systems themselves must change fundamentally. Moving from a centralized system of a few large and rather similar institutions to one of many small and diverse organizations would increase the ability of any one program to achieve its goals and would enhance the overall success of the system.

The coercive, semibureaucratic organization of massive congregate prisons and large though campus-like training schools has served long enough as the model for systems of corrections. Whatever its responsibility for the failure to rehabilitate prisoners, this organizational style has directly contributed to the development and persistence of disorderly, destructive, and debilitating inmate responses to confinement. Alternative modes of organization exist, however, that can do much to secure humane living conditions for prisoners and order for correctional administrators. The adoption of any of these alternatives rests on the development of far more egalitarian relationships between prisoners and their captors than the coercive and hierarchical model of penal institutions now encourages or envisions.

Ultimately, organizational change rests upon an adjustment in our perception of the meaning of punishment and correction. We are apparently in the midst of a decade of such readjustment, but it is by no means certain that the new vision will foster the organizational changes described and advocated here. I hope that the battle in each of us and in the society as a whole between the impulses toward harsh punishment and humane concern will be won by the latter forces. There is historic precedent if not great immediate hope for such victory. Only with it, however, will come the changes in correctional organization needed to overcome the most remediable of the failures of corrections in the United States.

NOTES

1. Although only of peripheral interest given the purposes of this book, recidivism data were painstakingly gathered nonetheless. They proved to be so flawed, however, that they are not reported here. Three problems in particular reduced the meaningfulness of the data, especially those from the community-based programs. First, over one third of the youths in the community-based programs had been in at least one other program immediately prior to or after their experience in the programs where we observed them. Separating the effects on recidivism of one program from another was impossible. Second, the quality of centralized record-keeping was low during the initial years of the community-based system, and as a result in about one-fifth of the cases we could not learn the departure date of youths from the programs we had observed them in. Setting a starting time for calculating recidivism rates during the six months or one year *after release* was thus often difficult. Third, one of the larger

programs we observed was out-of-state, and we had no assurance that persons recidivating from that program in particular would do so in Massachusetts, the only state where we had access—under strict guidelines—to criminal record information. None of these problems affected Feld's data as seriously, and he reports recidivism rates for the ten training school cottages analyzed here in his volume in this series, *Neutralizing Inmate Violence.* Nor do the second and third problems arise in the cohort study of DYS youths (see Preface), which followed youths closely (through a series of interviews) during and after their commitment to DYS and thus avoided reliance on sketchy official records. The first problem still affects the analysis and interpretation of recidivism rates and as here, prevents clear conclusions about the effectiveness of *individual* programs. Recidivism rates for types of programs and for types of sequences through several programs as well as for the state and various regions within it are available in that study, however. That research is reported in Coates, Miller, and Ohlin, *Diversity in a Youth Correctional System,* in this series.

2. Quoted in Gordon Hawkins, *The Prison: Policy and Practice* (Chicago: University of Chicago Press, 1975); Gresham Sykes, *The Society of Captives: A Study of a Maximum Security Prison* (Princeton, N.J.: Princeton University Press, 1958), p. 53.

3. Once again Walter Miller's work on status classes and their attendant subcultures has strongly shaped my thinking. See Walter B. Miller, "Subcultures, Social Reform, and the 'Culture of Poverty,'" *Human Organization* 30 (Summer 1971):111-25.

4. Sykes, *Society of Captives,* pp. 40-62.

5. The apparently paradoxical fact that reform efforts in prisons for men often lead to riots can be understood in terms of the failure of such attempts to substitute new, official opportunities for inmate leadership and achievement for the unofficial ones that so frequently are denied or disrupted in the change process. Prison reform itself need not cause unrest if new opportunities are substituted for the old ones.

6. Rose Giallombardo, *Society of Women: A Study of a Women's Prison* (New York: Wiley, 1966).

7. Maureen Kelleher, "Review of *The Social World of Imprisoned Girls,*" *Contemporary Sociology: A Journal of Reviews* 4 (November 1975):384.

8. See Hawkins's review of this scanty literature, in *The Prison,* pp. 81-107.

9. Don C. Gibbons, *Society, Crime, and Criminal Careers: An Introduction to Criminology,* 3d ed. (Englewood Cliffs, N.J.: Prentice-Hall, 1972), p. 491. It is evident that these checks are not always adequate, as the Report of the Special Commission on Attica, (reprinted in *Attica: The Official Report of the New York Special Commission on Attica* (New York: Bantam, 1972), among other documents, makes clear. Nevertheless, despite continuing abuses, brutal coercion by officials in contemporary U.S. prisons is severely curtailed in comparison to its historic uses. Twenty-four-hour lock-ups are occasionally resorted to in times of crisis, but typically there is considerable pressure to return to a normal routine as quickly as possible.

10. See, for example, the description of a moderately successful experiment in equality in one wing of a fairly traditional reformatory in Elliot Studt,

Sheldon Messinger, and Thomas Wilson, *C-Unit: Search for Community in Prisons* (New York: Russell Sage Foundation, 1968).

11. See David Fogel, *We Are the Living Proof: The Justice Model for Corrections* (Cincinnati: Anderson, 1975), pp. 263–66, for an example of such a design for a decentralized unit for adults.

12. Although I strongly believe that significantly shorter prison sentences are essential to a fair and effective penal system, my research does not bear on this issue, and I shall not digress to argue for shorter sentences. As a matter of policy, however, I would not want more humane conditions of incarceration to justify long sentences for juveniles and adults. During Commissioner Miller's administration of DYS, the length of stay in training school cottages and then community programs was supposed to be about three months, a significant reduction from past expectations. Such a reduction is nearly inseparable, it seems to me, from other reforms in the correctional system.

13. I am assuming that likelihood of a punishment (some loss of freedom) is a more potent deterrent than severity of punishment (the harshness of life experience by persons who lose their freedom). See, for example, Johannes Andenaes, *Punishment and Deterrence* (Ann Arbor: University of Michigan Press, 1974), p. 54.

14. For a criticism of community corrections and decarceration that highlights this problem, see Anthony Scull, *Decarceration: Community Treatment and the Deviant—A Radical View* (Englewood Cliffs, N.J.: Prentice-Hall, 1976).

15. Fogel, *We Are Living Proof*, p. 209.

16. The organizational traits indicating staff equalization have much more to do with shared decision-making and responsibility than do the indicators of staff-inmate equality. Participation has been isolated as a distinctive dimension for inmates.

17. See Hawkins, *The Prison*, pp. 81–107.

18. James Q. Wilson, *Varieties of Police Behavior: The Management of Law and Order in Eight Communities* (Cambridge: Harvard University Press, 1968).

19. For a discussion of the nature and effectiveness of the full range of community programs, see Robert Coates, Alden Miller, and Lloyd Ohlin, *Diversity in a Youth Correctional System: Handling Delinquents in Massachusetts*, in this series.

20. In theory, higher community contact may also carry less stigma for the offender, and therefore have fewer debilitating effects on self-conception and opportunities than more closed programs. Similarly, in theory at least, programs with high community contact—especially nonresidential programs— should be considerably cheaper to run than closed programs.

21. Although, almost by definition, programs with high community contact are less punitive, that does not necessarily mean that their capacity for deterrence is seriously jeopardized. Unfortunately, we have no evidence on that issue. Our observations gave no indication that community protection was lowered by community contact, however. The problem in open programs was not so much to protect citizens from delinquents on the loose as it was to protect program members from evil influences in the community. Obviously

community contact could jeopardize community protection if there were not moderate care exercised in selecting the people to have such contact.

22. We observed the use of such techniques at several programs in the community system such as Regiment and Group, but none of these was among the programs with highest community contact. Similarly, the Probation Subsidy Program and the Community Treatment Project in California (see Norval Morris, *The Future of Imprisonment* [Chicago: University of Chicago Press, 1974], pp. 11–12) and the Pinehills project (see Lamar Empey and Maynard Erickson, *The Provo Experiment: Evaluating Community Control of Delinquency* [Lexington, Mass.: D.C. Health, 1973]) used coercive techniques as a back-up control.

23. "Intensive" means a case load closer to five to ten youths (or adults) than to the fifty and up that typically burden probation and probation and parole officers.

24. Participation with the counselor in planning a course of individual activities, goals, and relationships would have obvious personal meaning to the individual offender whose life is being charted. One cannot expect the same commitment to and participation in the planning of activities for an artificially constructed group (such as Drop-in or Pick-up) when the continuing individual ties of program members are likely to be far more inviting and important. Decisions about collective welfare in programs with high community contact are not very important because the collectivity is of little concern to the individual.

25. See, for example, Edgar Schein, "Reaction Patterns to Severe, Chronic Stress in American Army Prisoners of War of the Chinese," in *Basic Studies in Social Psychology*, ed. Harold Proshansky and Bernard Seidenberg (New York: Holt, Rinehart, and Winston, 1965), pp. 638–45; and Bao Ruo-Wang (Jean Pasqualini) and Rudolph Chelminski, *Prisoner of Mao* (New York: Coward, McCann and Geoghegan, 1973).

26. It is interesting to note that three of the eleven youths removed ran away while or after being returned home and went back to Primal on their own.

27. Hawkins, *The Prison*, p. 26.

28. For a general review of the history of inmate self-government, see J.E. Baker, "Inmate Self-Government and the Right to Participate," in *Correctional Institutions*, ed. Robert Carter, Daniel Glaser, and Leslie Wilkins, 2nd ed. (Philadelphia: Lippincott, 1977), pp. 320–32.

29. John L. Gillin, *Criminology and Penology*, 3rd ed. (New York: Appleton-Century, 1945), p. 392. See also Fred Haynes, *Criminology* (New York: McGraw-Hill, 1930), pp. 281–300.

30. Haynes, *Criminology*, p. 285.

31. Fred Haynes, *The American Prison System* (New York: McGraw-Hill, 1939), pp. 59–87.

32. Lawrence Kohlberg, Peter Scharf, and Joseph Hickey, "The Justice Structure of the Prison," *Beyond Time: Connecticut Journal of Criminal Justice* 1 (Fall 1973):1–8.

33. See, for example, Fogel's discussion of the resistance to the idea, in *We Are Living Proof*, pp. 214–15.

34. Many other ideologies might be transmitted to inmates through participatory organization, including other political beliefs or religious dogmas. The success of the Nation of Islam in prisons—although not officially sponsored—appears to depend in part on its participatory organizational style.

35. Our observation suggested, however, that in very small closed programs (under 10), staff could quite readily keep track of youths despite a lack of activities; the youths, however, disliked the boredom.

36. National Criminal Justice Information and Statistics Service, *Prisoners in State and Federal Institutions on December 31, 1974* (Washington, D.C.: U.S. Government Printing Office, 1975).

37. I do not wish here to enter a debate about how much programs should reinforce conventional sex-role definitions or try to liberate people from them. Although I personally believe there should be some pressure toward liberation, I also recognize that programs must work with people already socialized into sex roles, and my impression of the youths we observed in 1973 was that there views were generally quite conventional.

38. Fogel, *We Are Living Proof*, p. 214.

39. Leo Carroll, *Hacks, Blacks and Cons* (Lexington, Mass.: D.C. Heath, 1974); and R. Theodore Davidson, *Chicano Prisoners: The Key to San Quentin* (New York: Holt, Rinehart and Winston, 1974).

40. The data show populations with higher proportions of blacks to be generally less cohesive than those with lower proportions, but blacks as individuals express no less or more affection for their peers as a whole (including whites) than do whites. This finding thus is not inconsistent with our strong observational evidence of higher cohesion among blacks within those general populations. In fact, one might surmise that it is that higher cohesion among blacks as well as white fears and perceptions that make for lower overall inmate cohesion where blacks are more numerous.

41. Six states have, for example, only one prison for adults, and nine others utilize two to four massive institutions. National Criminal Justice Information and Statistics Service, *Census of State Correctional Facilities, 1974, Advance Report* (Washington, D.C.: U.S. Government Printing Office, 1975). For juvenile delinquents the situation is similar; twenty states had one or two training schools in 1973, occasionally supplemented by forestry camps, group homes, and the like. National Criminal Justice Information and Statistics Service, *Children in Custody: Advance Report on the Juvenile Detention and Correctional Facility Census of 1972–73* (Washington, D.C.: U.S. Government Printing Office, 1975).

42. "Meaningful" implies that the choices, though limited by some independent assessment of the offender's "danger to the community" and capability for self-assessment, be among a real variety of programs. It also implies that the decision should not be indirectly coerced through anticipation of what a parole board might look upon with favor.

✳ *Appendix*

Descriptions of Community-Based Programs Observed in the 1973 Subculture Study

The brief descriptions in Chapter 1 of the thirteen community-based programs for delinquents included in the 1973 subculture study can only begin to depict the character and variety of these settings. This appendix contains somewhat lengthier descriptions of these programs in order to fill some of the gaps in the descriptions in the text and to complement the more detailed portraits of the ten training school cottages that are available in Feld's volume in this series, *Neutralizing Inmate Violence.* For readers unfamiliar with the enormous variety of possibilities for handling delinquent youths that a community-based system helps to make available, these descriptions provide a more detailed introduction. For other readers it should serve to highlight some of the features that made each of these programs distinctive.

INSTITUTIONAL PROGRAMS

Warning

According to its brochure, Warning was "a secure intensive care program for hardcore juvenile offenders," and its location on the second floor of a three-story brick building built and still used in part as a juvenile detention center did nothing to belie that description. From thirty to forty 14- to 17-year-old boys who were committed to DYS by the courts from a large section of the state made their homes for three to six months in the small, individually decorated double rooms that lined both sides of the second-floor corridor.

The boys, half of whom were black, spent their time in a variety of loosely structured activities. Many wandered around, talked in small groups, and listented to radios, watched television, or played pool in the two large common rooms. Some boys took advantage of the individualized teaching program in a downstairs classroom, and most boys participated in occasional basketball games in an upstairs gym or outdoor activities in the fenced-in yard at the back of the building. Although the doors of the building were locked, the program was focused on developing or rebuilding ties between boys and their communities. So some of the residents went out daily to work, and others if in good standing could leave to visit family or friends on passes for a weekend, an evening, or an afternoon.

Of the nearly thirty staff people, at least one-third were ex-offenders who could, it was thought, talk the boys' language, gain their respect, and, by describing the horrors of prison life and the futility of crime, warn them away from continued law breaking. They and other staff members "rapped" with the boys individually, exhorted them in groups, played pool and basketball with them, and accompanied them singly or in groups on excusions into the community. One staff member devoted all his time to the criminal cases still pending against a number of the Warning residents, and he and several administrators often spoke up for the boys in court. The five aftercare workers and teachers were the only women on the full-time staff.

Fatigue

Operated for over forty years by a charitable agency, Fatigue was located in a battle-scarred, four-story, three-wing brick building in the middle of an urban neighborhood of frame three-deckers. Of the twenty-five 12- to 16-year-old boys who lived at Fatigue during the summer,[1] seven were placed there by DYS, and the remainder by other state social-service agencies. All the boys had some kind of family problem that caused the typical placements at Fatigue to exceed one year. There were nearly equal numbers of blacks and whites in both the youth population and on the staff.

The boys lived in one wing, dispersed among three units where each resident occupied a single or double room furnished with desks, book shelves (uniformly bare), and bedrooms were decorated, with few restrictions, by the boys themselves. Each floor had a two-room apartment for the child-care counselor who lived in on a 72-hour shift, alternating with a partner.

Functional lines clearly divided the seventeen summer staff into five distinct groups—administrators, social workers, teachers, child-care workers, and support personnel (in declining order of professional credentials and prestige). Acting on the philosophy that idle hands are mischievous ones, the young men who were the child-care workers carried the heaviest burden in the summer because the four individualized classes of six to eight students lasted only from 9–11:30 a.m. The remainder of the time had to be filled by these men who used $10–$20 of recreation money daily, two vans, and considerable energy and ingenuity in an attempt to exhaust their charges in boating and picnics, bingo, drive-in movies, rides, swimming, miniature golf, and go-kart racing. Boys often opted not to go on these outings and would sign out from the unlocked building to somewhere in the city or occasionally would stay behind to do some work around the building for $1.50/hour. On weekends, boys who had accumulated enough points through promptness and cooperativeness in school and cleanliness in their living units could go home if arrangements could be made with their parents or relatives.

Mother

The water tower and the imposing, turn-of-the-century brick-and-frame architecture of the sprawling set of buildings suggested to the passerby that an old state hospital occupied the spacious grounds of Mother on the fringes of a small town. Instead, a visitor would have discovered the unusual combination of a nursing home on one side of the connected main buildings and a residential program for about twenty-five 12- to 17-year-old girls on the other. The girls, three-fifths of whom came to Mother through the Department of Youth Services, lived in three comfortable, remodeled units, each with its own kitchen, lounge, and sleeping areas to accommodate eight to nine girls in single, double, and triple rooms. Fourteen nonprofessional house mothers divided the three daily shifts in these three units; one woman was on duty in each unit at all times.

The self-conscious tradition at Mother was for house mothers to grant the girls "unconditional love," showing immense tolerance for verbal abuse, failure to do chores, runaways, and miscellaneous rule-breaking. To reduce this pattern of tolerance by the "upstairs" staff, the "downstairs" professionals (three social workers and two teachers) tried to put into practice a token economy using a point system and a regulated distribution of cigarettes as rewards. Disagreement and uncertainty about the system and inconsistency in its implementation by all staff members led to its demise soon after the end of our observation.

The accredited school program was in recess during the summer months, leaving the girls to spend their time in a variety of ways.

Planned group recreation ranged from a camping trip lasting several days to a haunted-house game, and most regularly was composed of a visit to a nearby beach. The girls were not required to join in group activities and often chose to watch TV, listen to records, play cards, crochet, or nap instead. These pastimes also filled the gaps between the irregularly scheduled group activities. In addition, five or six girls spent part of each weekday working in a nearby day-care center.

Behind Mother was a modern house where a young couple lived with and supervised four girls whom the Mother social workers deemed responsible enough to have the greater freedoms (such as to date) this house allowed. All these girls attended a local high school during the year and worked in some capacity during the summer, and thus were not fully involved in the group life of the program.

Reward

Eighty adolescent girls shared Reward's sprawling complex of modern brick buildings with several dozen nuns who had retired from the order that operated and, in part, staffed the program. Pervading the operation of Reward was the perspective expressed in an official statement of objectives: individual growth and change "is effected through the girl's increasing sense of personal worth." To achieve this goal staff members self-consciously but warmly praised the girls on their work, appearance, and disposition, and, in addition, had periodic official award ceremonies during which every girl was recognized in some way.

The residents lived in units of about twelve where each girl had her own room and shared a common room with the whole unit. Each unit was supervised by a nun who served as a group mother. Girls from the various units intermingled in the busy round of daily activities, which each girl planned at the beginning of the summer, but they spent a major part of their time in the evenings with other girls in the unit. Because of the size of the institution and the limited length of our observation, we followed the girls in only one unit, four of whom were commitments or referrals from DYS (approximately the same proportion as in the population as a whole).

Since Reward's accredited school (staffed by lay teachers) was in summer recess, only a few of the girls took academic courses, while others worked during the morning in a day-care program for retarded children, and almost all participated in some combination of classes in arts and crafts, dance and drama, guitar, swimming, tennis, beauty culture, sewing, and cooking. In addition, the girls worked for $1.85

per hour in preparing meals and serving them and in general house-keeping. Together these activities consumed almost every hour of the day; the evenings were spent in the group or unit. Girls did many of their own chores there—washing and ironing clothes, sewing, and letter writing. In addition, they found time to play card games together and to have occasional parties on birthdays or visits by recent graduates of Reward.

Each girl was encouraged to go home for a weekend once or twice a month. A staff of social workers arranged these visits and worked closely with the familes of the girls; parental agreement to cooperate with the staff was required before girls were accepted into the program. Residents remained at Reward for about a year on the average.

Regiment

Regiment utilized the upper floor of a large recreation building to house in single rooms twenty teen-age boys who were being detained for two weeks to a month while their cases were adjudicated and placements were made for those who were committed or referred to DYS. Almost all the boys at Regiment were white (there was one black on the staff), reflecting the makeup of the large working- and middle-class suburban area from which they came. The swimming pool, gym, and game room as well as the film projection equipment contained in the building Regiment used proved to be the major resources for a closely supervised round of daily activities. These were supplemented by the instruction of an arts and crafts teacher—the only woman on the staff—in one of several common rooms interspersed among the boys' rooms. Weekly outings to play softball or to drive-in movies in Regiment's decrepit van varied the regimen somewhat. During their limited free time boys watched TV in a supervised setting or visited with one another as long as no more than three boys entered a single, unsupervised room.

All boys were expected to participate in activities unless they were grounded for misbehavior or had a valid excuse (illness, court appearance, and so on). Locked doors did not bar the way of an escape, but close supervision did—the boys lined up before any group movement and marched together to the activity with one staff member at the head and one at the rear of the line. The same procedure followed for the trip down to the public cafeteria where the boys got their meals. Staff participated fully with the boys in the games and activities and talked with them informally when the boys sought them out. Several of the seventeen staff members devoted much of their time to court appearances on behalf of the youths or to seeking out placements for the boys who needed them, but they kept the rest of the staff informed about each boy through weekly staff meetings.

Shelter

Located in one of the aging four-story townhouses on a busy city street, Shelter detained up to seven teen-age girls for periods of two weeks to two months while their cases were heard in the juvenile court and placements made for them if they were committed or referred to DYS. In the same building and run by the same inter-dominational religious group were several other activities—a women's group, a religious fellowship, a neighborhood youth group. The third floor of the house was devoted to Shelter, however, and one was likely to find there several girls lounging about the large room they all shared, listening to records or the radio, napping, or crocheting. Much of the girls' time was spent in such activities, although, if the privilege had not been suspended by staff for misbehavior, girls could go out unescorted for brief periods during the day to a sub shop around the corner or for a walk in the immediate vicinity of Shelter. When the girls complained about boredom a typical staff response was, "You're here to think about yourselves and where you're going. . . ."

The group-living situation required some involvement of the girls in housekeeping and preparing food, although staff members often pitched in when girls balked at their responsibilities. Periodically the staff called community meetings to make announcements, discuss problems (failure to make beds or to empty ash trays; the disappearance of items of clothing), or to confront the girls with their misbehavior (taking obscene pictures of one another and showing them to workmen next door).

At any one time during the day several of the four to five part- or full-time professional (social workers and ministers) counselors were busy accompanying girls to medical examinations, court-appearances, and visits to possible placements; contacting the girls' social workers or probation officers; or talking individually with their counselees. The constant drain of staff time and energy in these activities tended to limit the scope and frequency of planned recreation. In the evenings and over night two of the six nonprofessional night staff attempted to keep order, get the girls to bed after watching TV, and get some rest themselves.

GROUP-TREATMENT PROGRAMS

Confront

A large parking area separated the old and new large frame houses and a modern one-floor officebuilding, symbolizing the divisions within Confront. In the two houses, nine young nonprofessional staff people worked with residential clients using group-therapy techniques, while the half dozen professional psychologists and psychiatrists in the offices worked individually with nonresidential clients and some of the residents.

During our observation the approximately twenty-five male and female residents were divided between the two unlocked houses that operated fairly autonomously. In House II seven of the fourteen residents were private patients, five of whom were adults, whereas in House I nine of the ten residents were DYS commitments.[2] This division followed a staff decision earlier in the summer that some of the DYS youths were not ready for the heavy group confrontations in House II; they were therefore moved to the vacant House I along with four staff members (leaving five staff people in House II) who led milder group confrontations—shorter ones without much screaming. Despite the division, the treatment strategies and programs were similar in the two Houses.

Weekdays began with an 8 a.m. breakfast prepared by a kitchen crew of residents and there followed a 9 a.m. meeting in which the house concept was recited, announcements were made, and residents described their "learning experiences" (punishments such as wearing a sign around one's neck). From then until lunch youths acting as crew heads and "ramrods" closely supervised a variety of housekeeping chores, including, at the extreme, picking the lint out of a rug by hand. After lunch, a two-hour seminar was scheduled that ranged in content from a discussion and recitation of nicknames to angry confrontations. An hour of free time preceded and followed the evening meal and the day was closed with a two- to three-hour group confrontation session, at which people let out their hostilities toward one another at varying decibel levels. Weekly psychodramas and a looser weekend schedule including volleyball or a beach trip varied this routine somewhat.

Staff members, all of whom had been through the program themselves, remained aloof from much of this activity, although they participated vigorously in the group confrontations and were available to talk privately with residents.

The DYS residents came from a large metropolitan area, but only two of the youths (and none of the staff) at Confront were black. During their approximately six-month stay (few DYS youths officially graduated; they just left), youths went home infrequently. Toward the end of their stay these visits increased, however, and some youths got nearby jobs in order to ease the transition to the community.

Primal

Perched on a wooded hillside in an out-of-state resort area, a square, two-story frame building with attached cement-block dormitory housed the sixty to seventy residents who participated in Primal. Since the full-time staff consisted only of eight paraprofessionals (plus several maintenance and service workers), it is not surprising that the residents had many organizational responsibilities.

A small second-floor room contained the elaborate organizational chart that classified residents by function (the departments included service, maintenance, communications, finance, business office, kitchen, and expediter (a police/watchdog role), and by position in a hierarchy (from worker up to coordinator). While part of every resident's day was devoted to carrying out these responsibilities under close supervision, a large portion of it was taken up by encounter groups, "primals" (primal scream therapy groups), and verbal "haircuts" (short sessions in which a youth was dressed down for a failure to carry out responsibilities), which went on almost nonstop. The record for "haircuts" was 75 in one day. When there was time (at meals, for example) people were required to move around and "relate" to one another. Doors were not locked, but runaways were rare; cross-country staff pursuit and capture of several runners was legend within Primal.

The residents were a mix of private patients (some of whom were in their twenties) from upper- and middle-income homes and of DYS commitments in about a 2-to-1 ratio, and they lived side by side in several men's and women's dormitories—large rooms with bunks and upright metal lockers for each resident. Primal was typically home for these young people for over a year, at which time they began reentry by taking a job in a nearby town and proving they could make it on their own. Visits home were rare during the period of their residence.

Group

A glance at the modern, ranch-style house in a mixed residential-industrial area of a residential suburb would have revealed no evidence that it housed Group, a program for nine to eleven boys or young men from 16–20 years of age. Most of these residents came to Group from DYS, but, during our observation, two clients were privately supported and one was sponsored by welfare. Although one of the seven male staff members occasionally took some or all of the boys to a nearby beach or a drive-in movie, daily morning and tri-weekly evening group meetings were the major focus of collective activity. The staff members sat with the boys in a large circle in the comfortable living room, and together they talked about the difficulties people were having with one another in the house, and the personal feelings and problems of individuals. The residents were asked to participate in decisions about restricting the privileges of residents for rule violations or for bad attitudes, and were encouraged to praise their peers for progress or friendliness.

In between these group meetings, activities varied immensely— one resident worked full-time as an apprentice in a neighboring factory, three others attended local summer high school courses part-time, and a fourth commuted to a private technical school. Contacts outside the house were prohibited during the first month of the expected six-month residence, but, after this ground was lifted by majority vote of all present at group meeting, boys could go out unescorted, with staff permission, to specific destinations for limited times. Because none of the boys was from the community where Group was located, the most attractive destination for many was a neighborhood store. Lifting the ground also opened the possibility of carefully planned one-day or weekend trips home to supplement the Wednesday visits of parents to Group. Typically the boys spent their time around the house doing chores (they prepared most of their own meals and did their own cleaning and laundry), watching TV in the living room, or listening to records in one of the three small individually decorated rooms where the boys slept. In addition, they frequently talked seriously or kidded around with one another or with staff members in pairs or in groups.

The nonhierarchical, all-male staff included a professional psychologist, two former program members, and another counselor who were all in their twenties; it was one of the latter three who slept overnight in one of the staff rooms. A Catholic priest, a psychiatric nurse, and the residence director were all in their thirties. In addition to serving as counselors, they tried to find jobs or make school arrangements for the boys.

Open House
Open House was one of nineteen halfway houses of various kinds within an eight-block area of large, old frame homes and tree-lined

streets. The eight 15- to 17-year-olds (four boys and four girls) who occupied the house came mostly from the city in which the program was located, and were expected to be in the program for three to four months. Two of the eight residents and one of the seven staff members were black.

Although the staff cited positive peer pressure as one tool of the program, the residents were rarely together in the roomy house or in group activities. Coming and going with considerable freedom, they attended local schools, worked in nearby jobs, or visited with local friends. The freedom to come and go was congruent with an official program description which noted, "We view the community as an essential testing ground for each youth." Several residents without local ties, however, were left to their own devices in the house where the TV and a pool table were strong attractions.

The five, young, long-haired, college-educated staff counseled "their kids" individually and also met with them as a group several evenings a week. In the brief group meetings they made announcements and let one of the older residents take the lead in identifying the failures of residents in doing the housekeeping chores that were divided among them. Occasional trips to a drive-in movie and the daily evening meal were other times when the Open House residents were all together.

OPEN-COMMUNITY PROGRAMS

Drop-in

Two flights up and next to O'Hara's Gym in a row of commercial buildings was a long room overlooking and overhearing a noisy street in an urban, white working-class neighborhood. This room was the home of Drop-in, and the neighborhood was the source of its clients who were placed there after being referred or committed to DYS. About fifteen to twenty boys and girls between the ages of 13 and 17 were expected to drop by Drop-in regularly during the afternoon or evening to talk with their counselors, to shoot pool (about the only item of furniture in the room was a pool table), and to participate in the occasional group activities, which ranged from a trip to a distant beach to a downtown movie. Despite a new rule that the irregularly distributed $5 weekly allowances were contingent upon fifteen hours a week of participation, staff still found it difficult to induce all their clients to take part regularly in program activities.

Two case workers (one man and one woman) met with youths at the center but spent much of their time in court, locating jobs, talking to school officials, and, less often, working with families. In addition, they supervised the work of four college student counselors who planned and supervised group activities and when possible talked with the youths individually or in groups. Drop-in's brochure contended that such "horizontal, nonprofessional, informal relationships create a rapport conductive [*sic*] to effective counseling."

Pick-up

Pick-up was a program that could be identified only with people since it had no physical home in the small city in which it operated. After a number of evening phone calls to make the arrangements, staff members converged the following morning in a coffee shop in a suburban shopping center to make their plans for the day. Three days a week several of these men would disperse to locate as many of the fifteen or so 12- to 17-year-old boys in their program as they could and take them to the planned activity for the day. On the other two days, staff members would make home visits, go to court with their own clients, or interview prospective members. Three of the men who made up the staff (two full- and one part-time) were ex-salesmen; of the three other staff, one was a college student, and two were, to quote one of them, "grown-up street kids." All the staff members and boys were white.

Activities were specifically planned to appeal to the boys and to give them opportunities they did not otherwise have: visiting an amusement park, fishing, boating, swimming, building bicycles from spare parts, and refurbishing a wooden boat.

During these activities staff casually engaged the boys in conversation when possible to try to establish rapport with them and to challenge them to think about their lives. In addition, the staff members worked to find jobs for some of the older boys and to iron out conflicts between the boys and their families, their school teachers, and the police.

Pair

In one of the houses in the middle of fraternity row on a small-town university campus lived from ten to sixteen young people who were paired off into four to seven student-advocate teams. College students took the summer job as advocates at $70 per week plus room, and were matched by sex and race with "students" who were youths over sixteen committed to DYS from the surrounding communities.[3] Three full-time adminstrator-coordinator-supervisors were not paired off with the students, but they occasionally participated in the daily life of the program. Together these people comprised the open and loosely structured Pair program.

To manage the group-living situation, daily chores were assigned on a rotating basis to advocate-student pairs, and occasional community meetings were held for announcements and some decision-making (whether or not to have a keg of beer for of-age staff and guests but not DYS youths at an upcoming open-house; the decision: unanimously no—unfair and too tempting). But the real program activity revolved around the pairings as each advocate tried to keep his student active and motivated. Spur-of-the-moment decisions to go swimming or to a movie, to attempt a several-day camping trip, and to visit with friends of the advocates comprised the organized program.

Some of the youths had part-time jobs obtained through the Neighborhood Youth Corps, and one was finishing the school year in a local public school. Talking, watching TV, shooting baskets, reading comics, going shopping (spending $5 weekly allowance or earnings) occupied many of the hours of both youths and their advocates. The key to the program and its attempt to guide and control its participants was supposed to be the close relationship between each youth and his or her advocate, a relationship that was intended to grow from the time of the initial interview between a DYS youngster and an advocate at the regional detention center.

NOTES

1. During the summer when Fatigue was observed that the usual population of 50–60 had been divided so that about half of the boys lived at a rural camp owned by the agency and half remained in the city.

2. At the start of our observation, the residents were all boys, but three girls were added about two weeks later to moderate the "male chauvinism" that had become rampant in House I. The three girls raised the House I population from seven to ten.

3. During the academic year, Pair drew its advocates by offering them course credit, and the "students" shared rooms with their advocates in college dormitories. The summer group-living experience was thus different from the program during the remainder of the year.

Selected Bibliography

Adamek, Raymond, and Dager, Edward. "Social Structure, Identification and Change in a Treatment-Oriented Institution." *American Sociological Review* 33 (1968): 931-44.

Akers, Ronald; Hayner, Norman; and Gruninger, Werner. "Homosexual and Drug Behavior in Prison: A Test of the Functional and Importation Models of the Inmate System." *Social Problems* 21 (1974): 410-22.

American Friends Service Committee. *Struggle for Justice.* New York: Hill and Wang, 1971.

Andenaes, Johannes. *Punishment and Deterrence.* Ann Arbor: University of Michigan Press, 1974.

Angell, Robert. "Integration: Social Integration." *International Encyclopedia of the Social Sciences.* 1968. Vol. 7.

Arnold, David, ed. *Subcultures.* Berkeley, Calif.: Glendessary Press, 1970.

Atchley, Robert, and McCabe, M. Patrick. "Socialization in Correctional Communities: A Replication." *American Sociological Review* 33 (1968): 774-85.

Baker, J.E. "Inmate Self-Government and the Right to Participate." In *Correctional Institutions,* edited by Robert Carter, Daniel Glaser, and Leslie Wilkins. 2d ed. Philadelphia: Lippincott, 1977.

Bartollas, Clemens; Dinitz, Simon; and Miller, Stuart. *Juvenile Victimization: The Institutional Paradox.* New York: Wiley, 1977.

Berk, Bernard. "Organizational Goals and Inmate Organization." *American Journal of Sociology* 71 (1966): 522-34.

Bondeson, Ulla. "Argot Knowledge as an Indicator of Criminal Socialization: A Study of a Training School for Girls." In *Scandinavian Studies in Criminology,* edited by Nils Christie, Vol. 2. London: Tavistock, 1968.

Bowker, Lee. *Prisoner Subcultures.* Lexington, Mass.: D.C. Heath, 1978.

Carlson, Norman. "A More Balanced Correctional Philosophy." *FBI Law Enforcement Bulletin* 46 (January 1977): 22-24.

Carroll, Leo. *Hacks, Blacks and Cons.* Lexington, Mass.: D.C. Heath, 1974.

Carter, Barbara. "Reform School Families." *Society* 11 (November–December 1973), 36–43.

Casper, Jonathan. *American Criminal Justice: The Defendant's Perspective.* Englewood Cliffs, N.J.: Prentice-Hall, 1972.

Clemmer, Donald. "Observations on Imprisonment as a Source of Criminality." *Journal of Criminal Law, Criminology, and Police Science,* 41 (1950): 311-19.

———. *The Prison Community.* New York: Holt, Rinehart, and Winston, 1940.

Cline, Hugh. "The Determinants of Normative Patterns in Correctional Institutions." In *Scandinavian Studies in Criminology,* edited by Nils Christie, Vol. 2. London: Tavistock, 1968.

Cloward, Richard. "Social Control in the Prison." In Richard Cloward, et al. *Theoretical Studies in Social Organization of the Prison.* New York: Social Science Research Council, 1960.

Coates, Robert. "Community-Based Corrections: Concept, Impact, Dangers." In Lloyd Ohlin, Alden Miller, and Robert Coates, *Juvenile Correctional Reform in Massachusetts.* Washington, D.C.: U.S. Government Printing Office, 1977.

Cohen, Harold, and Filipczak, James. *A New Learning Experiment.* San Francisco: Jossey-Bass, 1971.

Cressey, Donald. "Limitations on Organization of Treatment in the Modern Prison." In Richard Cloward, et al., *Theoretical Studies in Social Organization of the Prison.* New York: Social Science Research Council, 1960.

Cressey, Donald, and Krassowski, Witold. "Inmate Organization and Anomie in American Prisons and Soviet Labor Camps." *Social Problems* 5 (1957-58): 217-23.

Dahrendorf, Ralf. *Class and Class Conflict in Industrial Society.* Stanford Calif.: Stanford University Press, 1959.

Davidson, R. Theodore. *Chicano Prisoners: The Key to San Quentin.* New York: Holt, Rinehart and Winston, 1974.

Durkheim, Emile. *The Division of Labor in Society,* translated by George Simpson. Glencoe, Ill.: Free Press, 1952.

Ellis, Desmond; Grasmick, Harold; and Gilman, Bernard. "Violence in Prisons: A Sociological Analysis." *American Journal of Sociology* 80 (1974): 16-43.

Empey, Lamar, and Erickson, Maynard. *The Provo Experiment: Evaluating Community Control of Delinquency.* Lexington, Mass.: D.C. Heath, 1972.

Empey, Lamar, and Lubeck, Stephen. *The Silverlake Experiment: Testing Delinquency Theory and Community Intervention.* Chicago: Aldine, 1971.

Etzioni, Amitai. *A Comparative Analysis of Complex Organization: On Power, Involvement, and Their Correlates.* Glencoe, Ill.: Free Press, 1961.

Feld, Barry. *The Professional Ideology of Correctional Pathologists: Goal Operationalization in Juvenile Corrections.* Ph.D. dissertation, Harvard University, 1974.

———. *Subcultures of Selected Boys' Cottages in Massachusetts Department* of Youth Services Institutions in 1971. Mimeographed. Cambridge, Mass.: Harvard Law School, Center for Criminal Justice, 1972.

———. *Neutralizing Inmate Violence: Juvenile Offenders in Institutions.* Cambridge, Mass.: Ballinger, 1977.

Fisher, Sethard. "Social Organization in a Correctional Community." *Pacific Sociological Review* 4 (1961): 87-93.

Fogel, David. *"We Are the Living Proof": The Justice Model for Corrections.* Cincinnati: Anderson, 1975.

Garabedian, Peter. "Social Roles and Processes and Socialization in the Prison Community." *Social Problems* 11 (1963): 139-52.

Garrity, Donald. "The Prison as a Rehabilitation Agency." In *The Prison: Studies in Institutional Organization and Change,* edited by Donald Cressey. New York: Holt, Rinehart, and Winston, 1961.

Giallombardo, Rose. *The Social World of Imprisoned Girls: A Comparative Study of Institutions for Juvenile Delinquents.* New York: Wiley, 1974.

———. *Society of Women: A Study of a Women's Prison.* New York: Wiley, 1966.

Gibbons, Don. *Society, Crime, and Criminal Careers: An Introduction to Criminology.* 2nd ed. Englewood Cliffs, N.J.: Prentice-Hall, 1972.

Gillin, John. *Criminology and Penology.* 3d ed. New York: Appleton-Century, 1945.

Glaser, Daniel. *The Effectiveness of a Prison and Parole System.* Indianapolis, Ind.: Bobbs-Merrill, 1964.

Goffman, Erving. "On the Characteristics of Total Institutions." In *Asylums: Essays on the Social Situation of Mental Patients and Other Inmates,* Erving Goffman. Garden City, N.J.: Anchor, 1961.

Goldenberg, Ira. *Build Me a Mountain: Youth Poverty and the Creation of New Settings.* Cambridge, Mass.: MIT Press, 1971.

Grosser, George. "External Settings and Internal Relations of the Prison." In Richard Cloward, et al., *Theoretical Studies in Social Organization of the Prison.* New York: Social Science Research Council, 1960.

Grusky, Oscar. "Organizational Goals and the Behavior of Informal Leaders." *American Journal of Sociology* 65 (1959): 59-67.

Guenther, Anthony. "Compensations in a Total Institution: The Forms and Functions of Contraband." *Crime and Delinquency* 21 (1975): 243-54.

Haney, Craig; Banks, Curtis; and Zimbardo, Philip. "Interpersonal Dynamics in a Simulated Prison." *International Journal of Criminology and Penology* 1 (1973): 69-97.

Hawkins, Gordon. *The Prison: Policy and Practice.* Chicago: University of Chicago Press, 1976.

Hayner, Norman. "Washington State Correctional Institutions as Communities." *Social Forces* 21 (1943): 316-22.

Hayner, Norman, and Ash, Ellis. "The Prison as a Community." *American Sociological Review* 5 (1940): 577-83.

———. "The Prisoner Community as a Social Group." *American Sociological Review* 4 (1939): 362-69.

Haynes, Fred. *The American Prison System.* New York: McGraw-Hill, 1939.
——. *Criminology.* New York: McGraw-Hill, 1930.
Heffernan, Esther. *Making It in Prison: The Square, the Cool, and the Life.* Chicago: Aldine, 1965.
Heydebrand, Wolf, ed. *Comparative Organizations: The Results of Empirical Research.* Englewood Cliffs, N.J.: Prentice-Hall, 1973.
——. "The Study of Organizations." In *Comparative Organizations: The Results of Empirical Research,* edited by Wolf Heydebrand. Englewood Cliffs, N.J.: Prentice-Hall, 1973.
Irwin, John. *The Felon.* Englewood Cliffs, N.J.: Prentice-Hall, 1970.
Irwin, John, and Cressey, Donald. "Thieves, Convicts and the Inmate Culture." In *The Other Side: Perspectives on Deviance,* edited by Howard Becker. New York: Free Press, 1964.
Jacobs, James. *Stateville: The Penitentiary in Mass Society.* Chicago: University of Chicago Press, 1977.
——. "Stratification and Conflict among Prison Inmates." *Journal of Criminal Law and Criminology,* 66 (1975): 476–82.
——. "Street Gangs Behind Bars." *Social Problems* 21 (1974): 395–409.
Jensen, Gary and Jones, Dorothy. "Perspectives on Inmate Culture: A Study of Women in Prison." *Social Forces* 54 (1976): 590–603.
Kassebaum, Gene; Ward, David; and Wilner, Daniel. *Prison Treatment and Parole Survival: An Empirical Assessment.* New York: Wiley, 1971.
Kelleher, Maureen. "Review of the Social World of Imprisoned Girls." *Contemporary Sociology: A Journal of Reviews* 4 (1975):384.
Kobrin, Solomon. "The Chicago Area Project—A 25-Year Assessment." *Annals of the American Academy of Political and Social Science* 322 (1959): 20–29.
Kohlberg, Lawrence; Scharf, Peter; and Hickey, Joseph. "The Justice Structure of the Prison." *Beyond Time: Connecticut Journal of Criminal Justice* 1 (1973): 1–8.
McCleery, Richard. "Communication Patterns as Bases of Systems of Authority and Power." In Richard Cloward, et al., *Theoretical Studies in Social Organization of the Prison.* New York: Social Science Research Council, 1960.
McCorkle, Lloyd; Elias, Albert; and Bixby, F. Lovell. *The Highfields Story: An Experimental Treatment Project for Youthful Offenders.* New York: Holt, Reinhart, and Winston, 1958.
McEwen, Craig. "Subculture, Social Structure, and Behavior in Community-Based Correctional Settings: A Comparative Analysis of Thirteen Programs for Juveniles." Ph.D. dissertation, Harvard University, 1975.
Martinson, Robert. "What Works?—Questions and Answers about Prison Reform." *The Public Interest,* Spring 1974, pp. 22–50.
Mathiesen, Thomas; Colin, Marcel; Eisenberg, Ulrich; and Taylor, R. *Aspects of the Prison Community.* Strasbourg: Council of Europe, 1973.
Mattick, Hans. "The Prosaic Sources of Prison Violence." In *Criminal Behavior and Social Systems,* edited by Anthony Guenther. 2nd ed. Chicago: Rand McNally, 1976.

Messinger, Sheldon. "Issues in the Study of the Social System of Prison Inmates." *Issues in Criminology* 4 (1969): 133–44.

Miller, Walter. "Subculture, Social Reform and the 'Culture of Poverty.'" *Human Organization* 30 (1971): 111–25.

Mitford, Jessica. *Kind and Usual Punishment: The Prison Business.* New York: Knopf, 1973.

Morris, Norval. *The Future of Imprisonment.* Chicago: University of Chicago Press, 1974.

Morris, Terence, and Morris, Pauline. *Pentonville: A Sociological Study of an English Prison.* London: Routledge, Kegan and Paul, 1963.

National Criminal Justice Information and Statistics Service. *Census of State Correctional Facilities, 1974, Advance Report.* Washington, D.C.: U.S. Government Printing Office, 1975.

——. *Children in Custody: Advance Report on the Juvenile Detention and Correctional Facility Census of 1972–73.* Washington, D.C.: U.S. Government Printing Office, 1975.

——. *Prisoners in State and Federal Institutions on December 31, 1974.* Washington, D.C.: U.S. Government Printing Office, 1975.

New York State Special Commission on Attica. *Attica: The Official Report of the New York State Special Commission on Attica.* New York: Bantam Books, 1972.

Ohlin, Lloyd. "Correctional Strategies in Conflict." *Proceedings of the American Philosophical Society* 118 (1974): 248–53.

——. "Organizational Reform in Correctional Agencies." In *Handbook of Criminology*, edited by Daniel Glaser. Chicago: Rand McNally, 1974.

——. "Reform of Correctional Services for Youth: A Research Proposal." Cambridge, Mass.: Center for Criminal Justice, Harvard Law School, 1970. Mimeographed.

——. *Sociology and the Field of Corrections.* New York: Russell Sage Foundation, 1956.

Ohlin, Lloyd; Coates, Robert; and Miller, Alden. "Radical Correctional Reform: A Case Study of the Massachusetts Youth Correctional System." *Harvard Educational Review*, 44 (1974): 74–111.

Parsons, Talcott. *The Structure of Social Action.* Vol. I. New York: McGraw-Hill, 1937.

Polsky, Howard. *Cottage Six—The Social System of Delinquent Boys in Residential Treatment.* New York: Russell Sage Foundation, 1962.

President's Commisson on Law Enforcement and the Administration of Justice. *Task Force Report: Corrections.* Washington, D.C.: U.S. Government Printing Office, 1967.

Pugh, D.S.; Hickson, P.J.; Hinings, C.R.; Turner, C. "Dimensions of Organizational Structure." In *Comparative Organizations: The Results of Empirical Research*, edited by Wolf Heydebrand. Englewood Cliffs, N.J.: Prentice-Hall, 1973.

Raab, Selwyn, "City Prison Reform Plan Called Failure." *New York Times*, August 18, 1975, p. 1.

Reimer, Hans. "Socialization in the Prison Community." *Proceedings of the American Prison Association.* 1937.

Roebuck, Julian. "A Critique of 'Thieves, Convicts and the Inmate Subculture.'" *Social Problems* 11 (1963): 193-200.

Rothman, David. *The Discovery of the Asylum: Social Order and Disorder in the New Republic.* Boston: Little, Brown, 1970.

Ruo-Wang, Bao, and Chelminski, Rudolph. *Prisoner of Mao.* New York: Coward McCann and Geoghegan, 1973.

Schachter, Stanley. "Cohesion, Social." *International Encyclopedia of the Social Sciences.* Vol. 2. 1968.

Schein, Edgar. "Reaction Patterns to Severe Chronic Stress in American Army Prisoners of War of the Chinese." In *Basic Studies in Social Psychology,* edited by Harold Proshansky and Bernard Seidenberg. New York: Holt, Rinehart, and Winston, 1965.

Schwartz, Barry. "Peer Versus Authority Effects in a Correctional Community." *Criminology* 11 (1973): 233-57.

———. "Pre-institutional vs. Situational Influence in a Correctional Community." *Journal of Criminal Law, Criminology and Police Science.* 62 (1971): 532-43.

Scull, Anthony. *Decarceration: Community Treatment and the Deviant— A Radical View.* Englewood Cliffs, N.J.: Prentice-Hall, 1976.

Stephenson, Richard, and Scarpatti, Frank. "Essexfields: A Non-Residential Experiment in Group-Centered Rehabilitation of Delinquents." *American Journal of Corrections* 31 (1969): 12-18.

Strange, Heather, and McCrory, Joseph. "Bulls and Bears." *Society* 11 (July-August, 1974): 51-59.

Street, David; Vinter, Robert; and Perrow, Charles. *Organization for Treatment: A Comparative Study of Institutions for Delinquents.* New York: Free Press, 1966.

Studt, Elliot; Messinger, Sheldon; and Wilson, Thomas. *C-Unit: Search for Community in Prison.* New York: Russell Sage Foundation, 1968.

Sugarman, Barry. *Daytop Village: A Therapeutic Community.* New York: Holt, Rinehart, and Winston, 1974.

Sutherland, Edwin, and Cressey, Donald. *Criminology.* 8th ed. Philadelphia: Lippincott, 1970.

Sykes, Gresham. *The Society of Captives: A Study of a Maximum Security Prison.* Princeton, N.J.: Princeton University Press, 1958.

Sykes, Gresham, and Messinger, Sheldon. "The Inmate Social System." In Richard Cloward, et al., *Theoretical Studies in Social Organization of the Prison.* New York: Social Science Research Council, 1960.

Taft, Donald. "The Group and Community Organization Approach to Prison Administration." *Proceedings of the American Prison Association.* 1942.

Tagiuri, Renato. "Differential Adjustment to Internment Camp Life." *Journal of Social Psychology* 48 (1958): 103-109.

Thomas, Charles. "Theoretical Perspectives on Prisonization: A Comparison of the Importation and Deprivation Models." *The Journal of Criminal Law and Criminology* 68 (1977): 135-45.

———. "Toward a More Inclusive Model of the Inmate Contraculture." *Criminology* 9 (1970): 251–62.

Thomas, Charles, and Foster, Samuel. "Prisonization in the Inmate Contraculture." *Social Problems* 20 (1972): 229–39.

Thomas, Charles and Peterson, David. *Prison Organization and Inmate Subcultures.* Indianapolis, Ind.: Bobbs-Merrill, 1977.

Tittle, Charles. *Society of Subordinates: Inmate Organization in a Narcotic Hospital.* Bloomington: University of Indiana Press, 1972.

Tittle, Charles, and Tittle, Drollene. "Social Organization of Prisoners: An Empirical Test." *Social Forces* 43 (1964): 216–21.

Van den Haag, Ernst. *Punishing Criminals: Concerning a Very Old and Painful Question.* New York: Basic Books, 1975.

Ward, David, and Kassebaum, Gene. *Women's Prison: Sex and Social Structure.* Chicago: Aldine, 1965.

Weinberg, Kirson. "Aspects of the Prison's Social Structure." *American Journal of Sociology* 47 (1942): 717–26.

Wellford, Charles. "Factors Associated with Adoption of the Inmate Code: A Study of Normative Socialization." *Journal of Criminal Law, Criminology, and Police Science* 58 (1967): 197–203.

Wheeler, Stanton. "Socialization in Correctional Communities." *American Sociological Review* 26 (1961): 697–712.

———. "Socialization in Correctional Institutions." In *Crime and Justice: The Criminal in Confinement,* edited by Leon Radzinowicz and Marvin Wolfgang. New York: Basic Books, 1971.

Whyte, William. *Street Corner Society: The Social Structure of an Italian Slum.* Chicago: University of Chicago Press, 1955.

Williams, Vergil, and Fish, Mary. *Convicts, Codes and Contraband: The Prison Life of Men and Women.* Cambridge, Mass.: Ballinger, 1974.

Wilsnack, Richard. "Explaining Collective Violence in Prisons: Problems and Possibilities." In *Prison Violence,* edited by Albert Cohen, George Cole, and Robert Bailey. Lexington, Mass.: D.C. Heath, 1976.

Wilson, James Q. *Varieties of Police Behavior: The Management of Law and Order in Eight Communities.* Cambridge, Mass.: Harvard University Press, 1968.

Wilson, John, and Snodgrass, Jon. "The Prison Code in a Therapeutic Community." *Journal of Criminal Law, Criminology, and Police Science* 60 (1969): 472–78.

Wilson, Thomas P. "Patterns of Management and Adaptations to Organizational Roles: A Study of Prison Inmates." *American Journal of Sociology* 74 (1968): 146–57.

Index

New York Times, 3
Normative organizations, 36, 85
  defined, 29-30
Norms
  and social structure, 154, 179
  in subcultures, 117-26, 143-46

Offenses, 45-47, 208-209
Ohlin, Lloyd, xviii, 22
Open-community programs, 24, 28-29, 226-28
  cohesion in, 156-59
  community contact in, 40-43
  and equality, 64-70, 72-75, 90-93
  and participation, 102-107
  population, 47
  and program equality, 77
  sex subculture in, 134-38
  staff, 64-70, 72-75, 90-93
  subculture in, 127-29, 134-38, 146
  and supervision, 108-11
Open House program, 27-29, 225-26
  community contact, 39-42, 90
  and equality, 66, 74
  leadership, 167
  negative behavior, 174, 178
  and participation, 103, 105
  population, 46, 163
  staff, 66, 74
  subculture, 124, 127, 138-41
  and supervision, 108-109
Organizational factors, 31-33, 36, 112-15
  changes in, 38-43, 53, 184-97, 197-209, 209-12
  for community contact, 31, 92, 112-13, 183-84, 192-97, 210-12
  and diverse programs, 209-12
  equality, 72-79
  ideology, 115-16
  vs. inmate systems, 13-15, 44
  and leadership, 164-70
  and negative behavior, 171-78
  and norms, 36
  of participation, 101-107, 184, 197-201
  and population, 113-15, 183, 204-209
  for program equality, 76-79
  and self-concept, 130-34
  and social structure, 151-53, 155-59, 178-79
  and sociological theory, 13-15
  for staff equality, 72-76
  for staff-inmate relations, 63-70, 78, 92-93
  for staff perceptions, 79-83, 115-16

  and subculture, 99-101, 117, 121-22, 130-34, 143-47
  of supervision, 107-13, 184, 201-203
  and youth perceptions, 84-89
Organizations, formal
  characteristics of, 31-33, 36
  vs. goals, 33-35
  and practice, 29-35
  and sociological theory, 10-15
  and structure, 29-35
  types of, 29-30, 60, 93-95
Osborne, Thomas, 199

Pair program, 28, 227-28
  community contact, 40-41, 90
  and equality, 66-67, 75
  leadership, 167, 169
  negative behavior, 174, 178
  and participation, 103
  population, 47
  staff, 66-67, 75
  subculture, 127
  and supervision, 108-109
Participation, 14-15, 101-107, 114, 143-46
  and age, 205-207
  and cohesion, 156-59, 162-64
  and community contact, 194, 197, 201
  and friendship, 160-61
  and inmate perceptions, 83-89
  and leadership, 165-66, 168-70
  and negative behavior, 174, 177
  organizational factors of, 32, 53, 184, 188, 194, 197-201, 210
  and population, 162-64, 205-207
  and runaways, 176-78
  and self-concept, 131-34
  and sex subculture, 134-38
  and social structure, 153, 156-61, 179, 194
  and staff perceptions, 81-83
  -supervision, 112-15
  values, 197-99
  and youth perceptions, 83-89
Perceptions
  inmate, 13-14, 30-34, 61-63, 83-90, 94, 205
  of organizations, 36
  staff, 79-83
Perrow, Charles, 9
Philadelphia Society for Alleviating the Miseries of Public Prisons, 5
Pick-up program, 28, 227
  community contact, 40-41, 90
  and equality, 66-67, 75

About the Author

Craig A. McEwen is Assistant Professor of Sociology at Bowdoin College and has taught previously at Morgan State and Harvard Universities. He earned degrees from Oberlin and from Harvard, where he developed his research interests in corrections, police organization, and the courts.